CRUSADE TEXTS
IN TRANSLATION

About the volume:

This is the first English translation of Robert the Monk's *Historia Iherosolimitana*, a Latin prose chronicle describing the First Crusade. In addition to providing new and unique information on the Crusade (Robert claims to have been an eyewitness of the Council of Clermont in 1095), its particular interest lies in the great popularity it enjoyed in the Middle Ages.

The text has close links with the vernacular literary tradition and is written in a racy style which would not disgrace a modern tabloid journalist. Its reflection of contemporary legends and anecdotes gives us insights into perceptions of the Crusade at that time and opens up interesting perspectives onto the relationship of history and fiction in the twelfth century. The introduction discusses what we know about Robert, his importance as a historical source and his place in the literary tradition of the First Crusade.

About the series:

The crusading movement bequeathed to its future historians a legacy of sources unrivalled in their range and variety. *Crusade Texts in Translation* presents these sources document in fascinating detail as well as the motivations and viewpoints, military efforts and spiritual lives, of the participants in the crusades. They narrate the internal histories of the states and societies which crusaders established or supported in the many regions where they fought. Some sources have been translated in the past but the vast majority have been available only in their original language. *Crusade Texts in Translation* provides a wide ranging corpus of texts, most of them translated for the first time, which illuminate the history of the crusades and the crusader-states from every angle, including that of their principal adversaries, the Muslim powers of the Middle East.

About the author:

Dr Carol Sweetenham is an Associate Research Fellow at Warwick University, UK.

Robert the Monk's History of the First Crusade

Crusade Texts in Translation

Editorial Board

Malcolm Barber (Reading), Peter Edbury (Cardiff),
Bernard Hamilton (Nottingham), Norman Housley (Leicester)

Titles in this series include:

Robert the Monk's History of the First Crusade

Historia Iherosolimitana

Translated by

CAROL SWEETENHAM

ASHGATE

Published by
Ashgate Publishing Limited
Gower House
Croft Road
Aldershot
Hants GU11 3HR
England

Ashgate Publishing Company
Suite 420
101 Cherry Street
Burlington
Vermont, 05401–4405
USA

Ashgate website: http://www.ashgate.com

Paperback edition published 2006
Hardback edition reprinted 2006

British Library Cataloguing in Publication Data
Robert the Monk's History of the First Crusade = Historia Iherosolimitana – (Crusade Texts in Translation
    1. Robert, the Monk. 2. Crusades – First, 1096–1099 – Early works to 1800.
    I. Title. II. Sweetenham, Carol. III. History of the First Crusade. IV. Historia Iherosolimitana
    956'.014

US Library of Congress Cataloging in Publication Data
Robert the Monk's History of the First Crusade = Historia Iherosolimitana / translated by Carol Sweetenham.
        p.   cm. – (Crusade Texts in Translation; 11)
    Includes bibliographical references and index.
    1. Crusades – First, 1096–1099 – Sources. I. Title: Historia Iherosolimitana.
    II. Sweetenham, Carol. III. Title. IV. Series.
    D161.1.R614 2004
    956'.014–dc22   2004010537

ISBN-10: 0-7546-0471-3 (Hardback)   ISBN-10: 0-7546-5862-7 (Paperback)
ISBN-13: 978-0-7546-0471-6 (Hardback) ISBN-13: 978-0-7546-5862-7 (Paperback)

This book is printed on acid free paper.

Printed and bound in Great Britain by TJ International Ltd, Padstow, Cornwall

Contents

Preface

The success of the First Crusade at the end of the eleventh century had enormous repercussions. It led directly to the creation of the kingdom of Outremer, which was to last until the battle of Hattin in 1187 and whose remnants were to cling on until the fifteenth century.[1] It created a theological framework of holy war which took its origins in existing concepts of pilgrimage and just war but welded them into a new set of concepts.[2] It created a mythology of its own in the shape of the Old French Crusade Cycle and the fantastic legends around the first Advocate of the Holy Sepulchre, Godfrey of Bouillon;[3] the *chanson de geste* became an instrument not only for describing the past achievements of the Carolingians but for reflecting the glory of those still alive.[4] And it created a wave of historiography, with eyewitness accounts rippling out into later versions, compilations and adaptations: arguably the largest number of accounts dedicated to one single event.[5]

Amongst these accounts, that of Robert the Monk was far and away the most popular. It survives in some one hundred manuscripts, ten times more than any other work. It was one of the earliest chronicles to be translated into the vernacular. It was adapted numerous times and used as a source in compilations.[6] When Graindor de Douai produced the vernacular poem known as the *Chanson d'Antioche* for a late twelfth-century audience it was to Robert's chronicle that he

---

[1] S. Runciman, *A History of the Crusades* (Cambridge, 1951–4), 3 vols,: vol.III 468; henceforth Runciman. *History*.

[2] J. Riley-Smith, *The First Crusade and the Idea of Crusading* (London, 1986); henceforth *Idea*.

[3] The *Chanson d'Antioche,* ed. S. Duparc-Quioc, *La Chanson d'Antioche* (Paris, 1976–8), 2 vols: henceforth *Edition* (vol.I) and *Etude* (vol.II); the *Chanson de Jérusalem,* ed. N. Thorp, *La Chanson de Jérusalem* in *The Old French Crusade Cycle,* ed. J. A. Nelson and E. J. Mickel, 10 vols (Alabama, 1977–96), vol.VI (1992); and the *Chanson des Chétifs,* ed. G. M. Myers, *The Old French Crusade Cycle,* vol. V (1981) form the core of the cycle, although only the *Antioche* has any real historical value. Amongst the abundant literature see S. Duparc-Quioc, *Le Cycle de la Croisade* (Paris, 1955) (henceforth *Cycle*) for discussion of these three texts, and A. Hatem, *Les poèmes épiques des croisades: genèse – historicité – localisation* (Paris, 1932); for description of the full extent of the thirteenth and fourteenth century, increasingly fantastic, ramifications of the cycle see R. F. Cook and L. S. Crist, *Le deuxième cycle de la Croisade* (Geneva, 1972).

[4] See K.-H. Bender, 'Des chansons de geste à la première épopée de croisade. La présence de l'histoire contemporaine dans la littérature française du douzième siècle', *VIe Congrès International de la Société Rencesvals* (Aix-en-Provence, 1974) 485–500.

[5] For a modern overview see S. Edgington, 'The First Crusade: reviewing the evidence', in *The First Crusade: Origins and Impact*, ed. J. Phillips (Manchester, 1997) 55–77; N. Iorga, *Les narrateurs de la première Croisade* (Paris, 1928) is of some limited value.

[6] See Chapter One for discussion and references.

turned for historical authenticity.[7] So Robert's work shaped much of the perception of the Crusade in the Middle Ages.

However, modern scholarship has devoted little attention to Robert. The most recent edition remains that of the *Recueil*, done by Philippe le Bas and published in 1866.[8] The last translation of the work was Guizot's French version in 1825.[9] The only work solely dedicated to Robert is Marquardt's thesis for the University of Königsberg in 1895.[10] Kraft looked briefly at his work in his examination of the German translation by Heinrich Steinhöwels in 1905;[11] Haupt similarly examined him in the context of the fifteenth-century translation of the text, *Die Uzrustunge dez herezaugen Gotfrides von Bullion*.[12] Duparc-Quioc has identified the links between his text and the extant version of the *Antioche*,[13] and Knoch identified borrowings from his text in the 1108 *Magdeburger Aufruf*.[14] Riley-Smith has examined his theology in the context of the ideology of the Crusade.[15] Marcus Bull has examined his work in the context of the French court and the idealisation of Hugh of Vermandois.[16] But there is no complete study of his work.

The intention of this work is to make access to Robert's work easier for a modern audience and offer some starting points for an assessment of his position within the historiography of the First Crusade. I have aimed to translate into clear modern English to make his work more accessible both to historians and to students of literary history. The Introduction has five chapters. Chapter One provides an overview of the history of the text and its influence on later works. Chapter Two discusses its relationship with its main source, the anonymous *Gesta Francorum*.[17] Chapter Three contains an analysis of its links with other sources for the Crusade and discussion of its value as a historical source. Chapter Four assesses Robert's authorship as theologian, as historiographer and as literary stylist. Chapter Five sets out the principles followed in the translation. Explanatory

---

[7] Duparc-Quioc, *Etude*, 108–10, 119; borrowings flagged up in notes to the *Edition*.

[8] *Recueil des Historiens des Croisades: historiens occidentaux*, Académie des Inscriptions et Belles-lettres (Paris, 1841–1906), 16 volumes (henceforth *RHC Occ.* or *Recueil*) III.717–882.

[9] F. P. G. Guizot, *Collection des mémoires rélatifs à l'histoire de la France* (Paris, 1823–31), 30 vols: vol.XXIII (1825), 295–476.

[10] G. Marquardt, *Die 'Historia Hierosolymitana' des Robertus Monachus. Ein quellenkritischer Beitrag zur Geschichte des ersten Kreuzzugs* (Königsberg, 1892).

[11] F. Kraft, *Heinrich Steinhöwels Verdeutschung der 'Historia Hierosolimitana' des Robertus Monachus. Eine literarhistorische Untersuchung* (Strasbourg, 1905).

[12] B. Haupt, Historia Hierosolimitana *von Robertus Monachus in deutscher Ubersetzung* (Wiesbaden, 1972).

[13] See note 7.

[14] P. Knoch, 'Kreuzzug und Siedlung. Studien zum Aufruf der Magdeburger Kirche von 1108', *JGMOD*, 23 (1974), 1–33.

[15] *Idea* 135–52.

[16] M. J. Bull, 'The Capetian Monarchy and the Early Crusade movement: Hugh of Vermandois and Louis VII', *NMS*, 40 (1996), 25–46.

[17] *Gesta Francorum et aliorum Hierosolimitanorum*, ed. R. Hill (London, 1962); see also L. Bréhier's edition, *Histoire anonyme de la première Croisade* (Paris, 1924).

notes throughout the text give details of names, places and dates, biblical and literary allusions and other points of interest: these are intended to aid understanding for the reader and are not designed to be a full set of notes. To attempt any kind of edition is well beyond the scope of what I have set out to do and I have worked from the *Recueil* text as the only modern text currently available: the hundred-odd manuscripts extant await the attention of some future devoted editor.

I have added in an appendix translations of two letters which accompany Robert's work in around a third of the extant manuscripts: the apocryphal letter of Alexius to Robert of Flanders, and the letter from the Patriarch of Jerusalem to the Western Churches.[18]

---

[18] These are translated from the versions given by Hagenmeyer in *Die Kreuzzugsbriefe aus den Jahren 1088–1100*, ed. H. Hagenmeyer (Innsbruck, 1901); hereafter *Kreuzzugsbriefe*.

Acknowledgements

This work would not have been possible without the help of the Taylorian Institute, the Bodleian Library and the History Faculty Library in Oxford: I am grateful to all of them, and to Somerville College, Oxford, for access to a particularly elusive book. I owe particular thanks to two people. Linda Paterson in Warwick taught me everything I know in this area and has been an unfailing source of support, advice and ideas. Without Jonathan Phillips at Royal Holloway College of the University of London the translation would never have seen the light of day, and it has benefited considerably from discussion at his Crusade seminars. I am grateful to Professor Bernard Hamilton for the care with which he read the manuscript and the corrections he suggested. I am also grateful to Professor Jean Dunbabin and Dr Susan Edgington for helpful conversations, and to Professor Rees Davies for an opportunity to discuss the text at his seminar. Any mistakes are of course my own. I am grateful to Dr John Smedley of Ashgate for his advice during the preparation of the text. Finally I owe particular thanks to my husband Philip for his support, critical eye and ability to scare recalcitrant computers into submission, and to my children Oliver and William for tolerating (often) their mother's fascination with the twelfth century.

INTRODUCTION

Chapter 1

The textual history of the *Historia Iherosolimitana*

This chapter gives an overview of the textual history of the *Historia Iherosolimitana*. It starts by discussing the (sketchy) evidence on the author himself, and the probable circumstances surrounding the dating and commissioning of the work. It then briefly describes the manuscript tradition of the *Historia* and its later history in translation and in print.

i) Who was Robert?

We know little for certain about Robert. There is a certain amount of evidence in his text. An Abbot Robert of the Benedictine abbey of St-Rémi at Reims is well attested at around the same time. But there is no definitive evidence for identifying that abbot with our Robert.

Internal evidence

In the *Apologeticus Sermo* at the head of the text Robert tells us several things about the circumstances in which he composed his history and hence about himself. There is no obvious reason to disbelieve him.

His name was Robert; there are no significant variants in the *Recueil* text. The work was composed in 'claustrum cujusdam cellae Sancti Remigii',[1] in the episcopate of Reims. The Benedictine abbey of St-Rémi was large and prestigious, dominating the centre of Reims.[2] Two manuscripts, one thirteenth- and one fourteenth- century, specify that the relics of St Oriculus were kept where Robert wrote,[3] and if we accept this then that suggests the text was written at the priory of Sénuc in the diocese of Reims where these relics were housed. But that would be to place a lot of weight on two later manuscripts.

Robert was a monk. He was compelled to write 'per obedientiam',[4] in other words as part of his monastic vow. He was asked to write by his abbot, of whom he

---

[1] 'a cloister of a certain monastery of St-Rémi'.

[2] Bull, 'Capetian Monarchy', 40.

[3] *Recueil,* 722, n. 6. The manuscripts in question are D and E by the *Recueil*'s classification, respectively a fourteenth-century manuscript from St-Victor and a thirteenth-century one from Compiègne.

[4] *Sermo Apologeticus* ('by my vow of obedience').

speaks highly: 'litterarum scientia et morum probitate praeditus'.[5] Two manuscripts, both twelfth-century (Vatican 1795 and Turonensis) give the abbot's name as Bernardus, at least six others as Benedictus, others again simply as B or N.[6] Such commissioning was standard procedure: Orderic Vitalis was asked by his abbot to write about the restoration of the monastery of St Evroul; Henry of Huntingdon was commissioned to write by Bishop Alexander of Lincoln.[7]

Robert tells us that he was an eyewitness at the Council of Clermont, which was why the abbot picked him out to write the history: 'praecepit igitur mihi ut, qui Clari Montis concilio interfui, acephalae materiei caput praeponerem et lecturis eam accuratiori stilo componerem'.[8] His account of the Council is long and descriptive; given the importance placed on eyewitness testimony generally[9] and the emphasis Robert places on his presence as his justification for writing at all, there is no reason to think he was lying. However, there is no evidence in the rest of the text that he was a participant on Crusade.[10]

Robert emphasises that he wrote alone, without clerical help: 'notarium non habui alium nisi me, et dictavi et scripsi'.[11] This contrasts with what Guénée describes as standard practice for a monastic historian, supported by a team of note-takers and scribes,[12] and it is interesting that Robert is so emphatic about the circumstances under which he wrote. Given that he goes on to comment about the deliberate simplicity of his style, this may be nothing more than the standard modesty topos of the medieval historian. To detect a shadow of hurt pride would be sheer speculation.

---

[5] *Sermo Apologeticus* ('distinguished by his knowledge of literature and his upright behaviour').

[6] Bull, 'Capetian Monarchy', 39, suggests this may refer to Baudry of Bourgueil, of whom more later.

[7] *The Ecclesiastical History of Orderic Vitalis*, ed. M. Chibnall, 6 vols (Oxford, 1969–75); vol. I.130–131; henceforth OV. *Henry, Archdeacon of Huntingdon: Historia Anglorum: the History of the English people*, ed. and transl. D. Greenway (Oxford, 1996); henceforth HH.

[8] *Sermo Apologeticus:* 'so he instructed me, since I had been present at the Council of Clermont, to add the beginning which was missing and to improve its style for future readers.'

[9] See B. Guénée, *Histoire et culture historique dans l'Occident médiéval* (Paris, 1980), 78–84. William of Malmesbury (*Gesta Regum et Anglorum*, ed. and transl. R. A. B. Mynors, completed R. Thomson and M. Winterbottom, (Oxford, 1998), 2 vols., henceforth WM), for example, clearly states the importance of eyewitness testimony: 'quicquid vero de recentioribus aetatibus apposui, uel ipse vidi uel a viris fide dignis audivi' ('whatsoever I have added out of recent history, I have either seen myself or heard from men who can be trusted', Mynors' translation), 16–17.

[10] See discussion below in Chapter Three.

[11] *Sermo Apologeticus:* 'I dictated and wrote it unaided all myself, being my own scribe.'

[12] Guénée, 49–51.

External evidence

At the end of the eleventh century a Robert was briefly Abbot of St-Rémi. It is tempting to identify our Robert with this abbot. The link was already being made in the thirteenth century: at least three manuscripts, two thirteenth-century and one fourteenth-century, add the words 'quondam abbas Sancti Remigii', and two of these specify that Robert wrote his work in the priory at Sénuc.[13]

The historical Abbot Robert had a chequered career. He began as a novice at the abbey of St-Rémi before moving to the house of Marmoutier-lez-Tours. In 1096 he became Abbot of Saint-Rémi, to the discomfiture of Abbot Bernard of Marmoutier, who seems to have tried to ensure that Robert remained subject to him. In 1097 Robert was excommunicated at Reims. Over the next few years arguments as to his innocence went back and forth, with support from Baudry of Bourgueil, Bishop of Dol, well-known writer of Latin lyric who produced his own chronicle of the First Crusade; and from Bishop Lambert of Arras.[14] Although the excommunication was overturned by the Pope, Robert was obliged to retire to the priory of Sénuc as prior. He was eventually exonerated at Poitiers in 1100. Trouble continued to dog his footsteps. In 1122 he was formally destituted by Calixtus II on the grounds of maladministration and died in the same year.[15]

The case for identifying this Robert with our author is tempting and has been generally accepted.[16] Abbot Robert lived at exactly the same time as Robert the Monk produced his chronicle. Both lived in the area of Reims. Baudry of Bourgueil, who also produced a chronicle on the First Crusade,[17] supported Robert. If we accept the manuscript reading of 'Bernardus' there is a further link: on the assumption that Robert was in fact subject to Bernardus the work could well have been commissioned 'per obedientiam'.

However, there is no actual proof. Robert gives no indication other than that of being a monk. His description of writing 'per obedientiam' and receiving a clear command from his abbot as to what he should write and why further suggest that he is unlikely to have been an abbot (unless one argues that he is being deliberately disingenuous): he is quite clear on this. Kraft points out that one abbot, even a disgraced one, cannot be subject to another; and Robert fought hard to retain his position, taking his case all the way to Rome.[18] Neither does the link with Bernard seem convincing. Robert goes out of his way to praise Bernard in the *Sermo* in a way which does not sit well with the difficult relationship we may assume to have existed between the two; and it is as hard to imagine Bernard asking his defeated

---

[13] *Recueil*, 722, n.6. See note 2 above. Ottoboni 8, a thirteenth-century manuscript designated R by the *Recueil*, has the reference to Robert as abbot but not the reference to Sénuc.

[14] *Baudri de Bourgueil: Oeuvres Poétiques*, ed. P. Abrahams, (Paris, 1926), 329–32 poem CCXXXII; see especially 83–100.

[15] For fuller discussion and references see the discussion in the *Recueil*, III. xli-iii.

[16] See e.g. M. Manitius, *Geschichte der lateinischen Literatur des Mittelalters* (Munich, 1931), 3 vols, vol.III 425–6; Riley-Smith, *Idea*, 135–6; Bull, 'Capetian Monarchy', 39–40.

[17] *Historia Jerosolymitana*, RHC Occ. IV, 1–111.

[18] Kraft, 12–13.

opponent to undertake the work as it is to imagine ex-Abbot Robert being willing to do it in this terms. As pointed out above, only two manuscripts give the name Bernardus.[19]

Conclusion

So in sum the text points either to a deeply disingenous ex-abbot deliberately underlining his credentials as a humble monk or, more simply, to a monk. And the connection with Bernard is not supported by solid evidence. More generally Robert's style is more simple than that adopted by the chronicles of the Crusade produced by Baudry of Bourgueil and in particular Guibert of Nogent;[20] one might speculate whether the ex-abbot of such a large and prestigious abbey as St-Rémi would have deliberately set out to write a relatively unsophisticated account as he claims.[21]

In the end all we can safely conclude is exactly what Robert tells us: that he was a monk, that his abbot asked him to write a history as was so often the case, that he had sufficient skills to do the job and that he was additionally qualified by virtue of having attended the Council of Clermont. All else is speculation.

ii) The dating, purpose and commissioning of the *Historia Iherosolimitana*

In the immediate aftermath of the First Crusade the anonymous, intriguing and most probably eyewitness text known as the *Gesta Francorum* appeared. The author seems to have been a follower of Bohemond, who switched allegiance to Raymond IV once Bohemond established himself in Antioch.[22] Whilst forming a source of prime importance for the events of the Crusade and one which was heavily drawn on almost immediately, the *GF* was criticised by contemporaries on a number of grounds. Its style was seen as crude and unsophisticated: 'libellum super hac re nimis rusticanum' according to Baudry and 'verbis contexta plus equo simplicibus'[23] for Guibert. It did not describe the start of the Crusade. And its author was anonymous: 'nescio quis compilator, nomine suppresso'.[24]

In the first decade or so of the twelfth century the *GF* was extended and improved by a number of authors. Peter Tudebode, a Poitevin priest of whom we

---

[19] Vatican 1795 and Turonensis, both twelfth-century; not the same as the manuscripts which refer to Sénuc.

[20] *Gesta Dei per Francos*, ed. R. B. C. Huygens (Turnhout, 1996); transl. *The Deeds of God through the Franks. A translation of Guibert de Nogent's Gesta Dei per Francos*, R. Levine (Woodbridge, 1997).

[21] See Kraft, 13–14, for another tradition according to which Robert would have been the Abbot Robert of Mont St-Michel who died in 1186. As Kraft says, there is no evidence to support this.

[22] Hill, xi–xiii.

[23] BB 10: 'a little book on this matter which was excessively unsophisticated'; GN 79, 'pieced together in words more simple than was appropriate'.

[24] BB 10, 'some compiler who did not give his name'.

have no other record, followed it very closely, diverging only in the addition of some almost certainly eyewitness material and what is probably some material from oral tradition.[25] Guibert of Nogent, Abbot of Nogent-sous-Coucy and author *q·v·* of (amongst other things) an autobiography, a treatise on preaching and some now lost salacious verse, used it as the basis for his *Gesta Dei per Francos*, adding little historical detail but setting the Crusade firmly in a wider theological context and following its aftermath until 1107–8.[26] Baudry of Bourgueil, Archbishop of Dol and prolific humanist poet, produced another account.[27] Gilo of Paris drew on it for a poem in Latin hexameters.[28] The Occitan text known as the *Canso d'Antioca* was probably commissioned by Bishop Eustorge of Limoges at much the same time.[29]

Robert's account should be placed firmly in this context. Like the other texts it was produced using the *GF* as its primary source and in a clerical context; his description of his source as lacking a beginning and 'litteralium compositio dictionum inculta'[30] fits both the text of the *GF* and the comments of his contemporaries on it. As an eyewitness of the Council of Clermont, Robert brought particular credibility to the task.

It has been argued that this wave of texts takes its origin in Bohemond's trip to France in 1105–6.[31] Bohemond had recently been released from three years' captivity. He came to France in late 1105 and undertook an extensive tour from Poitou to the court of Philip I, to Flanders and back via the South of France. During the trip he married the daughter of Philip I, Constance, at the French court at Easter. Orderic Vitalis suggests that he missed no opportunity for propaganda about his own exploits on Crusade as a basis for raising enthusiasm for his projected new expedition: 'ubique tam a clero quam a plebe venerabiliter susceptus referebat varios eventus quibus ipse interfuit'.[32] Krey has built on this to suggest that the *GF* was re-edited for Bohemond's trip, emphasising his role and changing the description of the oath sworn to the Emperor to underline the legitimacy of

---

[25] *Petrus Tudebodus: Historia de Hierosolimitano Itinere*, ed. J. H. and L. L. Hill (Paris, 1977); transl. *Peter Tudebode: Historia de Hierosolimitano Itinere*, J. H. and L. L. Hill (Philadelphia, 1974).

[26] Op. cit.

[27] Op. cit.

[28] *The* Historia Vie Hierosolimitanae *of Gilo of Paris*, ed. and transl. C. W. Grocock and J. E. Siberry (Oxford, 1997).

[29] *The* Canso d'Antioca: *an Occitan Epic Chronicle of the First Crusade*, ed. L. M. Paterson and C. E. Sweetenham (Aldershot, 2003).

[30] *Sermo Apologeticus:* 'the composition was uncertain and unsophisticated in its style and expression'.

[31] For background see A. Poncelet, 'Boémond et St Léonard', *AB*, 31 (1912), 24–44; for discussion of how the *GF* might have been adapted as propaganda for such a trip see A. C. Krey, 'A neglected passage in the *Gesta* and its bearing on the literature of the First Crusade', in *The Crusades and other historical essays presented to D. C. Munro by his former students*, ed. L. J. Paetow (New York, 1928), 57–78. On Bohemond's problems at the time see *Byzantium and the Crusader States 1096–1204*, R. J. Lilie transl. J. C. Morris and J. E. Ridings (Oxford, 1993), 72–5.

[32] 'Everywhere he was honourably received by both clergy and people, and related the various adventures in which he had played a part': OV VI.68–71 (Chibnall's translation).

Bohemond's claim to Antioch.[33] The *GF* would thus have left a wake of texts behind it, inspired by the events it recounts and based on its account to greater or lesser degree. Two of these were in Poitou and the Limousin: the chronicle of Tudebode and the Occitan poem by Gregory Bechada.[34] The other four were in the orbit of the French court: the works by Gilo, Baudry, Guibert and Robert. All (with the exception of the Occitan poem, which survives only in a much later fragment) are heavily based on the account of the *GF*, Gilo somewhat less than the others. All place Bohemond centre stage, albeit with some ambivalence in some accounts. Events at Antioch, Bohemond's principality, dominate all the texts: Bohemond's main aim in his recruiting trip was to reinforce his position in Antioch and state the legitimacy of his claim to it despite the claims of the Byzantines, and it is hardly surprising to find his heroism stated explicitly, and the importance of Antioch to the Crusade implicitly.

If we accept that Robert's work, in common with that of his contemporaries, takes its origin in propaganda for a new Crusade linked to Bohemond's trip to France, the purpose of the work is clear: it would have been commissioned by his abbot to raise enthusiasm for a new expedition to the Holy Land. There is no evidence that the commission came from the French court, but Reims was the royal city where French monarchs were crowned and St-Rémi was the dominant abbey: there is a certain logic in commissioning a work about the husband of a French princess in the city intimately linked with the French court.

Several features of Robert's work support this hypothesis. In common with Baudry and Guibert he sets the First Crusade in a strong theological framework – stronger than its participants might have recognised – which explicitly casts it as the will of God and underlines the special role of the Franks in general and the French in particular.[35] The First Crusade is thus justified, glorified, and presented as a platform for future action. His comments about wanting to make his story clear ('probabilius est abscondita rusticando elucidare quam aperta philosophando obnubilare'[36]) suggest similarly a desire to spread the news of the Crusade as widely as possible.

This is backed up the presence of two letters serving as *excitatoria* to Crusade which accompany Robert's text in around a third of the extant manuscripts: the apocryphal letter of Alexius to the West, and part of the letter from the Patriarch of Jerusalem and bishops of the Eastern Church to the West.[37] Both encourage Christians in strong terms to come to the East, and the association further strengthens the case for Robert's text as encouragement for a new Crusade.

---

[33] Krey, op. cit. .

[34] *Canso*, Introduction 5–9.

[35] Riley-Smith, *Idea*, 135–52; for more detailed analysis see Chapter Four.

[36] *Sermo Apologeticus*: 'I thought it more appropriate to clarify obscure things by simplifying than to cloud over obvious things by philosophising'.

[37] Both edited in *Kreuzzugsbriefe*. See below for translation in Appendix. The Patriarch's letter is found in 34 manuscripts and the apocryphal letter of Alexius in at least 36.

A further pointer in this direction comes from the attitude to Byzantium. Robert constantly vilifies the Byzantines. The Emperor is described as cowardly and stupid and the worst possible interpretation is placed on his actions.[38] Allied to this is the close association between the apocryphal letter of Alexius and Robert's text.[39] Whether or not the letter is original (it is hard to believe that Alexius would have drafted something quite so clumsy, let alone invited the Christians in effect to plunder Byzantium), it makes very good propaganda for a Crusade in general and hostility towards Byzantium in particular. The Byzantines regarded Bohemond's position in Antioch as being in direct breach of his oath to the Emperor: conversely Bohemond's main aim was to shore up his claim to the principality.[40] So a letter portraying the Greeks as weak and desperate for help from the West was ideally suited to his purposes.[41] I discuss the letter in more detail in the Appendix.

In sum, Robert's work is much more than propaganda for a new Crusade. But it should be seen as having been commissioned in that context and with the clear purpose of shaping the story of the First Crusade as a basis for future action.

There is no internal evidence on dating. However, other texts in the *GF* tradition all date from roughly the first decade of the twelfth century. Huygens dates Guibert to 1109.[42] Baudry can probably be dated to c. 1107.[43] Gilo's editors suggest the first decade of the twelfth century.[44] The *Canso d'Antioca* was commissioned no earlier than 1106.[45] If we accept that Robert wrote as part of the wider wave of interest in the *GF* and that this was sparked by Bohemond's recruiting trip, we can similarly date his work to the first decade of the twelfth century. This is supported by the German text of 1108, the *Magdeburger Aufruf*, which is a call to crusade against the Saxons and which contains a few parallels with Robert's text.[46] If we accept that the *Aufruf* is not a forgery and that the textual parallels are both more than coincidence and do not derive from a common source, this suggests that Robert's text must have made its way to Germany no later than 1108 and must therefore have been written sufficiently before then to make the journey. This is consistent with the slight blurring of some of the detail in the account: Hugh of Vermandois is not only dead but has probably been dead for some time given the mistake Robert makes about the circumstances; Godfrey is already idealised as the hero-advocate of the Holy Sepulchre; Stéphen of Blois is rehabilitated in a way which may suggest knowledge of his death in the Holy Land in 1102.[47] None of this is definitive evidence, but there is a strong circumstantial case for dating Robert's text to 1106–7.

---

[38] See e.g. I.13, where Alexius is shown rejoicing over Peter the Hermit's defeat.
[39] Most notably in the accusation that the Turks defiled altars with the blood from circumcisions: Robert I.1, letter 131.
[40] Runciman, *History*, vol.II, 46–7.
[41] See translation and further comments in the Appendix.
[42] Introduction, 51–6.
[43] *Recueil* IV, vi. n. 5.
[44] Introduction, xxiv.
[45] *Canso*, Introduction, 8–9.
[46] Knoch, *Aufruf*, 6–21.
[47] VII.20; IX.10; VI.15.

iii) The manuscript tradition of the *Historia Iherosolimitana*

There is no modern edition of Robert, and it is not the purpose of this work to provide one. What follows is based on the variants and description of the *Recueil* and Kraft's later list of manuscripts.[48] The *Recueil* itself uses B.N. lat. 5129, a twelfth-century manuscript from Reims which also contains Gilo's work.[49] There is no detailed analysis of the relationship between the manuscripts and not all are complete. I will confine myself to noting that the variants listed in the *Recueil* (which come from around a quarter of the extant manuscripts) show little variation.

Robert's work is consistently found alongside a number of related texts. As well as the *Sermo Apologeticus* and *Prologus*, it is accompanied in at least 36 manuscripts by the apparent letter from Alexius to Robert, Count of Flanders, before the Crusade; and in 34 by the letter from the Patriarch of Jerusalem reporting on the events of the Crusade: this is particularly the case in the twelfth-century manuscripts. Some manuscripts also include Gilo. Not all the texts are found in all manuscripts, and the order shifts.[50]

One thing is immediately striking about the manuscript tradition of Robert's work. It survives in the best part of one hundred manuscripts, more by several orders of magnitude than any other First Crusade source: Guibert survives in 8,[51] the *GF* in 7,[52] Baudry in 7,[53] the *Chanson d'Antioche* in 9 manuscripts,[54] Ralph of Caen in 1.[55] William of Tyre survives in 9 and a fragment, but around 60 of the French translation.[56] The *Recueil* lists 26 manuscripts, airily commenting in a footnote that there are many others.[57] Kraft gives a very detailed and helpful list comprising 94 manuscripts;[58] a list apparently compiled by Riant could not be found.[59] This is powerful evidence of Robert's popularity compared to any other source for the Crusade.

The extant manuscripts display a large chronological spread: 37 are wholly or largely twelfth-century, the remainder span the period from the thirteenth to the

---

[48] Kraft, 16–20. See also 'Il cronista medievale e il suo pubblico: alcune osservazioniin margine alla storiografia delle crociate', R. Hiestand, *Annali della Facoltà di lettere e filosofia dell'Università di Napoli* 27 (1984–5) 207–27.

[49] *Recueil*, vol. III.xlvii.

[50] Kraft, 16–20.

[51] Introduction, 24.

[52] *GF* Introduction, xxxviii.

[53] *Recueil*, vol.IV xii.

[54] Duparc-Quioc, *Etude*, 43–80, for detailed analysis of manuscripts.

[55] *Gesta Tancredi*, Ralph of Caen, *RHC.Occ.*III, 587–716.

[56] *Willelmi Tyrensis Archiepiscopi Chronicon*, ed. R. B. C. Huygens, *Corpus Christianorum* 63 and 63a (1986); P. W. Edbury and J. G. Rowe, *William of Tyre: Historian of the Latin East* (Cambridge, 1988), 3–4; R. B. C. Huygens, 'La tradition manuscrite de Guillaume de Tyr', *SM* 5 (1964), 281–373.

[57] *Recueil*, III, xlvii–l, li n.2.

[58] Kraft, 153–164, Beilage 1.

[59] Kraft, 153.

seventeenth century. The two oldest printed versions probably date from around 1470 and 1530.[60]

The geographical spread is also striking. They are preserved in libraries all over Europe, ranging from Vienna to Uppsala, London, Paris, Rome and St Petersburg. We do not know the origins of many for certain. But again the evidence suggests that copies were widely made: for example Hamburg Stadtbibliotek Gm 31b was probably copied in the Netherlands in the fifteenth century;[61] Paris Bibl. Nat. Nouv acq.310 is from twelfth-century Germany;[62] Vatican 2001 was written before 1190 for Frederick Barbarossa in Germany.[63] Some fifty of the manuscripts are connected with Germany, suggesting a particular interest there in Robert.[64]

iv) The later history of the Historia Iherosolimitana

Adaptations

Robert's work was used as the basis for a number of adaptations. It was drawn on by the *Historia et Gesta Ducis Gotefridi*, a fifteenth-century compilation made in the Rhineland[65] and by the *Historia Nicaena et Antiochena* of 1146–7 under Baldwin III.[66] It was anonymously translated into 4000 leonine hexameters.[67] Graindor de Douai drew heavily on it in his reworking of the Old French *Chanson d'Antioche*.[68] The Alsacian monk Gunther of Pairis versified it in his *Solymarius*, a poem in hexameters on the First Crusade written between 1180–86, 232 lines of which survive.[69] Joseph of Exeter used it for his now lost *Antiochi Bella*.[70]

Translations

Robert's work is the only source for the Crusade to have been translated into the vernacular in the Middle Ages other than William of Tyre.[71] It seems to have been particularly popular in Germany; the nearness of Reims to the German border may be a factor. By the end of the sixteenth century the *Historia Iherosolimitana*

---

[60] Kraft, 165–71.

[61] Kraft no.15.

[62] Kraft no.38.

[63] Kraft no.51.

[64] Kraft 22.

[65] Discussed in *RHC Occ*.V, cxxviii–ix.

[66] See discussion in *RHC.Occ* V, xxxi.

[67] Manitius, 426–7; Haupt, 222; codex 267, Stiftsbibliothek Admunt.

[68] Duparc-Quioc, *Etude,* 108–10.

[69] Fr.A.28, Gymnasialbibliothek Cologne; ed. W.Wattenbach, 'Le *Solymarius* de Gunther de Pairis', *AOL* I.551–61 (Paris, 1881); see F. R. Swietek, 'Gunther of Pairis and the *Historia Constantinopolitana*', *S* 53 (1978), 49–79.

[70] Kraft, 5–6, n.4.

[71] Translated into Old French in the thirteenth century: *Estoire d'Eracles empereur et la conqueste de la terre d'Outremer, RHC Occ.*, I–II.

had been translated independently no fewer than five times into German. Kraft suggests that this reflects the very late arrival there of the legends of Godfrey as the Chevalier au Cygne, meaning a larger market for Robert's work;72 Haupt argues that this reflects the rise of towns and the influence of the preaching orders;73 it may also reflect an interest going back to Frederick Barbarossa, who was given a copy of the text. The following are extant:74

    a. *Die Uzrustunge dez herezaugen Gotfrides von Bullion*: this is extant in one fifteenth-century manuscript, Universitätsbibliothek Würzburg M.ch.f.38;[75]

    b. a mid-fifteenth-century translation extant in two fifteenth-century manuscripts, one at the Stiftsbibliothek St Gallen (ms 658) and the other at the Bayerischen Staatsbibliothek, Munich (cgm 224);

    c. a translation of 1466 by Peter Eschenloer, originally from Nuremberg and the Stadtschreiber of Breslau, now in Wroclaw;

    d. the *Reyssbuch des heyligen Lands* of 1584 in Sigmund Feyerabend's compilation of crusading texts;

    e. two manuscripts and a fragment of a translation which may be by Heinrich Steinhöwels, early Renaissance translator and scholar; versions were printed in Augsburg in 1482 and 1502.[76]

Haupt argues that these versions match manuscripts U and V, which may suggest a version in a compilation which was subsequently translated.[77]

A Dutch translation also appeared in the fifteenth century.[78] Three translations into Italian also appeared.[79] Guizot translated the text into elegant if occasionally inaccurate French in 1825.[80]

Editions

The Latin text was printed a number of times. It was one of the earliest texts of the First Crusade to be printed, appearing first at Cologne in 1472 and again at Basle in 1533. It was printed by Reuber in 1584, and again in 1619 and 1726. It was edited

---

[72] Kraft, 8.

[73] Haupt, 225.

[74] Kraft, 22–41.

[75] See ed. by Haupt, op. cit.

[76] Kraft, 150–51 for summary of arguments on Steinhöwels' authorship. By this stage the text was ascribed to a mysterious 'Doctor Guido'.

[77] Haupt, 234-42.

[78] *Scoenre historie hertoghe godeuarts van boloen* (Gouda, 1486).

[79] *Historia di Roberto Monaco della Guerra fatta da principi christiani contra Saracini per l'acquisto di terra Santa,* M. F. Baldelli (Florence, 1552); *La guerra per li principi cristiani guerregiata contra i Saracini corrente A.D.1095. Traslata in volgare per uno da Pistoia,* S. Ciampi (Florence, 1825); *La prima crociata ... di Roberto monaco, tradotta ... con nota e schiarimenti,* G. B. Cereseto (Nice, 1854).

[80] See Chapter Five for examples of one or two inaccuracies in a good translation.

by Bongars in 1611. Migne printed it in 1844. The most recent version remains the *Recueil* edition of 1866.[81]

Success

Guénée defines and discusses several criteria for assessing the success of a history: number of extant manuscripts, number of adaptations, geographical spread and historical period over which they were copied.[82] Judged by all of these, Robert's work was an outstanding success. His hundred-odd manuscripts stand comparison with Vincent of Beauvais (100 manuscripts) and defeat Gregory of Tours (50), although Valerius Maximus at 419 beats him by some distance.[83] He was copied and adapted repeatedly until the sixteenth century throughout Europe.

After the Renaissance interest in his text fell away. Modern authors have been less than complimentary, judging him purely from the standpoint of a primary source for the Crusade. Iorga comments: 'dans l'ensemble rien qui puisse se rapprocher le moins du monde de l'authenticité'. Runciman, slightly dismissively, describes him as 'popular and somewhat romantic'.[84] This ignores the wider interest of Robert's work as contributing to the creation of Crusade ideology and as a work of literature in its own right, and its consequent influence through adaptations and translations of our view of the Crusade.

v) Conclusion

We know nothing about Robert other than what he tells us: he was a monk from Reims asked to write by his abbot. Whilst it is tempting to identify him with the turbulent Abbot Robert of St-Rémi, the evidence is not really there. His work should be dated to 1106–7 as part of a wave of texts telling the story of the First Crusade to whip up enthusiasm for a new expedition. He wrote within the orbit of the French court.

What is clear is that his work was by some distance the most successful of the histories of the First Crusade. Since then he has fallen out of favour. But arguably his version of events has been one of the most persuasive in shaping our perceptions of the Crusade today.

---

[81] Cologne, possibly printed by Arnold Therhoeren; H. Petri, (Basle, 1533); *Veterum scriptorum, qui caesarum et imperatorum Germanicorum res per aliquot saecula gestas, litteris mandarunt*, Reuber, 217–71 (Frankfurt-am-Main, 1584), reprinted 1619 (Hanover) and again in 1726 (Frankfurt-am-Main), 303–98; I. Bongars, *Gesta Dei per Francos* (Hanover, 1611), 30–81; J. P. Migne, *Patrologiae cursus completus. Series latina* (Paris, 1844), vol.CLV, 669–758.

[82] Guénée, 48–74.

[83] Guénée, 250–252: interestingly he omits Robert from his list despite his popularity.

[84] Iorga, 84; Runciman, *History*, vol.I, 330.

Chapter 2

Robert and the *Gesta Francorum*

Chapter One situated Robert's work as part of the wave of texts probably generated by Bohemond's trip to Europe in 1106 and drawing to greater or lesser degree on the eyewitness account given by the *Gesta Francorum*, an anonymous text probably written by a follower of Bohemond. This chapter analyses the relationship between the two texts and argues that Robert, far from being a plagiariser, uses the *GF* with considerable subtlety and invention as a springboard for his own picture of the Crusade.

i) The *Gesta Francorum*

The *GF* is an intriguing and almost certainly eyewitness text. It shares with Raymond of Aguilers the privilege of being written shortly after the events of the Crusade and of being a first-hand account.[1] It plunges without introduction into a short account of the preaching of the Crusade, and describes events up to the battle of Antioch in nine short books. Bohemond is centre stage throughout, his on occasion dubious activities whitewashed,[2] other princes denigrated or sidelined, and with the emphasis firmly on Antioch (where he played a leading role) rather than the ostensible goal of Jerusalem (which he did not help to take).[3] The tenth book, taking the story up to the conquest of Jerusalem, is much longer and does not give the same prominence to Bohemond as the earlier books.

Several features set it apart from other Latin chronicles.[4] Its Latin is plain, with few quotes from Scripture, and the style paratactic, but there is evidence of more sophistication than the text is sometimes given credit for – not least by those

---

[1] *Le 'liber' de Raymond d'Aguilers*, ed. J. H. and L. L. Hill (Paris, 1969); transl. J. H. and L. L. Hill, *Historia Francorum qui ceperunt Jerusalem* (Transactions of the American Philosophical Society, 1968). For a recent analysis of relationships between the *GF* and Raymond see J. France, 'The Anonymous *GF* and the *Historia Francorum qui ceperunt Iherusalem* of Raymond of Aguilers and the *Historia de Hierosolymitano Itinere* of Peter Tudebode: an analysis of the textual relationship between primary sources for the First Crusade', *The Crusades and their sources. Essays presented to Bernard Hamilton*, ed. J. France, W. G. Zajac (Aldershot, 1998), 39–69: he argues that Raymond drew on the *GF* as an *aide-mémoire* and that the *GF* is an original source.

[2] For example, his taking of the oath to the Emperor is ascribed to desperation rather than duplicity (*GF* 12).

[3] H. Oehler, 'Studien zu den *Gesta Francorum*', *MJB* 6 (1970), 58–97; K. B. Wolf, 'Crusade and Narrative: Bohemond and the *Gesta Francorum*', *JMH* 17 (1991), 207–16.

[4] C. Morris, 'The *Gesta Francorum* as Narrative History', *RMS* 19 (1993), 55–71; henceforth '*GF* as Narrative'.

(hardly disinterested) critics who used it as a source.[5] Several passages, particularly around events at Antioch, are very reminiscent of the vernacular *chanson de geste* tradition; this is not unusual for chronicles of the period but particularly apparent in the *GF*.[6] And there is no prologue, meaning that we know neither the identity of the author nor his reasons for writing.

The text is generally thought to have been written by a Southern Norman with clerical training in the army of Bohemond, suggested alike by the favourable treatment of Bohemond, the details given on his followers,[7] the vilification of Byzantium[8] and some shading of Southern Italian forms in the Latin.[9] The repeated use of the first person ('nos' and 'nostri') and the details given suggest very strongly that the author was an eyewitness to the Crusade.[10] We do not have an exact date for its production, but it cannot have been later than 1105 and may well have been produced within months of the end of the Crusade.[11]

ii) The use made of the *Gesta Francorum* by contemporaries

The *GF* was undoubtedly the most influential source for the events of the Crusade in the years which immediately followed it. The texts derived from it follow it in a variety of ways: word for word, following it closely, or drawing on some of its material.

The text which follows it most closely is Peter Tudebode's account. He was an eyewitness of the Crusade, and adds a small amount of unique information.[12] However, most of his text is taken from the *GF* almost verbatim, to the point where

---

[5] Oehler, 67–74.

[6] The French editor of the text, Bréhier, argued strongly that the *chanson de geste*-style passages were interpolations by a later author. H.-J. Witzel, 'Le problème de l'auteur des *Gesta Francorum et aliorum Hierosolymitanorum*', *MA* 61 (1955), 319–28 analysed the language in detail and argues that there are no visible differences in style. Morris, 61: 'in a real if limited sense the *GF* is a *chanson de geste*'. For another example see OV VI.112–16, and Chibnall's comments at xxiii. For more general discussion of links between the *chanson de geste* and history see R. Lejeune, *Les chansons de geste et l'histoire* (Liège, 1948).

[7] See for example the list at *GF*, 7–8 or those referred to at Dorylaeum at *GF*, 20.

[8] B. Skoulatos, 'L'auteur anonyme des *Gesta* et le monde byzantin', *B* 50 (1980), 504–32.

[9] See Oehler, 60, n.15.

[10] Morris, '*GF* as narrative', 67–8: '[the] fluctuating use expresses a powerful *wir-gefühl*' (68).

[11] Ekkehard of Aura famously saw a 'libellus' at Jerusalem in 1101 which told the story of the Crusade up to Jerusalem, *Ekkehardi Uraugiensis Abbatis Hierosolymita nach der Waitz'schen Recension*, ed. H. Hagenmeyer (Tübingen, 1877); Hagenmeyer identified this with the *GF* (135, n.13), but there is not definite proof. Opinions differ: amongst the more recent Morris ('*GF* as narrative', 66) sees it as virtually contemporary with the Crusade whilst Oehler, 81 sees it as written at the time of Bohemond's recruiting trip. Hill, ix dates it to no later than early 1101.

[12] For example his description of the procession round the walls of Jerusalem (PT 138) in which he claims to have participated.

the *Recueil* printed the *GF* as a later derivative of his work.[13] Hill and Hill have argued that he should be seen as an independent source, but it is hard to see his text as much more than a close copy of his source, with information added where he had it.[14] Tudebode makes no attempt to impose his own theological or historical framework and does not identify himself in a prologue; neither does he explicitly acknowledge the *GF* as his source.

The accounts by Baudry, Guibert and Robert all take the *GF* as their base text but edit it freely. Their works share a striking number of features. All three are written by Benedictine monks, two with some status in the Church, particularly Baudry who was to become Archbishop of Dol. Guibert and Robert wrote for patrons: Robert for the mysterious Abbot B. and Guibert for Lisiardus Bishop of Soissons.[15] All three were from Northern France, within the Capetian sphere of influence: Robert from Reims, Guibert from the Abbey of Nogent-sous-Coucy in the Ile de France and Baudry from Bourgueil.[16] All have prologues and clearly identify themselves as the author of the work. All add a considerable amount of additional detail to their source.[17] All set the story of the Crusade in a clear theological framework. And all rewrite the *GF* substantially, using rhetorical techniques and changing the vocabulary; all three comment on what they saw as the poor quality of the Latin and the need to improve it so as to give fitting expression to the events of the Crusade.[18] It is hard not to see these three works as forming part of a deliberate attempt to create an official version, historical and theological, of the events of the Crusade, driven perhaps by Cluny. I have commented above on the probable links with Bohemond's recruiting drive of 1106.

The attitude taken by the three towards their source is particularly interesting. It was unusual to mention a contemporary source, which did not confer the same *auctoritas* as a classical one or as eyewitness testimony.[19] All three authors here go out of their way to mention their source and to criticise its poor style: other criticisms such as its anonymity or incompleteness are not common to all. Whilst this could simply reflect a shared Benedictine mindset and genuine discontent with the quality of their source, it is tempting to speculate that some kind of shared policy line lies behind their comments. The implication of their comments is that the author was not clever enough to understand the true story of the Crusade; by inference their accounts give a fuller and more accurate picture. In particular they redress the balance of the Crusade from Antioch to Jerusalem; Bohemond remains the hero but his actions are set within a clear crusading ideology; and the

---

[13] *RHC Occ.* III, 121–63.

[14] Hill and Hill, Introduction to translation, 10–12

[15] *Sermo Apologeticus*; GN 77–8.

[16] Riley-Smith, *Idea*, 136, points out that Nogent-sous-Coucy was a foundation of St-Rémi. My arguments here draw heavily on his.

[17] France, 'Use of anonymous *GF*' 38–9, 'the earlier [derivatives of the *GF*] were written in an age when there were survivors of the First Crusade, and the additional information they contain may be more credible than we have supposed'.

[18] GN 79, BB 10

[19] Guénée, 116.

Byzantines are blackened. All this is already in the *GF*; arguably, however, the three authors highlight particular themes to emphasise the legitimacy of the proposed Crusade of 1107.

The *GF* was used as a source, although with much more freedom, by another cleric: Gilo of Paris. Gilo was another Benedictine monk, later to achieve high office as the Cardinal-Bishop of Tusculum. At the time he wrote he seems to have been a cleric in Paris, and his work probably dates from the first decade of the twelfth century.[20] Like his prose-writing contemporaries, he clearly identifies himself as the author.[21] His text shows many parallels with that of the *GF*, and Books VIII and IX on events between Antioch and Jerusalem follow its narrative closely. His work differs from the other followers of Robert in several ways. Firstly, it is in verse rather than prose. Secondly, it omits large swathes of the action, starting at Nicaea, passing over in a sentence the events between victory at Dorylaeum and arrival at Antioch, closing its account with the election of Godfrey and not going on to describe the battle of Ascalon. A later continuator, the Charleville poet, filled in many of these perceived gaps. Thirdly, there is no mention of the *GF* as source.

Other writers also used the *GF* as a source although their work is independent of it. It is likely that the Occitan chronicler Raymond of Aguilers, chaplain to Raymond IV of Toulouse, drew on the *GF* for some details although he does not acknowledge it.[22] Fulcher of Chartres draws on it.[23] There are also resemblances between it and the early vernacular poetic accounts of the Crusade in both Northern and Southern France, in the forms respectively of the *Chanson d'Antioche* and the Occitan *Canso d'Antioca*: however, since both texts survive only in much later reworkings it is hard to discern quite which texts might have influenced which. Chapter Three discusses this issue.

Robert's use of the *GF* therefore needs to be set firmly in this context. Like many of his contemporaries he drew on the *GF*; like Baudry and Guibert he saw the text as defective and incomplete and set out to improve it.

iii) Robert's use of the *GF*

Robert's text is based on the structure and events of the *GF*. By his own account he made two major changes to the anonymous text he was shown: he added a

---

[20] Introduction, xxiv.

[21] IX, 374–5.

[22] France, 'Analysis of textual relationship', 45–51.

[23] *Fulcheri Carnotensis Historia Hierosolymitana (1095–1127)*, ed. H. Hagenmeyer (Heidelberg, 1913); transl. H. S. Fink and Sister F. R. Ryan, *Fulcher of Chartres: a history of the expedition to Jerusalem* (Knoxville, 1969). V. Epp, *Fulcher von Chartres: Studien zur Geschichtsschreibung des ersten Kreuzuges*, Studia Humaniora 15 (Düsseldorf, 1990), 145–6, argues that Fulcher based his original text on them then reread them as part of his re-editing of the text.

beginning by describing the Council of Clermont; and he improved the style.[24] These comments should be set against the wider perspective discussed above.

In fact his changes are much more extensive. Firstly, he changes the structure, adding a beginning, streamlining and editing. Secondly, he adds much material, not only by embroidering individual episodes but by bringing in new episodes and characters; at the same time he drops some of the details given by the *GF*, notably on the Southern Normans and the exploits of Baldwin and Tancred in Edessa. Thirdly, he makes changes to the attitudes and ethos of the text in three ways. He makes some changes to the heroes and villains of his story, moving away from the prominence given to Bohemond and the Normans given by the *GF*, laying stress instead on the heroism of others and if anything strengthening the criticism of Alexius. He sets the tale of the Crusade in a clear theological framework. He embellishes the style with consistent rhetorical additions and elaboration. Finally, on a few occasions he also seems to misread his source (or sources) and introduces some errors.

Structural changes

Robert retains the same storyline as his source and the same general balance of material: events at Antioch form the centrepiece to both texts. Indeed it is difficult to see how he could have done otherwise with such a clear sequence of events.

However, he takes no account of the book divisions in the *GF*. His Book III, for example, contains the end of *GF* II and all of *GF* III and IV, with the start of *GF* V in the middle of his last chapter. Book X of the *GF* starts in the middle of Robert's Book VII and covers the remainder of the text.

His text is much longer than its source. The *GF* has approximately 20,000 words. Robert's count is a rough 35,000 or so.

Robert also changes the centre of gravity of the text. The *GF* starts with a sketchy account of the preaching of the Crusade and ends with a short account of the taking of Jerusalem and the battle of Ascalon. The main emphasis lies very heavily on events at Antioch, which occupy 43 of the 97 pages of the text. The conquest of Jerusalem and the battle of Ascalon come as little more than an afterthought, occupying some ten pages. This is hardly surprising in a text with Bohemond centre stage: Bohemond took a leading role throughout events at the city and left the Crusade to become its ruler, an action which required some justifying. Robert keeps the central emphasis on events at Antioch: indeed it would have been hard not to given the structure of his source. If anything, Antioch is more central to his text, occupying the middle three books and the majority of the seventh.

However, he adds considerably more weight to the beginning and the end of his story. The Council of Clermont is described in detail at the start of Book I. Book IX is entirely devoted to Jerusalem, which becomes the climax of the whole history. Robert further emphasises its importance by casting events there as a kind of replay of the battle of Antioch which so strongly dominated his source. He

---

[24] *Sermo Apologeticus.*

builds up the character of Clemens as a second Kerbogha, lengthening the speech given him by the *GF* into a major set piece which parallels the speech of Urban at the start of the Crusade; his description of the battle of Ascalon deliberately echoes that of the battle of Antioch;[25] and he underlines the theological importance of the victory by following it with a description of the celebrations taken from Isaiah. He foreshadows these events at V.2, picking up the *GF*'s passing reference to envoys from the Emir of Cairo[26] and turning it into a full-scale description of an embassy reminiscent of the embassy to Kerbogha. In sum Robert was clear that Jerusalem was the goal of the Crusade, and carefully shifts the balance of the text to underline this.

Additions and omissions

Robert was not an eyewitness to most of what he recounts. But he adds significant extra material to the base text of the *GF* throughout:

Book I:
–   the Council of Clermont and role of Adhemar (I.1–4)
–   praise of Godfrey and criticism of Alexius (I.5, 6)
–   a reference to scouts and a fight with the Turks (I.7)
–   the heroism of Walter Sans Aveir (I.11)

Book II:
–   emphasis on the Crusaders' journey via Rome (II.2)
–   extra details (II.4)
–   the meeting of Godfrey and Hugh in Constantinople (II.7)
–   different terms of peace with the Emperor (II.10)
–   further criticism of Alexius (II.14)
–   a florid passage on the delight of the Christians at Bohemond's arrival in Constantinople and his speech (II.16)
–   Bohemond's leading role and the terms of the oaths taken to the Emperor (II.17–19)
–   the history of Constantinople (II.20)

Book III:
–   III.2–6: additional material on Nicaea
–   III.8–15: additional material on Dorylaeum including an exegesis of the victory at Dorylaeum (III.15)

Book IV:
–   extensive additional material on early events at Antioch (IV.1–7)
–   material on the skirmishes at Antioch (IV.14–16)
–   Godfrey's heroism and bisection of the Turk at Antioch (IV.20)
–   details on the death of Cassianus' son and the taking of prisoners (IV.21)

---

[25] For example the description of columns marching out is enumerated in the same way as for the battle of Antioch, whereas the *GF*'s description (95) is more vague.
[26] *GF* 37, 42.

Book V:
- the embassy from Babylon (V.1–2)
- the castle being given to Raymond IV and plundering (V.3)
- the truce and the death of Walo on the last day; lamentation of Walo's wife (V.5–7)
- lengthy dialogue of Bohemond and Pirrus (V.8–9)
- Fulcher as the first soldier into Antioch (V.12)
- Pirrus losing two brothers rather than one (V.13)
- a comet (V.14)

Book VI:
- an extra attack at Antioch in which Bohemond is wounded and a soldier commits spectacular suicide (VI.4–6)
- provocation by theTurks and the beheading of Roger of Barneville (VI.7–8)

Book VII:
- extra speeches for Kerbogha and Herluin (VII.6) and comments on Kerbogha's stupidity (VII.7)
- religious observances commanded by Adhemar before the battle of Antioch (VII.8)
- the Occitan apostate (VII.9)
- Adhemar's sermon (VII.10)
- the heroism of Hugh and Godfrey in battle (VII.11)
- Odo of Beaugency (VII.12)
- death of Gerard of Melun (VII.15)
- Adhemar's promise (VII.16)
- death of Hugh on mission to Constantinople (VII.20)

Book VIII:
- additional details on the fight at Ma'arrat-an-Nu'man and particularly the heroism of Golfier of Las Tours (VIII.4–6)
- the deaths of Pons Balazun and Warren of Petra Mora (VIII.18)
- description of Caesarea (VIII.20)

Book IX:
- reference to Wicher (IX.7–8) and Godfrey (IX.8)
- praise of Godfrey (IX.10)
- description of Ascalon (IX.14)
- first speech by Clemens (IX.18)
- the column of peasants (IX.23)
- musical celebration of the battle (IX.24)
- encomium of Jerusalem (IX.25–6)

Robert also omits some details given by the *GF*. To allow him to concentrate on the main narrative he abridges the *GF*'s detailed account of the activities of Baldwin and Tancred at Tarsus[27] and Tancred's refusal to take the oath to the

---

[27] III.20–21; *GF* 24–5.

Emperor;[28] at III.26 he drops the description of the Occitan knights who undertook Raymond IV's expedition.[29] On occasion he drops some of the circumstantial detail given by the *GF*: thus at I.8 in describing the thirst experienced by the Christians he drops the *GF*'s references to sewers and to the thirst lasting for eight days.[30] This might represent use of a different text of the *GF*, or more probably Robert's own taste. He also and strikingly drops much of the detail on the Southern Italian Normans given in the *GF*: for example, he omits the list of participants who set out on Crusade and the deaths of Godfrey of Montescaglioso and William Fitzmarquis.[31]

Heroes and villains

The *GF* has a simple pattern of characterisation. Bohemond and the Southern Italian Normans are centre stage until the battle of Antioch. With Bohemond's occupation of the city the focus shifts to Raymond IV. The Saracens are villains, the Byzantines ignoble cowards. Robert's cast of heroes and villains is slightly more complex.

Robert gives Hugh of Vermandois, brother of the King of France, considerably more prominence on the Crusade than seems to have been the case in real life, and inserts additional material on Crusaders from the Capetian kingdom.[32] Hugh played a secondary role on the First Crusade, returning to the Holy Land for the Crusade of 1101 where he died.[33] Robert goes out of his way to praise Hugh. He specifies that he was the standard-bearer of the whole Crusade, something not mentioned in other accounts.[34] When William of Melun is disgraced for fleeing from Antioch he is pardoned because Hugh is his relative.[35] Hugh is portrayed as a close friend of Godfrey and on several occasions as his companion in battle, sharing thereby in Godfrey's reflected glory.[36] He is first into battle at Antioch.[37] Given Robert's connection with Reims, the city where the Kings of France were crowned, it is not surprising that he should have chosen to glorify the King's brother in this way. What is surprising is the glaring error of placing Hugh's death on his mission to the Emperor after the taking of Antioch rather than on the crusade of 1101. Bull suggests this may be a deliberate lie to protect Hugh's posthumous reputation: if so it was a blatant one for an audience who might have been expected to know better.[38]

---

[28] *GF* 13.
[29] *GF* 26.
[30] *GF* 3–4.
[31] *GF* 7–8; 21
[32] Bull 'Capetian Monarchy', 40–42.
[33] Runciman, *History*, vol.II, 29.
[34] II.3.
[35] IV.12.
[36] II.7, III.11, VII.11.
[37] VII.11.
[38] Bull, 'Capetian Monarchy', 42.

More generally Robert shows an interest in the doings of Crusaders from the Ile de France. He describes in some detail the death of Walo II of Chaumont-en-Vexin and the mourning of his wife Humberge of Le Puiset:[39] the episode is alluded to in other accounts but considerably developed by Robert. Walo was the King's constable and his wife was from a prominent Ile de France family. Here again we see echoes of Robert's interest in the French court. He also inserts additional material on Odo of Beaugency and Gerard of Melun at Antioch, and refers to a group of French nobles (Clarenbald of Vendeuil, Pagan of Beauvais, Everard of Le Puiset and Thomas of Marle);[40] all were from the Ile de France.

Robert is more favourable towards Stephen of Blois than the *GF*. The *GF* is harsh towards his perceived cowardice at Antioch, vilifying his conduct and describing his illness as feigned.[41] Robert removes the criticism, softening it to a comment that Stephen began well and ended badly; and he describes the illness as genuine.[42] To some extent this may reflect the fact that by the time Robert wrote Stephen had died on the Crusade of 1101 and redeemed his name. It also reflects Robert's desire to emphasise the role played by those from the area of the Ile de France. Wolf suggests that Stephen was deliberately blackened as a foil to Bohemond's heroism;[43] Robert who, as described below, was ambivalent about Bohemond would therefore be redressing the balance.

On occasion Robert subtly praises the French. Particularly striking is the extraordinary comment on Bohemond at VIII.15, ascribing his best features to French ancestry. He also omits material less than complimentary to the French. At I.7 the *GF*'s reference to French arrogance is quietly removed.[44] His failure to name the escapees from Antioch enumerated by the *GF*, some of whom were French, may be for the same reason.[45]

Robert also places emphasis on the role of Godfrey. He devotes two sections to praising him at the beginning of the Crusade and again on his election as Advocate.[46] He stresses Godfrey's heroism in battle on a number of occasions.[47] In particular he describes in some detail Godfrey's bisection of a Turk on the bridge at Antioch: this does not appear in the *GF*.[48] Godfrey became increasingly mythologised as the hero of the Crusade, eclipsing Bohemond and ultimately becoming the nucleus of the whole epic cycle of the Crusade as the Chevalier au Cygne. Robert's portrayal represents an early stage in that sanctification.[49]

---

[39] V.6–7; see note in translation.

[40] Odo at VII.12; Gerard and the nobles at VII.15.

[41] *GF* 63.

[42] II.1, VI.15.

[43] Wolf, 214. Constance's first and divorced husband was Stephen's brother Hugh of Champagne.

[44] *GF* 3.

[45] The so-called *funambuli*: named by *GF* 56 as William and Aubrey of Grandmesnil near Lisieux, Guy Trousseau of Montlhéry and Lambert the Poor from near Liège.

[46] I.5, IX.10.

[47] E.g. III.11, VII.11.

[48] IV.20. See also BB 50, Gilo V.353–69, AA 385, RC 646.

[49] In commenting on this manuscript Professor Bernard Hamilton pointed out that Robert consistently refers to Robert, Duke of Normandy, as Count Robert: a further attempt

The other leaders of the Crusade receive less attention and their roles do not differ significantly from those in the *GF*. However they do on occasion act as a counterweight to Bohemond. Robert of Normandy is explicitly described as helping Bohemond to rally the troops at Dorylaeum.[50] Raymond IV's insistence on observing the terms of the oath to Alexius is implicitly contrasted with Bohemond's machinations.[51]

Robert gives a few additional details on the exploits of Occitan crusaders. In the earlier part of the text he omits details given by the *GF*: thus he does not give the names of the knights sent by Raymond IV on an abortive mission to Antioch.[52] However, he adds two passages to events after Antioch. The heroism of Golfier of Las Tours at the taking of Ma'arrat-an-Nu'man is heavily emphasised with much additional detail; and Raymond Pilet is singled out for praise.[53]

Robert's portrayal of the Saracens is not significantly different from the *GF*. Both texts place Kerbogha centre stage as the villain of the piece, although Robert also emphasises the role of the Emir of Babylon. Both describe the Saracens as variously innumerable, incomprehensible and of diverse races; however Robert adds some lurid rhetoric and does not reflect the *GF*'s grudging admiration.[54]

Similarly whilst the *GF* has little good to say about the Byzantines, Robert goes out of his way to vilify them. The Emperor is not only untrustworthy: he is stupid and cowardly.[55] Taticius is portrayed not only as unreliable: he is effeminate and lightweight.[56] The worst possible construction is put on every move of the Byzantines.[57] This reflects both the need for good villains in a story and the general Western perception of the Byzantine role on the crusade as unreliable at best and treacherous at worst.[58] It is likely also to reflect Bohemond's desire to seek help from the West against Byzantine opposition to his retention of Antioch; this point is discussed further in the Appendix.

---

to heighten Godfrey's prestige by badging him as the only Duke? See *Epp*, 265, for a similar procedure in FC.

[50] III.10.

[51] VIII.8.

[52] III.26; *GF* 26.

[53] VIII.4–6; IX.4.

[54] *GF* 21: 'eum [Christ] in caelo et in terra regnantem recta mente et fide credidissent, ipsis potentiores uel fortiores uel bellorum ingeniosissimos nullus inuenire potuisset' ('if only they had … believed … that he reigns in Heaven and earth, you could not find stronger or braver or more skilful soldiers'; Hill's translation). Robert's Saracens are cunning and cowardly (III.18); barely human, they jabber and grind their teeth (IV.21).

[55] See e.g. II.6, 8.

[56] *GF* 34–5; IV.13.

[57] At II.15, for example, the Emperor's friendly reception of Bohemond is ascribed to the most dastardly cunning and treachery.

[58] See e.g. Lilie, 60: 'the chroniclers …. tried to cover over the dubious rejection by the Crusaders of the Byzantine claims resulting from the feudal agreements by a systematic defamation of the Greek Empire'.

Robert does not share the *GF*'s interest in the Southern Italian Normans.[59] Bohemond is the central figure of the *GF*: the author is likely to have been in his army. As such Bohemond is repeatedly praised and placed at the centre of the action; the text centres around events at Antioch, implicitly justifying Bohemond's possession of it; other characters are played down or blackened in contrast, notably Stephen of Blois;[60] and whilst the author does recount some of Bohemond's more dubious actions, these are either justified or referred to in passing.[61]

Robert, writing some years later and with different aims, gives a more nuanced portrayal of Bohemond. He is described on several occasions as shrewd, intelligent and perceptive. There is a particular cluster of such references where Bohemond rouses the fervour of his men to go on Crusade. Robert specifies that Bohemond had crosses prepared before his speech, with the clear implication that he planned an outstanding piece of stage management. None of this is in the *GF*, which depicts a Bohemond wholly 'Sancto commotus Spiritu'.[62] Robert also comments on Bohemond's ability to make speeches:[63] historiographic practice required all good generals to have this ability: but Robert stresses the use Bohemond made of it to convince others: he is cast firmly as leader and inspirer. He is also cast as the representative of the ideology of the Crusade in three major speeches. At II.16 on arrival at Constantinople he sets out the justification of holy war and the support of God for the Crusaders. At IV.10 he bolsters morale by reinforcing the message of divine support. At V.8–9 his conversations with Pirrus stress the power given by God, embodied in the help given by the saints. Together these speeches set out much of the theological basis for the Crusade, with which Bohemond is firmly identified. This sits well with the context of Bohemond preaching a further crusade in 1106.

The Bohemond he portrays also engages, however, in some distinctly unheroic activities. On more than one occasion he bravely leads from the rear. Sometimes there is a very good excuse, such as the wound in the fighting outside Antioch which leads him to retreat and is followed immediately – and perhaps not coincidentally – by an account of the heroic suicide of a soldier who did not retreat.[64] On other occasions there seems to be no reason, most notably where he inexplicably hangs back at the taking of Antioch (this is in the *GF* but exaggerated by Robert).[65] All these elements come together in the lengthy episode of what one is tempted to describe as Bohemond's courtship of Pirrus:[66] Robert portrays Bohemond's shrewdness in finding and cultivating Pirrus, his eloquence and mastery of the situation in convincing him, and his inexplicable failure to appear at

---

[59] See above for material omitted.

[60] *GF* 63.

[61] For example, his taking of the oath to Alexius (*GF* 11–12) and his betrayal of the Saracens at Ma'arrat-an-Nu'man (*GF* 79–80).

[62] *GF* 7; II.3–5.

[63] E.g. II.16, IV.10.

[64] VI.5–6.

[65] *GF* 46; V.12.

[66] V.8–14.

the crucial moment. The whole passage is shot through with the fascination Bohemond clearly exercised on Pirrus, sufficient to make him sacrifice his city and risk his family. Bohemond's final appearance in Robert is at VIII.15, where he is described in a throwaway line as having excellent principles from a French father spoilt by the qualities inherited from his Italian mother, summing up admirably the complex response Bohemond seems to have inspired in his contemporaries. The ambiguity is already in the *GF*. But Robert lays far more emphasis on it. His Bohemond is undoubtedly a leader, sometimes a hero, shrewd but guilty of repeated dubious conduct. Above all he is charismatic: he exercised a fascination for contemporaries,[67] and Robert skilfully captures this in the relationship between him and Pirrus.

The theological landscape

The landscape of the *GF* is a largely secular one. The author is likely to have had clerical training, and his language carried biblical echoes.[68] However, there is little emphasis on the theology of the Crusade or the role of the Church. Robert creates a very different landscape, where the role of the Church is central, events are constantly related back to the Bible and Church history, and the religious identity of the Crusaders is underlined.[69]

The *GF* says little about Pope Urban's preaching of the Crusade, laying more emphasis on the role of Peter the Hermit.[70] Robert by contrast puts the Council of Clermont at the beginning of his account and is clear that it is the root or 'caput', of the Crusade: he makes this point clear in his prologue, stressing not only that he was commissioned to add details of the Council but that he was himself an eyewitness. He correspondingly criticises the role played by Peter the Hermit at the start of the Crusade: whereas the *GF* is neutral, Robert is at some pains to emphasise the sufferings and failure of Peter's Crusade as an implicit contrast to the success of the Church's own endeavour.[71] In the same vein Robert builds up considerably the role of Adhemar, Urban's legate. Adhemar is mentioned several times but given little prominence by the *GF*.[72] In contrast Robert places him firmly centre stage.[73] In sum Robert alters his source to give much greater prominence to and justification of the role played by the Papacy in launching the Crusade.

Robert constantly relates events back to the Bible in a way which is little emphasised in the *GF*. The *GF* ends the majority of its books with short doxologies and quotes the Creed.[74] Robert creates a much stronger Christian ethos.[75] Similarly

---

[67] See the lengthy description in Anna Comnena, 422 (*The Alexiad of Anna Comnena*, transl. E. R. A. Sewter (Harmondsworth, 1969); henceforth AC). Anna was in her early teens when she saw Bohemond, and was clearly both fascinated and repelled.

[68] Hill, Introduction, xiv–v.

[69] Discussed in detail in Chapter Four.

[70] *GF* 1–5.

[71] I.6–12.

[72] *GF* 5, 15–16, 18–20, 32, 46, 58, 68, 74.

[73] See discussion in Chapter Four.

[74] *GF* 21. The only books which do not conclude with doxologies are III and VIII.

Robert sets his story in a clear framework of Christian geography. The *GF* gives a detailed description of Antioch.[76] After the end of the main text comes a 'descriptio sanctorum locorum Hierusalem' or Itinerary, a rather baldly written tourist guide which is found in all complete manuscripts.[77] Robert retains the description of Antioch largely as written. He drops the Itinerary, choosing instead to close his text with two chapters relating the terrestrial and celestial history of Jerusalem: he also gives descriptions of Constantinople, Caesarea, Ramla and Ascalon.[78]

The *GF* generally refers to the Crusaders as 'nostri', and more specifically as soldiers: 'Christi militiam', 'fortissimi milites Christi', 'milites'.[79] Even though the Crusaders were described as pilgrims, the *GF* is clear that they were soldiers first and foremost. Robert emphasises (not always convincingly) the Crusaders' status as pilgrims: they are shown piously visiting Rome, compared to Charlemagne on his own pilgrimage to Jerusalem[80] and worshipping in the Holy Sepulchre as the climax of the Crusade.[81]

Adding artistic verisimilitude to an otherwise bald and unconvincing narrative

Robert rewrote and reshaped the text of the *GF* throughout. His stylistic changes have two main aims: to elaborate existing material with additional detail, heightening the intensity of the text by rhetoric and hyperbole; and improving the flow of the story by removing some extraneous detail and reordering events.

He adds detail constantly throughout the text, picking up and expanding material from the *GF*. For example, the *GF* describes how after the taking of Antioch the leaders held counsel, decided to wait until the rainy season to march on, split up and had arrangements for the maintenance of the poor of the army announced. Robert adds corroborative detail: reported speech, a thumbnail description of the heat and aridity, and an account not only of the finding of a herald but his need to stand on a high place to announce the decision.[82]

He also constantly elaborates language and rhetoric to heighten the tone and effect of the text. For example the speech of Clemens originates in the *GF*.[83] The themes there are the shame of being defeated by such a wretched army as the Christian pilgrims; their ingratitude; the cowardice of the Egyptian soldiers; the oath never to fight again; the reversal of the situation; and the scorn he will incur. All these themes recur in Robert and in the same order, but all are developed at more length and in lurid detail. Thus the concept of the ungrateful pilgrims is developed into deliberate spying and a resolve to win Saracen riches at all costs,

---

[75] See Chapter Four for detailed discussion.
[76] *GF* 76–7. Bréhier regarded this as an interpolation; Hill keeps it in the main text.
[77] Introduction, xxxviii–xl.
[78] IX.25–6; II.20, VIII.20, VIII.21, IX.14.
[79] *GF* 16, 18, 21.
[80] II.2, I.5.
[81] IX.9.
[82] *GF* 72; VII.21.
[83] *GF* 96–7, IX.21.

and the contrast of Clemens being attacked by those he had come to attack becomes a (doubtless deliberately) ludicrous complaint about the money he spent on siege engines to no purpose. Robert strengthens the rhetoric of the speech, mercilessly emphasising the contrasts between past and present and between Saracen and Christian, and making abundant use of hyperbole. He also brings a new theme, familiar from the *chansons de geste*: the rejection by the Saracens of the deity who has failed to deliver victory.

To the same end Robert expands considerably the number of speeches in the text, and embroiders the content of those already existing. The *GF* has some fourteen speeches or quasi-speeches: the highly abbreviated speech of Pope Urban,[84] the laments of Soliman and Clemens and Kerbogha's letter to the Caliph,[85] the offer of Taticius,[86] the speech of Stephen Valentine about his vision,[87] Stephen's report to the Emperor and Guy's lament for Bohemond,[88] the exchange of speeches between Sensadolus and Kerbogha and between the Christians and Kerbogha[89] and short speeches by Bohemond at Dorylaeum and Antioch.[90] Robert retains and expands most of these, and also adds a number of speeches: Bohemond is given speeches at the beginning of the Crusade and on his arrival at Constantinople,[91] although Robert does not retain the short speech at Dorylaeum, and a lengthy exchange with Pirrus;[92] an exchange of speeches between the Emir of Babylon and the Christian leaders;[93] the lament of Walo's wife Humberge;[94] Stephen Valentine's speech is put into narrative but a speech added for Peter Bartholomew;[95] there are additional speeches in the encounter between Kerbogha and the Christian envoys;[96] Adhemar gives a sermon before the battle of Antioch and a speech afterwards.[97] With the possible exception of Humberge's lament, all these additions mark and serve to emphasise key points in Robert's story.

His other main stylistic change is to reorder material to improve the flow of the narrative. Book I of the *GF*, for example, has a rather disorganised account of the Crusaders setting out: it refers to Raymond IV as leading one army and Bohemond, the Count of Flanders and Robert of Normandy and Hugh as leading another, describes the arrival of Hugh and Godfrey at Constantinople, then doubles back to describe (a second time, in much more detail) Bohemond's departure. Robert

---

[84] *GF* 1–2.
[85] *GF* 22, 96–7, 52–3.
[86] *GF* 34–5.
[87] *GF* 57–8.
[88] *GF* 63–5.
[89] *GF* 66–7.
[90] *GF* 18–19, 35.
[91] II.4, II.16.
[92] V.8–9.
[93] V.1–2.
[94] V.7.
[95] VII.1–2.
[96] VII.5–7.
[97] VII.10, 16.

considerably simplifies the line:[98] he describes the setting out of the northern then the southern armies, their arrival in Italy, Bohemond's interest and eventual departure, then the first arrivals at Constantinople. Robert puts the account of the finding of the Holy Lance immediately after the vision of Peter Bartholomew rather than separating the two events as in the *GF*.[99] He looks for connections and motivations which are absent in the *GF*: for example he attributes the raid on Tripoli to the boredom occasioned by the siege of Arqah, a motive absent in the *GF*.[100]

Mistakes in Robert's use of the GF

On occasion Robert seems to mistranslate his source. For example the *GF*'s description of the ferocious Agulani runs: '...neque lanceas neque sagittas neque ulla arma timebant, quia omnes erant undique cooperti ferro et equi eorum, ipsique nolebant in bellum ferre arma nisi solummodo gladios'.[101]

In Robert this becomes: '...nulla arma nisi solummodo enses gerebant: qui omnes undique ferro cooperti, nulla arma adversantia timebant. Equi eorum vexilla et lanceas ferre aspernabantur, et in eos qui ferebant, nimia ira succendebantur'.[102]

Duparc-Quioc picks up a further error: the Greek Emperor's order to retreat to Bulgaria and follow a scorched-earth policy becomes an incomprehensible order to devastate Bulgaria.[103] Riley-Smith suggests that a misreading may also lie behind the puzzling savagery of Raymond IV's forcible conversion of the inhabitants at Albara: Robert may have confused surrender ('reddiderant') with conversion ('crediderant'), a misreading which occurs in some manuscripts of Raymond of Aguilers.[104]

In a further two places Robert seems to have misread his source. At II.15 he seems to misinterpret the text of the *GF* to imply that Tancred's stomach was too delicate to cope with the local delicacies, something which defies the imagination.[105] At VI.9 he misreads (deliberately?) the *GF*'s reference to Corrosana as the biblical city Chorazin.[106]

---

[98] II.1–8.

[99] *GF* 59–60, 65; VII.23.

[100] *GF* 83; VIII.12.

[101] 'they fear neither spears nor arrows nor any other weapon, for they and their horses are covered all over with plates of iron. They will not use any weapons except swords when they are fighting' (Hill's translation); *GF* 49.

[102] '... who carried no arms, not even swords: completely covered with iron, they had no fear of enemy arms. Their horses flatly refused to carry standards and lances, and went berserk at those who did', VI.7. See R. Bossuat, 'Sur un fragment de la *Chanson d'Antioche*', *NM* 32 (1931), 110–18, 116, n.1.

[103] *Etude*, 108; *GF* 65, RM VI.16.

[104] *Idea*, 110.

[105] RM II.15, *GF* 11. See note to translation.

[106] RM VI.9, *GF* 50. But see R. K. Emmerson, *Antichrist in the Middle Ages: a study of Medieval Apocalypticism, Art and Literature* (Manchester, 1981), 80–81 for reference to Chorazin as one of the birthplaces of the Antichrist, and note to translation.

It is possible that Robert was simply careless. Equally he may have been using a defective copy or a variant version of the *GF*.

iv) Conclusion

The *GF* is compelling precisely because of its simplicity and closeness to the events it portrays.[107] Robert, working a few years later at second hand, works from a number of perspectives. As historian he adds further material, shaping and editing extensively. As commissioned writer he accentuates some aspects of the text and minimises others. As theologian he constructs a clear religious framework for the events of the Crusade. And as storyteller he cuts and shapes his material to accentuate the light and shade of his story, to improve its flow and to heighten its effect. His work takes the *GF* as its starting point but develops it into something new and different: a multi-layered variation of an existing theme.

---

[107] Hill, Introduction, xvii, comments on the similarity in tone between it and the letters her brother sent home from the Second World War.

Chapter 3

Robert's relationship with other sources and value as a historical source

This chapter analyses the extent to which Robert brings additional value as a historical source for the Crusade. It discusses his relationship with other sources, Latin and vernacular, and the extent to which he might have drawn on them. It concludes that he makes extensive use of another source also used by Gilo and no longer extant. Although he has some links with the vernacular tradition, these are probably stylistic and via the *GF* rather than direct. It discusses Robert's value as a source in his own right and offers some suggestions as to where he might have derived his additional material. It concludes that whilst Robert was not an eyewitness to the Crusade other than the Council of Clermont, his testimony – like that of most chroniclers of the Crusade – does have some independent value.

i) The other Latin sources based on the *GF*

Inevitably there are similarities between texts with a common source written in the same area at the same time. There is little evidence that Robert drew on the work of Tudebode, of Guibert or of Baudry. There are no clear parallels with Tudebode, and the small amount of unique information he adds, such as the death of Hugh of Lusignan's steward,[1] does not leave an imprint on Robert. Similarly there is no sign of Robert having been influenced by the considerable extra material added by Guibert on Church history or on events after the Crusade: details Robert gives are absent in Guibert, such as the attack on the tents at Dorylaeum[2] and vice versa.[3] There are slightly more similarities with the text of Baudry: the accounts of the Emperor's oath are close and in both Pirrus promises to send his son as hostage.[4] In short there is no evidence that Robert drew heavily on any of these accounts: there is the odd shared detail which may indicate that both used or talked to the same

---

[1] PT 135.

[2] III.9; compare GN III.

[3] For example, Guibert gives an anecdote about Hugh and a camel's foot (GN 236–7); despite Robert's interest in Hugh he does not have the same story.

[4] BB 25, 55. It is interesting that one manuscript of Baudry, the late twelfth-century G, adds a few episodes which are found in Robert: Wicher and the lion (50, n.15 and 92), a reference to an apostate (76, n.13) and material on Tancred and Eustace at Nablus (102, n.8). Given the date of the manuscript these are more likely to come from knowledge of Robert's work or a derivative than to reveal any closer relationship between the works of Baudry and Robert.

source and an occasional verbal reminiscence. But this probably shows simply that there are a limited number of ways to describe the same event.

ii) Parallels with Gilo's *Historia Vie Hierosolimitanae*

By contrast Robert's text shows extensive parallels with Gilo's work. Whilst his overall structure and approach is taken from the *GF*, substantial passages – particularly at Nicaea, Dorylaeum, the earlier events at Antioch and some of the battle of Antioch – are close to Gilo's work. Several episodes are found only in these two texts in detail. There are numerous details in common and shared wording, with one identical hexameter. Nearly all the hexameters in Robert coincide with these parallels.

Parallels with Gilo

Gilo's text begins with events at Nicaea. In Robert's account of Nicaea the order of events is initially the same as in Gilo, swapping to the *GF* halfway through.[5] The initial fighting round Nicaea (III.2–3) is close to Gilo's account, although the embassy to the Emperor is intercalated from *GF* 16–17. The arrival of the ships and the fall of the city (III.4–5) is taken from *GF*. The reference to the Council of Nicaea (III.6) is similar to Gilo (IV.14–19). Some elements of Robert's description are found in neither source: the role played by Raymond IV and Adhemar (III.3), and the catapulting of severed heads into the city (III.4; something of a favourite theme with Robert as will become apparent). The vividness of the description is Robert's own.

Immediately after Nicaea the description of Dorylaeum also shows strong similarities of order and emphasis with Gilo's text.[6] The story is recognisably that of the *GF* but its narrative is much closer to Gilo: the timing of the battle, the leading role of Hugh, the attack on the camp, the rallying by Robert of Normandy and the counter-attack by the Occitan forces are all in Gilo. Some of the details given by Gilo are absent: a cutting-out expedition by one thousand Turks in the mountains;[7] Godfrey's heroism;[8] a surprise attack by the Christians from the mountains;[9] and details of victory.[10] Again the vivid description and the exegesis is Robert's own. Gilo gives no details of events between the battle and arrival at Antioch, and for these Robert's account is close to the *GF*.

On arrival at Antioch Robert initially combines the *GF* with events in Gilo in a rather confused account of skirmish and plunder. IV.1–8 are a patchwork of resemblances with Gilo and borrowings from the *GF* with some unique material. The arrival at Antioch (IV.1) moves from Gilo V.1–12 to *GF* 28–9, back to Gilo

---

[5] RM III.2–6; Gilo IV 20–145.
[6] RM III.8–15; Gilo IV.151–344.
[7] Gilo IV.241–53.
[8] Gilo IV. 260–5.
[9] Gilo IV.276–321.
[10] Gilo IV.323–30.

V.14–31 then back again to *GF* 29–30, with a description of foraging brought
forward from Gilo V.118–21. IV.2–3, the attack on Harim, is recounted in Gilo
V.34–62: however the naming of the castle and the reference to beheading come
from *GF* 29. Christmas in IV.4 is expanded from *GF* 30; the details about winter
weather in IV.5 are also in Gilo V.87–90. The description of the foraging party in
IV.6 starts in parallel to Gilo V.104–112 but moves to *GF* 31; the description of
victory and plunder in IV.7 and 8 appears to be Robert's own. He then resumes
borrowing from *GF* 32 at IV.9. It seems clear that Robert is interweaving the *GF*
and the Gilo text to give the fullest possible picture. In practice this produces a
rather confused narrative with some repetition: the description of the harshness of
winter at IV.11 following *GF* is similar to the description in IV.5 paralleled in
Gilo.

Resemblances with Gilo start again at the end of IV.13. The desperation of the
Christians and their revitalisation under threat from the enemy in IV.14–15 follows
Gilo V.145–198. A short passage from *GF* 37–8 is inserted in IV.16 describing
severed heads (again) before returning to Gilo V.205–22 to describe the ambushes
of the natives and the castle on the bridge in IV.16–17. The Turkish ambush in
IV.18 has elements both of Gilo and *GF*. The description of the ensuing battle in
IV.19–21 follows the order of events of Gilo V.307–394, although with the odd
interpolation from the *GF* (the twelve emirs killed in IV.21 are from *GF* 41 as is
the Turkish loss of confidence). The desecration of the Turkish graves by the
Christians returns to the *GF* 42. It is interesting that IV.21 describes the death of
Cassianus' son, paralleled in Gilo V.381–2: unless he is miraculously resurrected
in between or has a brother, this directly contradicts his mission to Kerbogha in
VI.9. In this instance at least Robert has failed to reconcile his two sources.

Much of the description of the taking of Antioch in V follows the Gilo text.
V.1–2 is unique to Robert. The reference to destroying Turkish tombs in V.3 is
from *GF* 42. Thereafter much of the book runs parallel to Gilo V.394–460; in
particular the truce and the death of Walo are recounted only here and in Gilo. The
negotiations with Pirrus at V.8–9 are Robert's own and the description of
negotiations with the other princes at V.10–11 is from *GF* 44–5. Many details of
the taking of Antioch recur in Gilo: Bohemond's delay and the reference to dawn
(V.12; Gilo VII.83); the reference to Pirrus having two brothers (V.13; Gilo
VII.104); Bohemond's acknowledgement of Pirrus (V.14; Gilo VII.111–116); and
the comet (V.14; Gilo VII 64–7).

Once Antioch has fallen there are more resemblances with Gilo at VI.4–8,
covering Bohemond's wound, the suicide of a soldier, the speculation about
Kerbogha's arrival (VI.7, with the *GF*'s description of the Agulani interpolated)
and the death of Roger of Barneville; this sequence of episodes is close to Gilo
VII.167–277. From VI.9 Robert follows the *GF* again: I have commented above on
the apparent resurrection of Sensadolus in VI.9 after his death in IV.21. The
description of hunger in VI.14 interweaves elements from *GF* 62 and Gilo
VII.299–316: the donkey leg and starving babies are Gilo's, the flesh cooked with
hide still on and the weakness are from *GF*. The description of the deserters at

VI.14 and the following episodes about Stephen of Blois and Guy are again from *GF*.

The description of events in the run-up to the battle of Antioch is largely that of the *GF* with the order changed to improve narrative flow. The detail of Peter the Hermit refusing to bow to Kerbogha at VII.5 is found at Gilo VII.335–40; and whilst Gilo does not have the episode of the Occitan apostate, Kerbogha's threat to behead Peter at VII.357–60 is close in sentiment. Adhemar's sermon at VII.10 is in Gilo, VII.378. Thereafter Robert's description of the battle combines elements of the *GF* and the Gilo text. In VII.11 the formation of the seventh squadron is from the *GF*; the heroism of Hugh and Godfrey in Gilo (VII.369, 418 and 431–52); Odo of Beaugency is found at Gilo, VII.452–9. The celestial army and the grass fire (VII.13–14) come from *GF*; the death of Gerard of Melun (VII.15) is in Gilo VII.484–7 followed by the attack of Everard of Le Puiset and others (Gilo VII.468–75) and the description of plunder (VII.17; Gilo VII.490–91). Robert adds much vivid detail of his own such as the description of battle in VII.14 and Adhemar's thanksgiving at VII.16.

After the battle of Antioch Gilo and Robert both follow the order of the *GF* very closely, corresponding to the start of *GF* X and Gilo VIII. However, there are a few shared details between Gilo and Robert which do not appear in the *GF*: praise of Raymond Pilet (VII.22, Gilo VIII.10–13); the reference to the feast of St Peter ad Vincula at Adhemar's death (VII.23; Gilo VIII.78–81); some of the wording around the massacre at Albara (VII.24; Gilo VIII.85–91); the detailed description of Golfier of Las Tours at VIII.6–7 (Gilo VIII.188–211); the stranglings at Ma'arrat-an-Nu'man (VIII.7; Gilo VIII.259–63); the inhabitants throwing down food at Hisn-al-Akrad (VIII.10; Gilo VIII.356–7); the death of Warren of Petra Mora (VIII.18; Gilo IX.85); part of the description of thirst (IX.5; Gilo IX.231–4); the description of Eustace and Godfrey at Jerusalem and the reference to Wicher and the lion (IX.7; Gilo IX.274–5, 289–90). The final passage where the two texts run in tandem is at the taking of Jerusalem: Robert's description of the slaughter, the thanksgiving and the election of Godfrey at IX.8–10 is close to Gilo IX.317–71. At this point Gilo's text comes to an end, not going on to describe the battle of Ascalon.

Two particular episodes are found only in Gilo and Robert: the death of Walo and lamentation of his wife;[11] and the heroism of Golfier of Las Tours at Ma'arrat-an-Nu'man.[12] The death of Walo is referred to in passing by Guibert and in the second letter of Anselm of Ribemont to Manasses of Reims.[13] Both Gilo and Robert expand the episode considerably, giving details of the truce, Walo's death in an unguarded moment, and the lengthy lament of his wife Humberge. The accounts are not identical: Gilo gives the wife's name, unlike Robert; and his lament is reminiscent of Ovid's *Heroides* whereas Robert's is closer to the *planctus* form.[14]

---

[11] Gilo V.423–60; RM V.6–7.
[12] Gilo VIII.188–211; RM VIII.6–7.
[13] GN 332; for Anselm's letter see Hagenmeyer's edition, *Kreuzzugsbriefe*, 156–60.
[14] See note to translation.

Similarly both go into detail on the heroism of Golfier of Las Tours at the taking of Ma'arrat-an-Nu'man. Most sources refer to this in passing. Robert and Gilo are alone in developing it into a major episode.[15] Again the two give different details. Gilo describes Golfier being borne aloft on a siege ladder and compares him to a bear harried by dogs. Robert's account is much more detailed and lurid, depicting Golfier weighed down by a shield full of arrows, protecting his fellow soldiers, and finding a second wind when exhausted. So whilst both are alone in developing these two episodes, they do it in different ways.

The two texts also agree in numerous points of detail and wording not found in other texts. For example both describe poisoned arrows at Nicaea.[16] Both agree that the battle of Dorylaeum took place on the fourth day's march and that there were 300,000 Turks, and both describe mothers dragging in their sons' bodies.[17] Gilo reflects Robert's sentiment about tents being awash,[18] and the description of corpses being held upright by the crush of bodies.[19] Both give Pirrus two brothers.[20] Both assert that Fulcher of Chartres was the first into Antioch.[21] Both describe the Turks hurling insults and tossing their swords in the air.[22] Both describe how Peter the Hermit refused to bow to Kerbogha, although Gilo gives more detail.[23] Both specify that the booty after the battle of Antioch included 15,000 camels.[24] The play on Adhemar's death being on the feast of St Peter ad Vincula is common to both.[25] In the temple at Jerusalem both have a lurid description of body parts floating on a sea of blood.[26] Both describe Wicher as having killed a lion although in slightly different ways.[27]

The two texts show numerous verbal parallels. There is one exact coincidence: an identical hexameter, 'partim predati, partimque fuere necati'.[28] Beyond that are a number of close echoes. For example, both refer to 'hiemps glacialis' during the winter at Antioch;[29] describing those who fall off the walls at the taking of Ma'arrat-an-Nu'man Gilo's wording ('necem ... ad terram confracti repperiebant') is close to Robert's ('mortem, quam evadere putabant, confracti ad terram invenerunt').[30] At IX.274–5 Gilo comments that Eustace of Boulogne 'stans ... in

---

[15] Gilo VIII.188–211; RM VIII.6–7. For references in other texts see e.g. PT 123, RA 97.

[16] Gilo IV.45–6; RM III.2.

[17] Gilo IV.160, 166, 278; RM III 8–10.

[18] Gilo V.90, RM IV.5.

[19] Gilo V.331, RM IV.19.

[20] Gilo VII.104, RM V.13.

[21] Gilo VII.62, 86–93; RM V.12–13.

[22] Gilo VII.238–42; RM VI.7.

[23] Gilo VII.336–40, RM VII.5.

[24] Gilo VII.452–9, 484–8, 490; RM VII.12, 15, 17.

[25] Gilo VIII.77–81; RM VII.23.

[26] Gilo IX.317–23; RM IX.8.

[27] Gilo IX.289–90; RM IX.7.

[28] Gilo V.38; RM IV.1, first hexameter on 776.

[29] Gilo V.63; RM IV.5.

[30] Gilo VIII.222-3; RM VIII.6.

castro cum Godefrido/susceptos ictus reddit cum fenore duro', which is close to Robert's wording at IX.7: 'duros ictus jaculorum et lapidum suscipiebant, et quadruplici foenore recompensabant'.[31] Other examples are picked up in the notes to the translation.

Gilo's text is in hexameters; Robert's text is prosimetric, with hexameters inserted at various points. Virtually all Robert's hexameters are found in passages which are parallel with Gilo. There are eight in the description of Nicaea at III.2–6; 25 at Dorylaeum in III.8–14; 14 on arrival at Antioch at IV.1; six at the death of Walo in V.7; six at Albara in VII.24; six at Ma'arrat-an-Nu'man in VIII.4–6; and one at Desen in VIII.17 in a passage close to the *GF*. The only hexameters which do not coincide with a passage in Gilo are at IX.15 before the battle of Ascalon. Not all the parallels between Gilo and Robert contain hexameters; but virtually all Robert's hexameters coincide with such borrowings. None of the passages close to *GF* contain hexameters. The hexameters in Robert and Gilo also contain clear verbal parallels. I have commented above on the identical hexameter describing plundering at Antioch. At VIII.4 Robert has two hexameters, 'Tela, sudes, lapidesque volant, ignesque facesque/Ex quibus arderent introrsus tecta domorum'; this is close to Gilo's wording at VIII.136–7, 'Iactant saxa, faces flammas per inane ferentes/quas haerere solunt ad culmina suscipientes'.[32] There are, however, no obvious parallels between the hexameters at the head of some of Robert's chapters and Gilo's text.[33]

The relationship between Robert and Gilo

It is therefore fair to say that Robert appears to use Gilo or a text related to his work as a source second only to the *GF*. At times (Nicaea, Dorylaeum, early events at Antioch) he follows it in preference to the *GF*. On other occasions he weaves together an account from the two, for example on arrival at Antioch (IV.1). Elsewhere he inserts details from it in the middle of passages taken from the *GF*, such as the animals flung down from the battlements at VIII.10. He takes from it two episodes found nowhere else in the sources for the Crusade, Walo and Golfier; and he echoes the wording. Nearly all the hexameters in his text are found in these borrowings.

So what exactly is the relationship between Robert's text and Gilo's? There are significant differences between them as well as resemblances. The structure of the two is very different. Gilo is more selective with his material: he begins his narrative at Nicaea, omits the events between Dorylaeum and Antioch and stops

---

[31] Gilo: 'Count Eustace stood firm on the siege castle with Count Godfrey and paid back the blows he received with hard interest' (Grocock and Siberry's translation); RM: 'they withstood the hard blows of darts and stones and paid them back with fourfold interest'.

[32] RM: 'Weapons, stakes and stones fly, and fires and torches/Which set alight the rooves of the houses inside'; Gilo: 'They flung rocks and torches that carried flames through the void; they aimed them high, wanting them to stick to the battlements' (Grocock and Siberry's translation).

[33] I discuss these in more detail in Chapter Five. In my view they are later additions and have no connection with any parallels with Gilo.

before the battle of Ascalon, meaning that about a third of Robert's text has no parallel in Gilo. Conversely he gives details absent in Robert: for example he specifies that the second man into Antioch was a Venetian, and suggests that Kerbogha sent a special message to Bohemond before the battle.[34] There are also differences of approach: in particular Gilo praises Taticius,[35] in sharp contrast to Robert's sustained vilification.

The evidence is not therefore clear enough to suggest that either author borrowed directly from the other. The pattern of resemblances seems too piecemeal to suggest sustained borrowing: whilst some episodes and wording are shared, details are often different. The parallels, though, are undeniable. Gilo's editors suggest a lost shared source which would have been drawn on independently by both authors. I am reluctant to invent yet another supposed lost source for the events of the Crusade. But it is hard to see another convincing explanation.

If there was such a source, it must have been in Latin given the close resemblances of wording in places. And it must have been at least partly in verse: nearly all the hexameters come in passages resembling Gilo, and one hexameter is identical. A reference to it might also explain a puzzling reference in Robert's *Sermo Apologeticus*, where he comments on the 'levitas carminis': why call his work a poem when it is overwhelmingly prose? We do not know what material such a source might have covered. Gilo's use of it would suggest that it focussed particularly on events between Nicaea and Jerusalem. Equally the presence of hexameters in Robert's description of the battle of Ascalon and some of the material which Robert adds in Books I, II and IX might well come from the putative lost source. What does seem clear is that the source followed the *GF* much more closely after the battle of Antioch than before. The *GF* itself changes nature markedly at this point, with Book X being much longer than the others and focussed on Raymond IV more closely than Bohemond: this may be simple coincidence or may indicate that the end of the *GF* should be seen as different and separate in some way.

The First Crusade is a field stalked by the shadowy ghosts of supposed lost sources. But to postulate such a lost shared source in verse, which Robert would have used as a secondary source alongside the *GF*, explains the pattern of parallels with Gilo, the fact that many of them are in Robert's hexameters and possibly his reference to a poem. It is though a suggestion which raises as many questions as it answers. If such a source existed it would have had to be an early one as well as a sophisticated one: not impossible but surprising given the nature of the two earliest first-hand sources, the *GF* and Raymond of Aguilers, neither of which betray enormous literary sophistication. We would have to believe that Robert used the *GF* as his base text despite his criticisms of it, using the presumed higher quality verse text only as an ancillary text: again not impossible if we assume that, like Gilo, the verse text gave only selected highlights of the Crusade and that, as he says, Robert was specifically commissioned to re-edit the *GF*. We would also have to accept that Robert makes no mention of it, in contrast to his clear

---

[34] Gilo VII.191, 400–402.
[35] Gilo V.262.

acknowledgement of the *GF*: this is not necessarily a problem if we accept that there was a clear story about the quality of the *GF*; medieval historians routinely do not acknowledge contemporary sources.[36] And the text would have left no trace anywhere but Robert and Gilo despite its presumed quality. None of these are overwhelming objections. But the case for a lost shared Latin source remains unproven, albeit tempting.

iii) Sources contemporary with Robert not based on the *GF*

Robert's text shows a few similarities with Raymond of Aguilers. The two agree that Fulcher of Chartres was first into Antioch.[37] Both refer to the death of Roger of Barneville.[38] Robert has Kerbogha advised by an Occitan apostate, whilst Raymond assigns the role to the Saracen Mirdalis.[39] Both mention the death of Pons Balazun, Raymond's co-author.[40] It is likely that Raymond had finished his text by 1105.[41] Interestingly most of these details are also in Gilo.[42] We can therefore assume that Robert drew directly on Raymond for a few additional details; that Raymond knew and drew on the postulated lost verse source; or that both authors had access to similar sources and/or eyewitnesses.

iv) Vernacular poetic tradition

Several episodes in Robert's chronicle show strong links to vernacular poetic tradition, and the ethos of the *chanson de geste* permeates his work. There is nothing surprising in this: chroniclers routinely used material from vernacular poetry just as the writers of the *chanson de geste* liked to suggest reputable written sources for their work.[43] Arguably, though, Robert reflects more of this influence than many other sources for the Crusade.

Extant vernacular sources

The surviving vernacular poetic sources for the Crusade date from the end of the twelfth century or later and have been extensively reworked. They include the Northern French Old French Crusade Cycle, a set of *chansons de geste* centred

---

[36] Guénée, 116.

[37] RA 64, RM V.12.

[38] RA 66, RM VI.8.

[39] RA 80–81, RM VII.9.

[40] RA 107, RM VIII.18.

[41] Introduction, 11.

[42] Fulcher at V.62, 86–93; Roger at VII, 245–77; Pons at IX.82–5.

[43] For a claim by a *chanson de geste* to the auctoritas given by a named source see the *Roland*'s much-quoted reference to Turold, 'ci falt la geste que Turoldus declinet' ('here ends the story recounted by Turold') 4002: *La Chanson de Roland*, ed. I. Short (Paris, 1990). On the use of fictional material in Latin chronicle see e.g. N. Partner, *Serious Entertainments: the writing of history in twelfth-century England* (Chicago, 1977).

around Godfrey of Bouillon and containing largely legendary material; of interest to us here is the central text of the *Chanson d'Antioche* and to a lesser extent the heavily reworked *Chanson de Jérusalem*. There is the Occitan *Canso d'Antioca*. There is also a late twelfth-century Old French poem based on Baudry of Bourgueil but with substantial additions;[44] in the absence of an edition it is hard to comment on this further, but a quick examination of the manuscript shows no obvious relationship with Robert. In addition there is plenty of evidence of songs and poems contemporary with the Crusade, which may or may not have been *chansons de geste*.[45] It is difficult to construct exactly what the relationship between Robert and these sources might have been.

Potential (and puzzling) links with Occitan vernacular poetry

There is no clear textual link between the surviving fragments (probably themselves a later reworking) of the Occitan text and Robert. There are, however, two coincidences.

Robert's text, as discussed above, gives great prominence to the heroism of Golfier of Las Tours at Ma'arrat-an-Nu'man, devoting nearly two chapters to him and describing his achievements in terms redolent of the *chanson de geste*. The first version of the Occitan text was written by Gregory Bechada, who was in the household of Golfier; and Golfier is a prominent character in what we can reconstruct of his version.[46] Robert's account may simply reflect his consistent embroidery of events: Golfier's heroism is mentioned in most sources at this point.[47] This is not sufficient evidence to show that Robert borrowed from an early Occitan poem; Gilo gives similar prominence to Golfier.[48] It does suggest that he at least had some knowledge of a source or tradition in which Golfier was prominent and chose to echo it at the point where Golfier was acknowledged to have played a leading role. It would be tempting to argue that Robert's praise of the Occitan Raymond Pilet reflects the same source:[49] however, the evidence is insufficient.

There is a further coincidence. Robert describes Kerbogha being informed about the Christian forces by an Occitan apostate, who is then unappreciatively beheaded for misleading him.[50] The closest parallel to this is in the Occitan poem, where the interpreter Herluin similarly briefs and deliberately demoralises Kerbogha, and makes a quick exit before he can be executed;[51] Gilo has something

---

[44] Paul Meyer edited some extracts as 'Un récit en vers de la première Croisade fondé sur Baudri de Bourgueil', *R* 5 (1876), 1–63, *R* 6 (1877), 489–94. It is preserved in two English manuscripts in Oxford and London.

[45] GN comments 'nihil nisi quod publice cantitatur dicere libuit' (GN 83; 'it was not fitting to talk about things other than those already being sung in public').

[46] *Canso*, Introduction 9–17.

[47] For example RA 97, PT 123.

[48] Gilo VIII.188–211.

[49] VII.22, VIII.13, IX.4; he is mentioned but not praised in *GF* 73–4, 83, 87–9.

[50] VII.9.

[51] RA 80–81 has a similar episode but the briefer is the Saracen Mirdalis rather than a Christian and is not executed. Intriguingly the poem based on Baudry of Bourgueil has

similar in Kerbogha's threat to behead Peter the Hermit.[52] Robert may have remembered this episode and made the apostate Occitan in a vague memory of the source being Occitan; he may even have had some knowledge of the source; but there is not definite proof.

A third if tenuous link is worth mentioning. At the fall of Antioch Bohemond arrives very late to help take the city, and is bitterly criticised by the traitor Pirrus. The terms in which he does so evoke the coming of dawn and the need for a messenger. The theme and story are also in Gilo.[53] This reads very like an invocation of the lyric *alba* form, which at the time was attested in Occitan but much less in French or Latin.[54]

So in sum there are some links between the Occitan tradition and Robert's work which are also found in Gilo. This is intriguing. It would be tempting to ascribe them to a common knowledge of Gregory Bechada's *Canso d'Antioca*. However this was a vernacular text,[55] not a Latin one as suggested by the verbal parallels between Robert and Gilo; and it is unlikely to have been finished before Robert wrote his account[56]. So the resemblances prove nothing more than that the putative lost shared source had at least a passing acquaintance with the Occitan tradition which is reflected in Robert and Gilo, and possibly also in some of the parallels with RA.

Robert's relationship with the Northern French Old French Crusade Cycle

Robert's relationship with the Old French Crusade Cycle is more complex. The cycle was edited and compiled from earlier material by the northern French poet Graindor de Douai at the end of the twelfth century and acquired increasing accretions during the thirteenth century.[57] The nucleus of the cycle is formed by the *Chanson d'Antioche*, the *Chanson de Jérusalem* and the *Chanson des Chétifs*. The *Chétifs* is an almost entirely fantastical text very loosely based on the crusade of 1101; the *Jérusalem* contains some material which may reflect earlier sources but is for the most part a derivative rerun of events at Antioch. The *Antioche* is a rather different matter: it is a detailed and realistic account of events from the start of the Crusade up to the battle of Antioch, which not only shows abundant parallels with other sources but contains a substantial amount of apparently eyewitness testimony.

Mirdalis rescued later on by Raymond IV, a further Occitan connection for the episode. The *Antioche* copies the episode of the Occitan apostate (8382–90) after creating total confusion by introducing the embassy of Herluin, comments by the Saracen Mirdalis and comments by another Saracen Rouge Lion.

[52] Gilo VII. 357–60.
[53] RM V.12; Gilo VII.83.
[54] See V.12 and note to translation.
[55] See *Canso*, Introduction, 6.
[56] See *Canso*, Introduction, 8–9.
[57] See Duparc-Quioc, *Cycle*.

Graindor's text of the *Antioche* is a compilation from at least two sources. His use of both reflects the growing perception by the end of the twelfth century that a rhymed text was less 'true' than a prose text.[58]

Firstly, he claimed that his source was an earlier work by an otherwise unknown poet, Richard le Pèlerin, who was an eyewitness at least to the events of the battle of Antioch.[59] How literally one can take Richard's existence or Graindor's claims to be using eyewitness and therefore unimpeachable source material is a matter for debate.[60] But it seems beyond doubt that there was some earlier version of the *Antioche* which may have been near-contemporary with the events of the Crusade. Albert of Aix's chronicle shows strong parallels, suggesting that he had access to this earlier version of the *Antioche* in some form.[61]

Secondly, Graindor borrowed extensively from Robert, adding authenticity to his text by drawing on the most popular Latin chronicle of the Crusade at the time. Graindor's borrowings from Robert start in earnest with Kerbogha's arrival and continue throughout the remainder of the *Antioche*.[62] From 6565 onwards he translates sections of Robert faithfully.[63] He uses Robert as his base text, inserting

---

[58] See G. Spiegel, *Romancing the past: the rise of vernacular prose historiography in thirteenth-century France* (Berkeley and Los Angeles, 1993).

[59] *Antioche* 9014. The reference comes in the middle of the battle of Antioch and just before a list of fantastically named Saracen kings: it does not suggest explicitly that Richard described all the events of the Crusade.

[60] And has been debated, extensively, for the last 150 years. Until recently most opinion was in favour of the existence of the shadowy Richard and his value as an eyewitness; R. F. Cook. *Chanson d'Antioche, chanson de geste: le cycle de la croisade est-il épique?*, (Amsterdam, 1980), challenged this view in 1980, pointing out that we have only one reference to Richard in a part of a late twelfth century chanson de geste giving a list of legendary kings. H. Kleber, 'Wer ist der Verfasser der *Chanson d'Antioche*? Revision einer Streitfrage', *ZFSL* 94 (1984), 115–42, argues that whether or not Richard existed his name became a kind of talisman guaranteeing authenticity. For summary of arguments and further refs see *Canso*, Introduction 60–61. In my view the evidence for an earlier source of some kind stands up; its attribution to a historical – as opposed to a possibly legendary – Richard does not.

[61] *Historia Hierosolymitana*, Albert of Aix, *RHC Occ.*IV, 265–713. The new edition by Susan Edgington was not available at time of writing. Duparc-Quioc (*Etude,* 148–70) analyses the parallels in considerable detail. See also P. Knoch, *Studien zu Albert von Aachen* (Stuttgart, 1966).

[62] *Etude,* 107, 118–20

[63] See 6676–81, where he describes the Turks throwing and catching their weapons: 'Dont ce partent de l'ost li baceler legier/A Anthioce en vont por l'estor commencier/Mais n'en pueent fors traire serjant ne chevalier./Par le camp vont poignant, si mainent grant tempier,/La veissiés maint Turc se lance palmoier,/Envers le ciel jeter et au fer rempuigner' ('At this the lightly armed young knights ride out from the army to Antioch to provoke a fight, but were unable to tempt out any man-at-arms or knight. They go spurring over the field at a great pace; many Turks could be seen taking their lances, throwing them up to the sky and catching them again'). Compare Robert VI.7: 'cursores suos ante urbem direxerunt, qui nostros ad bellum provocarent et de civitate exire suaderent. Sed nostri ... salubrius esse

passages from his earlier source (who may or may not have been Richard le Pèlerin) where they bring additional information and often giving two accounts of the same episode.[64] The fact that Graindor chose to use Robert rather than another chronicle reflects not only Robert's popularity by this stage but the closeness of his style to that of a *chanson de geste*, making it easy to move material between them.

The net result of this complex process is that we do not know whether Robert had any knowledge of the primitive version ('Richard's') of the *Antioche* and cannot use the extant *Antioche* as a guide. There may be a clue in the fact that the *Antioche*'s borrowings from Robert only start at Kerbogha's arrival at Antioch.[65] Duparc-Quioc argues that this was because Robert only started borrowing from the primitive *Antioche* from this point and that his text would therefore not have matched sufficiently well for any earlier borrowings. In my view this is not sufficiently strong evidence that Robert did know the primitive *Antioche*.

It may, though, reflect Robert's borrowing of a number of *chanson de geste* style episodes from his source the *GF*. Most of these cluster around Kerbogha and the events at Antioch, where there is a sequence describing the embassy of Sensadolus to Kerbogha, the presentation of rusty supposed Christian arms, Kerbogha's letter to the Caliph and his long conversation with his fortune-telling mother;[66] Kerbogha is built up as the characteristically boastful Saracen. The speeches and portrayal of Soliman after Dorylaeum and of Clemens at Ascalon have similar hallmarks.[67] The embassy from the Emir of Cairo is also reminiscent of the *chansons de geste*.[68] The sequence of events at Antioch is almost identical in the *GF* and its derivatives. Soliman and Clemens are both in the *GF* although Robert has embroidered the episodes. The ambassadors from the Emir of Cairo are referred to in passing by the *GF* although the detailed portrayal is Robert's own.[69]

Whether the *GF* got these from the early version of the *Antioche* we do not know. Certainly they stand out from the rest of the text to the point where Bréhier dismisses many as interpolations, something which has been disproved by later

---

judicaverunt inter moenia remanere, quam extra bella movere. Illi vero per campos et plana currendo, nostros ad bella ciebant, diraque convicia eis improperabant. Lanceas et gladios in altum ejiciebant, et in manibus recipiebant'.

[64] *Etude* 108–10. For example both the *Antioche* and Robert include St Maurice in the holy forces (*Antioche* 9064; RM VII.13). For an example of a faithfully reproduced mistake compare *GF* 65, where the Emperor orders a retreat to Bulgaria backed up by a scorched-earth policy; in RM 816 this is telescoped into an order to lay waste Bulgaria, followed by the *Antioche* 7102. For an example of an episode recounted twice see the two flights of Stephen of Blois, the first with a feigned illness (5595–644) and the second, following Robert, with a genuine one (7021–53).

[65] Hatem, 331, argues from this that Robert must have been drawing on an earlier epic text; the borrowing cannot be by Graindor as it would have been illogical to start doing so only at this point. Duparc-Quioc's analysis (*Etude,* 118–119) proves clearly in my view that Graindor is the borrower.

[66] RM V.9–12.

[67] RM III.17, IX.21.

[68] RM V.1–2.

[69] *GF* 50–56; 22; 96–7; 42 for passing reference to the envoys.

stylistic analysis.[70] And the depiction of the Saracens is closely in line with their portrayal in vernacular *chansons de geste*.[71] Clearly these passages are rooted in the vernacular *chanson de geste* tradition. But there is no proof that they come from a primitive form of the *Antioche*. Moreover, the closeness of the texts and the fact that the same material appears in near-identical form in all derivatives[72] makes it clear that Robert derived his version from the *GF* rather than directly from any precursor of the *Antioche*. So their presence may have triggered Graindor to start borrowing from Robert at this point, but they are not proof that Robert knew 'Richard's' version of the *Antioche*.

Reconstructing any relationship with the *Jérusalem* is even harder. We know little about what an earlier text of the *Jérusalem* might have contained or when it would have been written.[73] Graindor's version casts the siege of Jerusalem and the battle of Ascalon as a rerun of events at Antioch,[74] and the few shreds of original material which might survive show no obvious resemblances with Robert. The most we can say is that Robert builds up Clemens as a kind of second Kerbogha and places considerable emphasis on the battle of Ascalon: whether this reflects some kind of early vernacular tradition or indeed whether it influenced Graindor de Douai's later treatment of the subject is impossible to say.

Other reminiscences of the chansons de geste

There are also episodes in Robert which do not come from other sources and could conceivably be traced back to an early epic tradition. Some of these give additional information on specific figures in a style very reminiscent of the *chanson de geste*: the death of Roger of Barneville, the death of Odo of Beaugency and the death of

---

[70] Bréhier, vi–vii. See Oehler, 62–66 and Witzel for detailed analysis.

[71] See N. Daniel, *Heroes and Saracens: a reinterpretation of the chansons de geste* (Edinburgh, 1984).

[72] See, for example, the description of the rusty weapons at VI.10: 'attulerunt ante eum Francigenam ensem, valde despicabilem et obtusum et foeda rubigine tectum. Attulerunt et lanceam eadem deformitate consimilem, quae etiam sua abjectione ensem faciebat praepollentem' ('they brought him a Frankish sword which was in abysmal condition, blunt and covered in filthy rust. They also brought a lance in equally bad state – indeed it made the sword look good in comparison'). See *GF* 51: 'quemdam uilissimum ensem rubigine tectum, et deterrimum arcum ligneum, et lanceam nimis inutilem' ('a very poor sword all covered with rust, and a thoroughly bad wooden bow, and a spear which was quite useless', Hill's translation). Compare GN 211: 'ensem scilicet diutina rubigine scabrum, nigrum ad instar fuliginis arcum et lanceam impolitam, multorum annorum fumo infectam' ('a sword flaking with rust from use, a bow black as soot and a lance tarnished and dirtied by years of smoke'); BB 61 'ensem videlicet rubiginosum, lanceam quoque satis inutilem et squalidum, et arcum aspernabilem' ('a rusty sword, a lance which was also filthy and past use, and a laughable bow').

[73] Duparc-Quioc, *Cycle*, 1–74; see *Canso*, Introduction, 43–44 for summary of passages from the original *Jérusalem* which may survive in the thirteenth-century Spanish compilation the *Gran Conquista de Ultramar* (ed. L. Cooper (Bogota, 1979), 4 vols).

[74] Duparc-Quioc, *Etude*, 130–31; *Cycle*, 46–75.

and vengeance for Gerard of Melun.[75] The *Antioche* copies all of these although misnaming Odo as Odo of Beauvais.[76] Presumably none of these can have been in the primitive *Antioche*: if they were, Graindor could have copied them from there and given Robert's version as a doublet of Richard's as he does elsewhere. The common thread is that most – though not all – are shared with Gilo.[77] Whilst the style of the episodes would not be out of place in a *chanson de geste*, the similarities with Gilo suggest that if anywhere they came from the possible lost shared Latin source.

More generally Robert's style is on occasion reminiscent of the techniques and language of the *chanson de geste*. The description of the arrival of the ambassadors from the Emir of Babylon shows resemblances with the Blancandrin embassy in the *Chanson de Roland*;[78] the description of Hugh killing a Saracen at the battle of Antioch (VII.11) is a standard topos from the *chanson de geste*.[79] These resemblances are discussed further in the next chapter. They prove nothing more than that Robert knew and echoed *chansons de geste* in his work: at most they show that the association of the First Crusade and vernacular epic represented by the Old French Crusade cycle was already forming in the first decade of the twelfth century.

Conclusion

Putting this together, we arrive at the following. The *GF* would have derived some of its material from an earlier *chanson de geste* focused on events at Antioch, which might be identified with an earlier version ('Richard''s) of the *Antioche*. Robert would have copied this *chanson de geste* style material from the *GF* rather than directly from a vernacular source. He would have added some material from an unknown source which might or might not have been a *chanson de geste* but, given the resemblances with Gilo, is more likely to have been the postulated lost shared source in Latin verse. He would also have used the language and topoi of the *chanson de geste* to add colour to his narrative. In a neat irony the later editor of the primitive *Antioche* would then have used Robert to add historical

---

[75] VI.8, VII.12, VII.15.

[76] 6682–724; 9145–76; 8648–60.

[77] Gilo VII.245–77, VII.452–9, VII.484–8.

[78] V.1; see *Roland* 110–13: 'sur palies blancs siedent cil cevaler,/As tables juent pur els esbaneier,/E as eschecs li plus saive e li veill,/E escremissent cil bacheler leger' ('the knights sit on white cloths. They are playing at tables for amusement; the oldest and wisest play chess whilst the young and energetic are skirmishing [with swords]').

[79] Chosen from innumerable examples, compare *Chanson de Guillaume*, ed. and transl. P. Bennett (London, 2000) 1829–33: 'Puis fiert un altre sur la targe novele;/Tote li fent e fruisse e escantele,/Et sun halberc li runt e desmaele,/Colpe le piz suz la large gonele/Que mort le trebuche des arçuns de la sele' ('Then he strikes another on his new, round shield: he splits it right through and smashes it to splinters, and tears rows of links from his halberk, cuts open his chest under his broad tunic with the result that he knocks him dead out of his saddle'; Bennett's translation).

authenticity, the epic material in his text lending itself well to the *chanson de geste* style of the *Antioche*.

v) Material in Robert not found elsewhere

The Council of Clermont

The most significant addition, and the only one for which Robert is now cited as a historical source, is his account of the Council of Clermont (I.1–3).[80] By his own account he was an eyewitness and was specifically commissioned to give an account of the Council. Most accounts of the Council are found in the *GF* and its derivatives: there is a brief account in the *GF*, and longer versions by Baudry and Robert (who were eyewitnesses) and Guibert (who was probably not).[81] Fulcher's account is independent and probably eyewitness.[82] Munro regards William of Malmesbury's later account as being derived from eyewitnesses.[83] Some points also recur in the supposed letter of Alexius to Count Robert of Flanders.[84] Raymond of Aguilers and Ralph of Caen make no reference to the Council, and Albert of Aix attributes the preaching of the Crusade to Peter the Hermit.[85]

Urban made three speeches during the Council: the first concerned reform of the clergy; the second was an exhortation to go on Crusade; and the third contained practical directions for the Crusade.[86] Robert acknowledges the first, gives the second in great detail and the third in somewhat less detail. No source gives a verbatim account of the speech: Munro compares sources and reconstructs what Urban is likely to have covered.[87]

---

[80] The only part of Robert which has been translated into English is Urban's speech (D. C. Munro, *Urban and the Crusades* (Philadelphia, 1895) 5–8; reprinted in A. C. Krey, *The First Crusade: the accounts of eye-witnesses and participants* (Princeton, 1958), 30–33. E. Peters, *The First Crusade: the chronicle of Fulcher of Chartres and other source materials* (Philadelphia, 1971), 1–16, assembles translations of the main accounts. On the Council itself see R. Somerville, *The Councils of Urban II, vol. I, Decreta Claromontensia* (Amsterdam, 1971). For discussion of Urban's speech see D. C.Munro, 'The Speech of Pope Urban II. at Clermont 1095', *AHR* 11 (1905), 231–42; H. E. J. Cowdrey, 'Pope Urban's preaching of the First Crusade', *H* 55 (1970), 177–88. P. J. Cole, *The Preaching of the Crusades to the Holy Land 1095–1270* (Massachusetts, 1991),1–36 analyses the reports of the speech in terms of oratory and argues (13–15) that Robert's account is 'valuable because he attempted to convey something of its oratorical form' (15).

[81] *GF* 1–2; GN 111–17; BB 12–15.

[82] FC I.2–3.

[83] Munro, 233–4; WM I.598–607.

[84] See Appendix.

[85] AA 272-4.

[86] Munro, 232–3, n.16; 241, 'undoubtedly his exhortation was longer than any of the brief reports which have been preserved'.

[87] Munro, 236-42.

Robert does not give a full account of the speech: no version does.[88] He picks out and highlights the themes of particular interest to him. The opening words place the French centre stage, backed up by a later reference to Charlemagne, and Pope Urban is made to refer twice to the glory given to the Franks by God and the obligation to help Jerusalem which comes with it: this reflects Robert's orientation towards the French court. Saracen antics in the Holy Land are described with relish. Jerusalem is presented both as the centre of the world and as the goal of the Crusade and culmination of the speech: this reflects Robert's shifting of gravity away from events at Antioch.[89] The account emphasises throughout that God is the source and inspiration of the Crusade: the Bible is quoted repeatedly, the Franks are presented as both privileged by and under an obligation to God, and Robert emphasises heavily the significance of the cry 'Deus vult!'.[90] Robert is at pains to point out, in one of his few references to sources, that he has consulted other authorities extensively and all agree the Crusade was inspired directly by God.[91] As reported by Robert the speech is a microcosm of the themes which run throughout his work, some of which recur in the apocryphal letter of Alexius.[92]

There is no reason to disbelieve Robert as an independent eyewitness source for Urban's speech. Like any witness he is selective in what he reports and fits it to his main themes: but that does not detract from his value as a primary source from a key episode of the Crusade.

Other episodes

Robert adds material in many places which is found neither in the *GF* nor in Gilo. I have commented above on his consistent vilification of the Byzantines and praise of Hugh and Godfrey. Much of the new material comes from his desire to construct an ideology of the Crusade, such as the descriptions of cities in the Holy Land and (probably) the three speeches given to Bohemond on the theology of the Crusade; in the latter part of the text he deliberately builds the taking of Jerusalem and battle of Ascalon into a rerun of events at Antioch, emphasising the importance of the

---

[88] RM I.1, 'haec et id genus plurima peroravit' ('when Pope Urban had eloquently spoken these words and many other things of the same kind'). Compare BB, 'his vel hujus modi aliis' (15) ('these and other words of this kind'); see also WM's comments at I.606.

[89] See Cowdrey for a helpful summary of the arguments around whether Urban intended the liberation of Jerusalem to be the goal of the Crusade or whether it served as a means to another end, releasing the Eastern church from Turkish domination. Cowdrey's view is that the liberation of Jerusalem was Urban's central aim. Certainly this is what is reflected in Robert, who gives considerable detail on the suffering of the Eastern Christians but is clear that Jerusalem is the main goal: 'Praesertim moveat vos sanctum Domini Salvatoris nostri Sepulcrum' (I.1, 'most especially let the Holy Sepulchre of Our Lord move you').

[90] See B. Lacroix, '*Deus le volt! La théologie d'un cri*', *Etudes de Civilisation Médiévale: Mélanges offerts à Edmond-René Labande* (Poitiers, 1974), 461–70.

[91] 'ut cunctis clarescat fidelibus quod haec via a Deo, non ab homine, sit constituta, sicut a multis postea comperimus' (I.3, 'to make it quite clear to all believers that this pilgrimage had been set in train by God rather than men – as we have since established from many sources').

[92] See Appendix for further discussion of these links.

former. On occasion it can also be hard to distinguish between new material and Robert's desire to tell a good story: thus he embroiders considerably Godfrey's exploit bisecting the Turk at Antioch but it is not clear how far this is poetic licence and how far more detailed information;[93] the same could be said of the crossing of the mountains on the way to Antioch.[94] Leaving these additions aside, the main new factual material comprises the following.

In events up to arrival at Antioch Robert adds material on the sending out of scouts and a fight with the Turks (I.7). He also emphasises the heroism of Walter Sans Aveir (I.11). The crusaders travel via Rome (II.2). He gives different details on the negotiations with the Emperor, in which Bohemond plays a leading role (II.17): the account differs in virtually every text. At Nicaea the role of Raymond IV and Adhemar (III.3) and the lobbing of severed heads (III.4) are not in either the *GF* or Gilo. At III.24 the spontaneous surrender of Caesarea is not in *GF* 25.

At Antioch he gives additional material on the initial fighting at IV.7–8 (intercalated between *GF* 31–2) and IV.18, although this is general description which might be imaginative rather than real. The visit by the envoys from the Emir of Babylon at V.1–2 is Robert's own, probably developing what is a passing reference in *GF*. The link of the truce to Tancred's blocking from his castle is Robert's own (V.5), probably an example of a linking device. The long conversation of Bohemond and Pirrus at V.8–9 is Robert's, again developing a short reference from his sources. He lengthens the negotiations between Kerbogha and the crusaders at VII.5–7, building on existing material. The episode of the Occitan apostate at VII.9 is unique to Robert, though elements of it are found in other texts. Adhemar's speech at VII.16 is Robert's own.

After the fall of Antioch the death of Hugh is not found elsewhere (VII.20). At IX.17 the description of marching out to the battle of Ascalon is close to the description for the battle of Antioch, reflecting Robert's desire to emphasise events at the end of the Crusade. The role of Clemens is heavily emphasised and ascribed to an apostate eyewitness source conveniently in Jerusalem: this reflects both Robert's liking for a good story and his concern to create a villain equivalent to Kerbogha for the battle of Ascalon. The slaughter of the peasants at IX.23 is not in his sources. The climax in IX.24–26 is Robert's own, placing the focus firmly on the terrestrial and celestial Jerusalem as the culmination of the Crusade.

We do not know where this material came from. It may well be from eyewitnesses. There is no reason to disbelieve or discard it, but it does not add a great deal to our knowledge of events. And it is hard to draw the line between imaginative addition, theological embroidery, propaganda and historical fact.

Mistakes by Robert

Robert makes two identifiable errors of fact. Firstly, he puts the death of Hugh of Vermandois on the embassy to Constantinople.[95] Hugh in fact died on the crusade

---

[93] IV.20.
[94] III.28.
[95] VII.20.

of 1101.[96] There is no obvious explanation for this in a text which magnifies Hugh's role and was written in the orbit of the Capetian kings. Bull[97] suggests that this was a deliberate lie to rehabilitate Hugh's reputation, his failure to return to the Crusade having given rise to accusations of cowardice; if so it was a glaring distortion of the truth aimed at an audience who would have been likely to know the truth of the case better than most, but none the less likely for that.

Robert also suggests that Baldwin was at the taking of Jerusalem: in fact Baldwin came on pilgrimage later in the year.[98] This may reflect a desire to glorify the man who by the time Robert wrote had become King of Jerusalem.

Robert also makes some apparent errors in the process of editing and translating. I have commented above on several errors in his adaptation of the *GF*.[99] At III.9 he seems to make a similar error translating from the source shared with Gilo, translating Gilo's 150,000 Turks as 150.[100] I have also commented above on the failure to reconcile his two sources over the death of Cassianus' son, leading to his apparent resurrection to negotiate with Kerbogha. At IX.11 Robert confuses 40 with 400, asserting that Jerusalem had been under pagan domination for only 40 years: this is in neither Gilo nor the *GF*, suggesting either misreading of another source or a faulty memory.

Was Robert an eyewitness?

Robert is quite clear that he was an eyewitness at the Council of Clermont, and implies that because of this he was a particularly suitable person to write an account of the Crusade: '[Bernardus] praecepit igitur mihi ut, qui Clari Montis concilio interfui, acephalae materiei caput praeponerem'.[101] Eyewitness testimony was the most valued form of historical evidence;[102] for a subject as important as the Council it is a claim Robert is unlikely to have made lightly. His account is consistent with other accounts of the Council and one of the fullest. Whilst he edited and summarised events, we may take his account as essentially accurate.

There is no evidence that he was an eyewitness to any of the other events of the Crusade. In adapting the *GF* he is always careful to write 'nostri' rather than 'nos', making it clear that he was not a participant. In IX.20 and IX.22 he attributes the speech of Clement to eyewitness testimony from an apostate living in Jerusalem:[103]

---

[96] Runciman, *History*, vol.II, 29.

[97] Bull, 'Capetian Monarchy', 42.

[98] IX.7; Runciman, *History*, vol.I, 302–3.

[99] See discussion above in Chapter Two.

[100] Gilo IV.174–5. Robert's number is probably nearer the mark in terms of strict realism, but out of kilter with the huge numbers generally given in Crusade texts.

[101] *Sermo Apologeticus*: '[Abbot Bernard] instructed me, since I had been present at the Council of Clermont, to add the beginning which was missing'.

[102] Guénée, 78–84.

[103] 'quid Clemens....dixerit audiamus: sicut supradictus proselytus Iherosolimis deinceps retulit, qui juxta illum erat, ut assecla et domesticus verna illius' ('let us hear what Clement ... said ... This story was told by the convert mentioned above at Jerusalem, who was beside Clement as his hanger-on and house slave', IX.20). This assertion is puzzling,

quite how he met this apostate we do not know (he may be relaying an account from a third party) but the implication that he was not himself an eyewitness is clear. His account of Urban's speech reports Urban's prohibition on clergy going on Crusade without express permission from their superiors: maybe Robert was one of those forbidden to go.

vi) Conclusion

Robert's starting point is the *GF*. The structure and much of the detail is from that source; and like his contemporaries Baudry and Guibert he tells a consistent story about the deficiencies of the text and his commission to improve them. As such he should clearly be classed with the other *GF* derivatives.

Like the other users of the *GF*, he adds some new material. Much though not all of that material is common with Gilo, though in a sufficiently different form to suggest that it is not directly borrowed; some elements of this also appear in Raymond of Aguilers. Virtually all the hexameters in Robert's text coincide with this material. The most likely explanation is that Robert drew extensive additional material from a now lost Latin verse source which Gilo also knew but which, surprisingly, has left no other traces; he used this alongside the *GF* and for some parts of his text in preference to it.

Whilst there are parallels with other texts such as Baudry, there is no clear relationship; they are more likely to reflect the difficulty of telling the same story in different words, and possibly talking to the same eyewitnesses and hearing the same stories.

There are clear echoes of the *chanson de geste*. However, much of the 'epic' material in Robert is borrowed directly from the *GF*, which may in turn have derived it from a primitive form of the *Antioche*. Many of the echoes are of style rather than substance. Of the other unascribed material it is impossible to discern under the *remaniement* of the *Antioche* and *Jérusalem* by Graindor what might have belonged to an earlier version.

Two episodes seem to suggest some knowledge of the Occitan tradition reflected in the later reworking of the *Canso d'Antioca*: the heroism of Golfier and the episode of the Occitan apostate. The first of these is in Gilo and the second has some echoes in his text. These are more likely to reflect the lost source than direct knowledge by Robert of the Occitan poem (which in any case is unlikely to have been completed by the time Robert wrote).[104] However, it is interesting that Robert praises Raymond Pilet from the Occitan contingent, on occasion adding references

---

coming as it does before a rhetorical speech by a Saracen which would be completely at home in a *chanson de geste*. Robert implicitly acknowledges this by describing his informant as an apostate, who could be assumed to understand what Clemens apparently said. This is the only part of the chronicle attributed to an eyewitness other than the Council of Clermont. Robert may have intended this as a framing device, opening and closing the chronicle with set-piece speeches both relayed by eyewitnesses.

[104] *Canso*, Introduction, 8–9.

to Raymond IV and Adhemar; and interesting too that he echoes the predominantly Occitan lyric form of the *alba*.

The remaining additions are unique to Robert. Many reflect his desire to construct a theology for the Crusade, to emphasise the role of French crusaders and simply to tell a good story. We do not know what his sources were for the few pieces of original material: it may reflect a now lost source or reliance on tradition and eyewitness accounts from returned Crusaders. Either way it is not without value but adds little substantial to our knowledge of events. We can be clear that, other than the account of the Council of Clermont, it is not eyewitness testimony from Robert himself.

As historian, Robert delivers exactly what he promises in his prologue: to supply an account of the Council and to improve his source text. His account is of interest to the historian because of what it says about the Council and because of the perceptions he brings; it adds little new historical fact.

Chapter 4

Robert as author: the theologian, the historiographer and the storyteller

Robert brings three different but linked perspectives to his history: those of the theologian, the historiographer and the literary craftsman. This chapter examines the three approaches in turn. It concludes that his work reflects a stage in a conscious effort to develop a theology and ideology of the Crusade alongside that of other authors; that he wrote as a serious historiographer and that accusations to the contrary are unfair; and that he possesses storytelling skills of a high order which probably account for his overwhelming popularity throughout the medieval era.

i) Robert as theologian of the Crusade

Robert's account of the Crusade is as much a spiritual odyssey as a temporal one. Along with Baudry and Guibert he creates a theological framework which justifies and explains the events of the Crusade.[1] As Riley-Smith comments, it is striking that all three were Benedictine monks (Urban was formerly the Prior of Cluny): 'in spite of natural differences in style and interest, the message that flowed from these three pens was already recognizably one message'.[2] The First Crusade was almost literally miraculous in its scope and its success against the odds: there was a need both to explain that success and to draw on it in stimulating enthusiasm for a new Crusade, and to underline the leading role of the Papacy and the church.

Robert and his Benedictine contemporaries did not create their theology from a void. They developed it from the ideas generated on the Crusade itself, giving 'an intellectual expression of the semi-popular ideology forged in the traumas of the expedition and with them the crusading idea as it had developed in the course of the crusade passed back into the province of theologians'.[3] These ideas stemmed directly from Urban's preaching and the experiences of the Crusade. Jerusalem was the central goal, apparent from charters.[4] The Crusaders were on alien territory, outnumbered and frequently starving: it seemed literally miraculous that they should have defeated the infidels, and this found explanation in the direct help of

---

[1] See the illuminating discussion by Riley-Smith, *Idea,* 135–52; also P. Alphandéry, 'Les citations bibliques chez les historiens de la première Croisade', *RHR* 99 (1929), 139–57; *La chrétienté et l'idée de croisade* (Paris, 1954).

[2] Riley-Smith, *Idea,* 139.

[3] Riley-Smith, *Idea,* 139.

[4] Cowdrey, 'Pope Urban II's preaching'.

God,[5] symbolised through visions and miracles (particularly at Antioch) and through divine intervention. There was some inkling that this represented what was foretold in Scripture.[6] The intense suffering on Crusade was integral to their penance, a punishment and a test of their faith.[7] Martyrdom expressed their love for God and the reward for the Crusade, as well as being a comfort in an environment where sudden death was frequent.[8] All of these are expanded in the theology developed by Robert and his contemporaries.

Goals of the Crusade and centrality of Jerusalem

The concept of holy war was clear.[9] The Crusade as preached by Urban had two aims: regaining the territory lost by Greek Christians and regaining Jerusalem. In a secular sense the war was a just one: property had been seized by violence and should be restored. But it was equally justified in spiritual terms. Jerusalem was at the centre of Christian doctrine as well as the centre of the world, full of memories of the physical presence of Jesus. Its sacredness and the pollution by the infidels added a spiritual dimension to the concept of just recovery of stolen land.[10]

Urban's speech as rendered by Robert sets out two clear goals for the Crusade: the liberation of the Eastern Christians from Turkish domination (the horrors of which he illustrates copiously and imaginatively) and the need to free Jerusalem, presented as the climax of the first speech. These are to be achieved through holy war: not only have the infidels stolen the territory, they have deliberately and sacrilegiously polluted it and prevented pilgrims from travelling there in peace. These themes are woven throughout the remainder of the history.

There is relatively little emphasis on the need to help Eastern Christianity. Whilst Robert is contemptuous of the Byzantines, his description of Byzantium[11] fully acknowledges its status as the head of the Eastern Church and refuge for

---

[5] See the second letter of Stephen of Blois (ed. Hagenmeyer, *Kreuzzugsbriefe,* 149–52): 'Deus autem pugnauit pro nobis suis fidelibus contra eos', ('moreover God fought for our faithful soldiers against them', 151).

[6] See *GF* 55: Kerbogha's mother comments 'inuentum est in nostra pagina et in gentilium uoluminibus, quoniam gens Christianam super nos foret uentura, et nos ubique uictura, ac super paganos regnatura' ('it was discovered in our Koran as well as in the books of the infidel, that the Christian people was destined to come upon us and to defeat us in every place, and that it should rule over the pagans', Hill's translation).

[7] *GF* 34: 'hanc paupertatem et miseriam pro nostris delictis concessit nos habere Deus' ('God granted that we should suffer this poverty and wretchedness because of our sins', Hill's translation).

[8] See the account of Rainald Porcet's martyrdom in PT 79–80: 'animam cuius angeli confestim suscipientes ante conspectum Dei pro cuius amore martyrium suscepit' ('angels immediately raised his soul into the sight of God for love of whom he had accepted martyrdom').

[9] See, for example, BB 14.

[10] Riley-Smith, *Idea,* 144–7; C. Erdmann, *The Origin of the Idea of Crusade,* transl. M. W. Baldwin, W. Goffart (Princeton, 1977).

[11] II.20.

Christians, subordinate only to Rome. There is a passing mention by the envoys from the Emir of Babylon and in the vision of Stephen Valentine.[12]

Jerusalem is by contrast present throughout. The Crusade is repeatedly presented as the voyage to the Holy Sepulchre or the pilgrimage to Jerusalem.[13] The goal is explicitly stated: 'nostra omnium una sit intentio, sancti scilicet Sepulcri deliberatio'.[14] Events at Jerusalem form the climax to the history, occupying the whole of the last book. Robert sets out its central place unequivocally: 'vero historicus sermo iste ab Iherosolima nominis sui sumpsit exordium, et finem retinet, sicut et medium'.[15] The finale of his story consists of two chapters describing the temporal and the spiritual Jerusalem.

Robert refers frequently to the justification underlying the Holy War. The pollution of the Holy Land by the Turks is luridly described: 'praesertim moveat vos sanctum Domini Salvatoris nostri Sepulcrum, quod ab immundis gentibus possidetur, et loca sancta, quae nunc inhoneste tractantur et irreverenter eorum immundiciis sordidantur'.[16] There are two sets of negotiations with the Turks, encapsulating two approaches: the refusal to restore what the Christians see as stolen territory, and the difficulties created by them for pilgrims. In neither case (inevitably) is there a meeting of minds. Herluin's discussions with Kerbogha throw into sharp relief the theme of land: 'tu et rex tuus gensque tua in eorum conspectu culpabiles estis, qui terras Christianorum immoderata cupiditate invasistis'.[17] The offer from the Emir of Babylon centres on restoring unfettered pilgrimage to Jerusalem: the Christians refuse because it cannot be an alternative to the divinely ordained regaining of Jerusalem. It can, though, be a useful adjunct, as in the agreement reached at Caesarea.[18] And once Jerusalem is regained the restoration of pilgrimage is celebrated as a central achievement: 'nunc peregrini sui portis apertis recipiuntur cum laudibus, qui olim cum magna difficultate in magnis injuriis suscipiebantur'.[19]

---

[12] V.2, VII.1.

[13] For example, I.3, 'etiam in maritimis Oceani insulis divulgatum esset quod Iherosolimitanum iter in concilio sic stabilitum fuisset' ('even in the islands of the sea it was common knowledge that a pilgrimage to Jerusalem had been launched at the Council'); V.7 'quantum desiderabat tuum videre Sepulcrum' ('he wanted so desperately to see Your tomb').

[14] V.11: 'We all have but one goal: the liberation of the Holy Sepulchre.'

[15] IX.25: 'This historical sermon took its beginning and its end and its middle from Jerusalem.'

[16] I.1: 'Most especially let the Holy Sepulchre of Our Lord the Redeemer move you – in the power as it is of foul races - and the holy places now abused and sacrilegiously defiled by their filthy practices.'

[17] VII.5: 'You and your king are guilty of invading Christian lands with unbridled covetousness.'

[18] V.1; VIII.9.

[19] IX.24: 'Now his pilgrims were received with open arms and encouragement, whereas before they had been received only with great difficulty.'

The Franks as chosen people

If the Crusade stemmed directly from the will of God, it was logical to see the Franks as his chosen instruments. Guibert enshrined this in the title of his work – *Gesta Dei per Francos*, the achievements of God through the Franks.

It is a recurrent theme in Robert that the Franks are the chosen people of God. It is set out in his prologue: 'Francorum *beata gens, cujus est Dominus Deus ejus, populus quem elegit in hereditatem sibi.*'[20] Urban's speech sets out that their achievements show the divine favour they enjoy. They are gifted by God with outstanding attributes: glory in arms, courage, physical strength and fitness.[21] The warcry 'Deus vult!' is attributed directly to divine inspiration, a concept explained in some detail: 'sit ergo vobis vox ista in rebus bellicis militare signum, quia verbum hoc a Deo est prolatum'.[22] Bohemond raises morale by asserting 'cui unquam genti praestitit Deus in tam brevi tempore tot bella committere, tot acerrimos hostes superare, tot spoliis gentium ditari, tot triumphantium palmis insigniri?'.[23] Robert's closing sentiment is that the Franks were chosen to liberate Jerusalem, and that this had been part of God's plan all along, foretold in Isaiah: 'haec et multa alia invenimus in propheticis libris, quae congruunt huic liberationi factae aetatibus nostris'.[24]

Robert pays lip service to Crusaders of other nationalities: Urban's speech starts with a reference to 'gens Francorum, gens transmontana'.[25] The focus then narrows almost immediately to the French. They are set apart by geography; they live in a land surrounded by sea and mountains. They are encouraged to leave behind the violent struggles of late eleventh-century French society. Their ancestry is brought in by reference to Charlemagne, a passing reference in the *GF* which Robert deliberately sites in Urban's speech.[26] Legends about Charlemagne's pilgrimage had been current since the ninth century:[27] Robert evokes at a stroke the noble ancestry of the Franks and the Frankish precedent for the Crusade. Similarly Godfrey of Bouillon is described as following Charlemagne's route on his way to Constantinople: the first Advocate of the Holy Sepulchre is seamlessly assimilated

---

[20] Prologue: '*the blessed nation* of the Franks *whose God is the LORD; and the people whom he hath chosen for his own inheritance.*'

[21] I.1.

[22] I.2: 'so let that cry be a warcry for you in battle because it came from God'.

[23] IV.10: 'to what race has God granted the privilege of fighting so many battles, beating so many terrible enemies, enriching themselves with so much spoil from races and being crowned with the palms of so many triumphs?'

[24] IX.26: 'We have found this and many other things in the books of the prophets which fit exactly the context of the liberation of the city in our era.'

[25] I.1: 'Frenchmen and men from across the mountains.'

[26] *GF* 2; RM I.1.

[27] J. Horrent, *Le Pèlerinage de Charlemagne. Essai d'explication littéraire avec des notes de critique textuelle* (Paris, 1961): 'la vaste tradition du voyage légendaire de Charlemagne à Jérusalem et à Constantinople, attestée depuis Benoît de St André du Mont-Soracte, existante à l'époque de la *Chanson de Roland* et plus tard encore' (22–3).

to the Carolingian dynasty.[28] Bohemond's French ancestry is evoked more than once: when setting off on Crusade he exhorts his forces with the words 'nonne et nos Francigenae sumus? Nonne parentes nostri de Francia venerunt ...?'.[29] In a remarkable comment Bohemond's less appealing traits are blithely ascribed to his partly Italian ancestry: 'habuitque a patre suo, qui Francigena fuit, optima principia; sed a matre, quae Apuliensis exstitit, retinuit vestigia'.[30]

The working out of God's will in the events of the Crusade: assertion, scripture and miracles

The Crusade was willed by God and its success is a direct result of his power. Robert sets out the theme in detail in his Prologue: 'post creationem mundi quid mirabilius factum est praeter salutiferae crucis mysterium, quam quod modernis temporibus actum est in hoc itinere nostrorum Iherosolimitanorum? ... non fuit humanum opus, sed divinum'.[31] As such it has been part of God's plan from the beginning and is foretold in Scripture: the events of the Crusade show prophecy coming true in reality. Guibert's exegesis comes from various parts of the Bible: Robert's is heavily concentrated on the prophecies of Isaiah.[32]

He consistently refers to God's will being displayed through the events of the Crusade. The news of the venture spreads immediately throughout the world.[33] God inspires the princes of Northern Europe to set out on Crusade.[34] Victory at Nicaea is with God's help;[35] he frustrates the attempts by the citizens to defend Ma'arrat-an-Nu'man.[36] At times God becomes almost a player in events in his own right: his hand repels the Turks, and personally provides supplies for the famished army.[37]

The Crusaders are identified with groups in the Bible. They are compared to the Israelites on their way to the Promised Land with Adhemar compared to Moses;[38] the hymn of praise at Dorylaeum is composed of phrases taken from the Book of Exodus;[39] and the prologue starts with reference to Moses. The Saracens are similarly compared to biblical characters: the Persians are described in the same

---

[28] I.5.

[29] II.4: 'after all are we not French? Didn't our parents come from France ...?'

[30] VIII.15: 'He had inherited the highest principles from his French father; but they were tainted by elements from his Apulian mother.' The comment is so crude that it is tempting to wonder whether it is a later marginalium which has become incorporated.

[31] *Prologue*: 'since the creation of the world what more miraculous undertaking has there been (other than the mystery of the redeeming Cross) than what was achieved in our own time by this journey of our own people to Jerusalem? ... this was not the work of men: it was the work of God'.

[32] Riley-Smith, *Idea*, 142.

[33] I.3.

[34] II.1.

[35] III.4, 6.

[36] VIII.5.

[37] IV.3, IV.8.

[38] I.1, II.16, IV.8, VI.12; I.4.

[39] III.14.

terms as renegade Israelites and the Turk killed by Godfrey on the bridge at Antioch as a second Goliath.[40] The disinheriting of Seon and Og in favour of the chosen people is evoked.[41] The Crusade thus becomes a replay of key Old Testament events, which in turn underline the predestined nature of its success.

The Crusaders are repeatedly depicted playing out in reality what is foretold in Scripture, with Robert making particular use of Isaiah: as he explains at the end of the story the Crusade is part of God's plan and foretold by the Prophets.[42] There is a long passage of exegesis setting victory at Dorylaeum in the context of both the Old and the New Testament.[43] A skirmish at Antioch is foretold in the Book of Proverbs.[44] The riddle of Samson is used to explain the treachery of Pirrus.[45] The sole mention of the Apocalypse comes when the Crusaders first see Jerusalem: Jesus' rising from the tomb evokes that of humanity in the Last Judgement.[46] After Ascalon the hillsides literally ring with jubilation as foretold in Isaiah.[47]

The story of the Crusade is punctuated by Christian festivals, whose import is sometimes symbolically reflected in the activities of the Crusaders. A particularly striking example is Ascension Day, which is played out in the ascent of a mountain path.[48] The feast of St Peter ad Vincula variously symbolises Adhemar's release from earthly bonds and the election of Arnulf as Patriarch of Jerusalem when the city is freed from its Saracen chains.[49] The defeat of the diabolically inspired Clemens happens on the same day as that on which Jesus defeated Satan, whilst the turning point of the battle of Ascalon is at the same hour as when He ascended the Cross.[50]

Robert highlights the two key symbols of the Crusade: the warcry of 'Deus vult!' and the taking of the Cross. At the Council of Clermont the cry of 'Deus vult!' is represented as coming directly from God, and Robert explains in some detail that it is a symbol of God's will in the enterprise.[51] In Robert's source the *GF* the cry is mentioned in the context of Bohemond's departure on Crusade; Robert places it at the centre of his Crusade ideology, thereby both emphasising the divine will and shifting the emphasis away from Bohemond towards Urban and the French. Similarly Robert retains Bohemond's dramatic stage management of the taking of the Cross by his own forces, but places the theology firmly in Urban's speech.[52]

---

[40] I.1, IV.20.
[41] VI.12.
[42] IX.26.
[43] III.15.
[44] IV.6.
[45] VI.1.
[46] IX.1.
[47] IX.24.
[48] VIII.19.
[49] VII.23; IX.11.
[50] IX.16, 20.
[51] I.2; see also II.3.
[52] *GF* 7; RM I.2, II.4. It is interesting however that much of the theological exposition by Robert is put in the mouth of Bohemond, notably the conversations with Pirrus in V.8–9.

Miracles were seen as the active intervention of God in human affairs, explaining the inexplicable and giving a tangible sign of God's approval.[53] Pre-eminent amongst these are the celestial white forces led by saints (often St George, St Demetrius and St Maurice) who feature particularly in *GF*-derived sources for the Crusade.[54] Robert lays heavy emphasis on their role. He puts them at the centre of discussions between Bohemond and Pirrus, giving a detailed description of how they are angels in human guise;[55] their role is further emphasised by being foretold in Adhemar's sermon; and their intervention is depicted as the turning point of the battle.[56] They are also the deciding factor in the conversion by the Turks in the citadel, the essential sequel to the victory in battle.[57] St George's role as standard-bearer is recalled when the Crusaders reach his sacred place of Ramla.[58] The cluster of miracles and visions around the battle of Antioch before the battle parallels closely the accounts in other chronicles, but the explanations are consistent with the picture Robert develops elsewhere: the emphasis on divine aid and the special status of the Franks symbolised by the comet.[59]

The status of the Crusaders: milites Christi, pilgrims and martyrs

The status of Crusaders was ambiguous. They were pilgrims to the Holy Sepulchre as many had been before them. They were also soldiers. The description at II.3 sums this up: despite the magnificence of the army, the soldiers buy their provisions as if they were pilgrims. Robert refers repeatedly to the Crusaders as 'peregrini', pilgrims, and to the Crusade as 'viam sancti Sepulcri'. He pointedly describes the Crusaders travelling via Rome to visit the holy sites there.[60] Their expedition is twice compared to the pilgrimage of Charlemagne to Jerusalem and Constantinople.[61] Equally he is clear that they are soldiers.[62] On occasions they are addressed or described as both.[63] The envoys from the Emir of Babylon contrast the military status of the Crusaders with their apparent status as pilgrims, offering them safe passage if they lay down their arms.

Robert portrays the Crusaders as Christian superheroes. The ethos is summed up at II.2: they are utterly committed to the cause, fearless, splendidly equipped and united in their aim. (This can make for some interesting gymnastics where events have to be portrayed which show them as neither committed, fearless nor

---

[53] B. Ward, *Miracles and the Medieval Mind* (London, 1982).

[54] V.9; *GF* 69, PT 112, BB 77, GN 240.

[55] V.8–9; VI.12.

[56] VII.10, 13.

[57] VII.18.

[58] VIII.21.

[59] VII.1, 4.

[60] II.2.

[61] The best-known version of this is the parodic *chanson de geste Le Pèlerinage de Charlemagne,* ed. G. S. Burgess and A. E. Cobby, *The Pilgrimage of Charlemagne and Aucassin and Nicolette* (New York and London, 1988).

[62] II.14.

[63] II.16, VI.16.

united, notably in Book VIII.) They cannot be defeated because God has made them stronger than any Saracen opponent.[64] The picture is reinforced in mirror image by the descriptions the Saracens are made to give of their opponents: thus the defeated Soliman's speech at III.17 highlights the same features of fearlessness, glittering arms and unconquerability.

As well as being secular heroes, they are also models of Christian unity and humility. They are disciplined and pious, buying food rather than pillaging. Following Jesus' command in the New Testament, they renounce family and home to follow the Crusade. They are united in purpose. The ethos is that of 'a monastery in motion'[65] – although a monastery whose discipline would buckle repeatedly under the stress of privation and attack.

Robert makes it clear that the Crusaders have been transformed from mere soldiers to soldiers of God. Through their sufferings on Crusade they do penance for their sins.[66] When they die their reward is spiritual, Paradise and the status of martyrs: this is implicit in the *GF* but developed in more detail by Robert: 'Ibunt consanguinei et fratres nostri sine nobis ad martyrium, imo ad Paradisum?'[67] They also gain temporal rewards, with the poor finding themselves rich.[68] Adhemar's sermon before the battle of Antioch develops this theme in more detail and it recurs at the fall of Jerusalem.[69]

However, heroism is tempered by the realities both of the suffering on the Crusade and fallible human nature. The suffering of the Crusaders is a major theme and one Robert could hardly avoid. He offers various explanations as to why God should have allowed it. One is that he is testing their faith: at IV.10 he reduces the Franks to a state of abject misery before intervening to help them. Another is that he does not want them to become complacent in relying on divine help: at VI.6 he is described as deliberately impeding the taking of Antioch. At VII.1 the suffering is seen as punishment for sin, in this case fornication.

There is also a hint of ambivalence in his attitude to some of the worst excesses of the Crusade. This is particularly clear at the taking of Ma'arrat-an-Nu'man. The events – the massacre and the treachery of Bohemond towards his prisoners – are all in Robert's source.[70] Robert, though, spares no detail in his description: children are killed, citizens strung up several at a time, corpses cut open to retrieve gold coins: and his comments about 'detestanda auri cupiditas' and the description of the 'maceratio' as well as the emphasis on the fact it was the Sabbath all betray a certain unease. At VIII.14 there is implicit criticism of the leaders of the Crusade.

---

[64] II.16, V.9, VI.12.

[65] Riley-Smith, *Idea*, 150.

[66] II.16.

[67] II.4: 'Are our relatives and brothers to head for martyrdom – indeed for Paradise – without us?'

[68] III.15. This is a standard theme in Crusade rhetoric. Compare, famously, FC III.37.6–7: 'qui enim illic erant inopes, hic facit eos Deus locupletes' ('for God made rich those who had been poor').

[69] VII.10, IX.8.

[70] *GF* 79–80.

The status of the Turks

If God's will is that the Crusaders should be victorious, the Turks by definition are creatures of the devil, destined to be defeated as a race alien to God. So the Turks are represented as a mirror image of the Crusaders, with Mahommed as a less powerful version of Jesus and the Caliph as the Pope.[71] Robert is quite clear that the Turks are, by definition as the enemies of the Crusaders, literally diabolical: the diabolical legion and sons of the Devil.[72] In a piece of heavy symbolism they slaughter a priest in the middle of Mass.[73] In contrast to the certainties of God's power, they rely on divination, spells and astrology.[74] At IX.13 Clemens is stirred up against the Christians by the Devil, acting as his instrument in just the same way as the Crusaders are instruments of God. Like the Christians they suffer reverses in battle: unlike the Christians they turn on Mahommed as a failed deity.[75]

Apostasy and conversion

Apostasy is the worst thing a Christian can do on Crusade. In I.9 Rainald is consigned to Hell for his apostasy. At VII.6–7 the dialogue of Herluin and Kerbogha sets out the arguments in sharp relief: God's power is overwhelming and apostasy unthinkable. The fate of the apostate at VII.9 stands as a sharp reminder of the foolishness of apostasy: far from being rewarded he is decapitated at the whim of Kerbogha.

Conversion to Christianity is naturally a completely different matter. Pirrus converts to Christianity at V.10. At VII.18 those in the citadel of Antioch who do not wish to convert are allowed safe passage back home. This is in sharp contrast to events at the taking of Albara, where those who refuse to convert are beheaded;[76] the implication is similar at the taking of Ma'arrat-an-Nu'man. Riley-Smith suggests that Robert may have misrendered events at Albara as a result of textual corruption, and that the well-documented events at Ma'arrat-an-Nu'man may in fact reflect involvement in local politics.[77] The two are isolated instances: but there is no hint that they represented outrageous or unexpected behaviour. There is a hint of ambivalence at VIII.11: the Emir of Tripoli is offered peace if he will convert, but Robert comments that Raymond was more interested in his lands; perhaps unsurprisingly the Emir offers to convert.[78] The only eyewitness acknowledged by Robert other than himself is a convert:[79] it is hard to know whether this is more than a convenient fiction.

---

[71] IV.22, IX.21, VI.11. On the similarity of this to treatment of Saracens in the *chanson de geste* see Daniel, *passim*.

[72] I.10, IV.16.

[73] I.12: this is from *GF* but embroidered by Robert.

[74] VI.12.

[75] IX.21.

[76] VII.24.

[77] Riley-Smith, *Idea*, 110–11.

[78] VIII.19.

[79] IX.18, 20.

The role of the Church and her representatives

The position of Pope Urban as the inspiration of the Crusade sets the tone of Robert's work. His speech sets out the theological framework of divine justification and approval on which the Crusade is based. It also sets out the practicalities of how it is to be conducted. His speech refers to Charlemagne, setting the Crusade firmly in the context of Carolingian glories of the past. There is no doubt in Robert's mind about the pre-eminent position of his fellow Cluniac.[80] Interestingly he is alone amongst the chroniclers of the Crusade both in the long and detailed speech he gives to the Emir of Cairo and in calling him Clemens.[81] The Antipope Wibert of Ravenna took the name of Clemens, and was a bitter opponent of Urban throughout his Papacy.[82] This suggests that Robert's glowing portrayal of Urban may not be without a hint of propaganda on behalf of the legitimate Papacy.

Adhemar becomes the personification of the Church Militant. He appears in a number of roles. He is compared to Moses leading his people to the Promised Land. His role is particularly prominent during events round the battle of Antioch, where he seems to take command of the Crusade, underlining the spiritual importance of the battle. At VII.1 he takes steps to ascertain the truth of Stephen Valentine's vision; at VII.8 he gives orders for spiritual preparations for battle; and he embodies the role of the warrior bishop by giving a pre-battle sermon and carrying the Holy Lance out to battle.[83] The battle itself is as much a spiritual as a temporal one: the priests and clerics march out with the soldiers whilst the soldiers sing psalms with them, and the pre-battle speech is a sermon by Adhemar who foretells the divine help which will be the deciding factor. He greets victory with a further speech at VII.16. His death is represented as the worst calamity yet to befall the army.[84]

By contrast Robert blackens the picture of Peter the Hermit's Crusade in book I. Some accounts of the Crusade attributed its genesis to Peter; Robert makes it clear not only that the inspiration was Urban but that Peter's Crusade was not part of the mainstream movement. Peter is implicitly accused of lack of leadership, leaving the direction of the Crusade to the apostate Rainald and slipping away to Constantinople. Rainald is the leader of what one is tempted to call the anti-Crusade: he is depicted as cowardly and treacherous, and eventually as the antithesis of a Crusade leader when he apostasises and passes to the side of the Devil. The success of the main Crusade was seen as a sign of God's favour: equally the failure of this pre-Crusade suggests that it did not find favour with God. The legitimacy and divine approval of Urban's crusade gains by contrast.

---

[80] H. E. J. Cowdrey, 'Cluny and the First Crusade', *RB* 83 (1973), 285–311.

[81] RM IX.21

[82] G. Tellenbach, *Church, State and Christian Society at the time of the Investiture Contest*, transl. R. F. Bennett (Oxford, 1959); C. Morris, *The Papal Monarchy: the Western Church from 1050 to 1250* (Oxford, 1989); I. S. Robinson, *The Papacy 1073–1198: Continuity and Innovation* (Cambridge, 1990).

[83] VII.8–10 for Adhemar's role in the battle.

[84] VII.23.

Towards the end of the account as the Crusaders take cities near Jerusalem, the question of establishing the Church assumes more prominence. The first priority at Albara is to ordain a bishop as at Ramla.[85] Godfrey's election is immediately followed by the election of Arnulf as Patriarch: Robert casts him as a kind of second version of Adhemar in the battle of Ascalon, giving instructions on religious observance beforehand, riding out to battle and warning against premature plundering.[86]

The description of the Holy Land

The Crusaders would have long been familiar with the place names of the Holy Land through the Bible and through accounts of pilgrimage, both from written itineraries and returning eyewitnesses: 'the Holy Land was itself a relic, glowing with the power imparted to it by physical contact with the prophets and apostles and particularly with Christ'.[87] To this might be added the resonances of early Church history. Different chroniclers of the Crusade approach this in different ways. Guibert begins his work with a full description of the history of the Church.[88] Fulcher, perhaps reflecting the fact that he lived in the Holy Land, offers a literal description of the sites.[89]

Robert combines history, geography and theology in his landscape. A detailed description of Byzantium evokes its key role in the founding of the early Church.[90] The mention of Nicaea evokes memories of the Council of Nicaea: the saving of the Church from heretics then parallels its wresting from the Turks now. Iconium evokes the memory of the Apostle Paul as does Antioch.[91] The links between Antioch and St Peter are highlighted.[92] The description of Antioch itself is something of an outlier, focusing on the physical city and its history rather than its spiritual significance: this is the only passage of description which Robert took from the *GF* and occurs in other *GF*-derived accounts.[93] Caesarea is the home of the Apostle Philip, evoking the events recounted in the Acts of the Apostles.[94]

Conclusion

Like his Benedictine contemporaries Guibert and Baudry, Robert creates a theological framework for the events of the Crusade. It takes its starting point in the holy war preached by Urban. It develops the events of the Crusade and the beliefs of the Crusaders themselves, setting them in a clear spiritual context which

---

[85] VII.24, VII.21.
[86] IX.11, IX.14–16.
[87] Riley-Smith, *Idea*, 94.
[88] GN I.
[89] See e.g. his description of Jerusalem at I.26.
[90] II.20.
[91] III.19, III.29.
[92] IV.4, VIII.2.
[93] VIII.3; see e.g. GN 249–50; PT 119–20.
[94] VIII.20.

illuminates whilst not ignoring the course of events and the all too evident human frailties. The success of the Crusade was both explained and justified by the will of God, part of his timeless divine plan and therefore unshakeably preordained.

ii) Robert as historiographer

Surprisingly for the most popular chronicler of the Crusades during the Middle Ages, Robert has not found favour as a historian with modern authorities. He has been criticised as inaccurate and over-romanticised.[95] This misses the point. What is striking about his text is not the differences from contemporary historical disciplines but the similarities. Along with his Benedictine contemporaries Guibert and Baudry, he takes the raw events of the Crusade and places them in the framework of universal history, exploring and developing their meaning as part of a wider canvas.

Robert's *Prologue* and *Sermo Apologeticus* follow familiar lines. His reasons for writing start from the familiar concept of moral example:[96] the events of the Crusade are exemplary for the rest of the world and therefore need to be as widely known as possible: 'revera Deo fit acceptabile ut ad notitiam fidelium suorum litteris commendetur, quum in terra peragit … aliquod opus mirabile'.[97] Truth and authenticity are therefore crucial: 'nihil frivoli, nihil mendacii, nihil nugarum, nisi quod verum est enarrabimus'.[98]

The events need to be explained simply so that a diverse audience can learn from them and so that the style does not obscure the truth: 'probabilius est abscondita rusticando elucidare quam aperta philosophando obnubilare'.[99] But equally they need to be expressed in a style which befits their moral significance, 'lecturis eam accuratiori stilo componerem'.[100] This fits entirely the context of promoting a new Crusade: constructing a coherent framework for the events of the previous Crusade and expressing it in a simple and compelling style.

Robert places heavy emphasis on the familiar modesty topos.[101] He was commissioned to write by his abbot and wrote only 'per obedientiam', because of his monastic vow. He is insistent that he had no help.[102] He emphasises the deliberate simplicity of his work. This is ascribed in part to the haste of composition, and in part to specific intention to write in 'pedestri sermone', to ensure understanding. He dwells on this in some detail, justifying his approach. He

---

[95] See Chapter One.

[96] See e.g. HH 2–5 and compare GN 82.

[97] *Prologue*: 'How pleasing it is to God that an account should be written for the faithful of any miraculous deed he has brought to pass on Earth.'

[98] *Prologue*: 'our story will contain nothing frivolous, misleading or trivial – nothing but the truth'.

[99] *Sermo Apologeticus*: 'I thought it more appropriate to clarify obscure things by simplifying than to cloud over the obvious by philosophising.'

[100] *Sermo Apologeticus*: 'improve its style for future readers.'

[101] See for example WM 16–17.

[102] Guénée, 48–50.

attacks an unknown scholar who takes the opposite view and writes in a highly academic style. We do not know who this is: it would be tempting to guess at Guibert, who makes a virtue out of his own convoluted style, but if so there is no corresponding reference in Guibert's work.[103] Robert rather pointedly quotes from Horace to prove that he too knows his classics.[104] There is a clear implication that his work is truer because more simple.

Other than the reference to Bernard, Robert says little about the circumstances of commissioning. His task was to improve the style and add an account of the Council of Clermont, supplying a theological underpinning to the Crusade. However the references to the haste with which he seems to have written and the emphasis on explaining events simply to a wide audience, allied to the emphasis on the French as chosen people and the divine inspiration of the Crusade, are all consistent with a work written c. 1106–8 in the context of the preaching of a new Crusade.[105]

Robert's use of source material is conventional. He follows the hierarchy of 'visa, audita, lecta';[106] the one section of the text for which he was an eyewitness is clearly marked as is (rather dubiously) a section he claims to have had from an eyewitness convert in Jerusalem; there is also a vague reference to implied eyewitness sources for the speed with which the message of the Crusade spread.[107] His procedure as a historian, as explained in Chapters Two and Three above, can be clearly followed.[108] The *GF* was his source text, with order and material for the most part faithfully reproduced: this is the only source he mentions assuming – as is almost certain - it is to be identified with the text mentioned in the prologue. He drew extensively on a second source, probably now lost but held in common with Gilo; at one point his use of the two introduces an inconsistency.[109] Whatever this second source may have been, it was not acknowledged. This is standard procedure for a medieval historian;[110] it may also reflect Robert's desire to follow the prevailing orthodoxy on the *GF*. A few further elements are likely to have come

---

[103] Guibert was not exactly backward in attacking another chronicler of the Crusade, Fulcher of Chartres (GN 329–31). For discussion of style see his *Praefatio* 79–84. For discussion of his attack on Fulcher see Epp 71–6. It is interesting that Guibert criticises Fulcher for an over-elaborate and lurid style, something hardly justified by Fulcher's actual work; the unknown critic Robert refers to is similarly credited with an over-emphasis on style and by implication under-emphasis on accuracy. There are the echoes here of some lost dispute which we are unlikely to recapture.

[104] See note to translation.

[105] See discussion in Chapter One.

[106] For an expression see e.g. WM 16–17: 'quicquid vero de recentioribus aetatibus apposui, uel ipse vidi uel a viris fide dignis audivi', ('whatsoever I have added out of recent history, I have either seen myself or heard from men who can be trusted', Mynors' translation).

[107] *Sermo Apologeticus*: I.3; IX.18, 20.

[108] Guénée, 211–14.

[109] See discussion above in Chapter Three of the mysterious resurrection of Cassianus' son.

[110] Guénée, 116.

from other sources, returning Crusaders, vernacular literature or simply his own imagination.

Robert's thinking is in line with the tenets of universal history. History plays out as part of God's overall plan for the world, where events are foretold by the prophets and the Bible is central: 'le christianisme imposait une conception linéaire du temps'.[111] This was given expression in universal chronicles such as that of Otto of Freisingen. Guibert starts his work with a discussion of Church history. Whilst Robert focuses more sharply on the events of the Crusade, he is equally clear about the providential framework in which they exist: 'post creationem mundi quid mirabilius factum est praeter salutiferae crucis mysterium, quam quod modernis temporibus actum est in hoc itinere nostrorum Iherosolimitanorum?'.[112] Just as the Old Testament patriarchs wrote to record God's doings for posterity, so will he.

As historiographer, Robert is notable only – and precisely – for his conventionality. He uses the standard techniques and topoi of other Latin historians. It is fair to say that his work contains little new for the historian of the Crusade. But he approaches his work with the same seriousness as other historiographers and there is no reason to accord him less respect.

iii) Robert as literary craftsman

Robert works within literary tradition. His account is full of literary reminiscences, with heavy use of the conventions and language of the vernacular *chanson de geste*. He is a good craftsman who makes full use of stylistic techniques to heighten the effect.[113] Beyond this he has a rare skill: that of the storyteller, able to portray characters and scenes with a few deft strokes and keep the reader enthralled till the end.

Literary sources

The *chanson de geste* is by far the dominant literary influence in the *Historia*. *Chansons de geste* were the fictionalisation of Carolingian battles, notably against pagan enemies; written down from orally transmitted originals and formulaic in style, they recount and glorify the process of battle in minute detail. The First Crusade brought a new sense of immediacy; just as the events of the Old Testament suddenly came to pass, heroic fights against the Saracens became immediate and eyewitness reality. The events and ethos of the Crusade permeated the *chanson de geste*, most famously the *Chanson de Roland*.[114] Conversely the

---

[111] Guénée, 20

[112] *Prologus*: 'since the creation of the world what more miraculous undertaking has there been (other than the mystery of the redeeming Cross) than what was achieved in our own time by this journey of our own people to Jerusalem?'

[113] Marquardt, 7, sums up neatly: 'alles in viel grellerem Lichte darzustellen'.

[114] For analysis of the relationship between the *chanson de geste* and the Crusade ethos see D. A. Trotter, *Medieval French Literature and the Crusades: 1100–1300* (Geneva, 1988), 72–125.

sometimes mundane and shocking reality of the Crusade was invested with a new glamour, its heroes and events placed on a par with those of the heroic past.

Robert draws extensively on the themes and techniques of the *chanson de geste*. Urban II is given a specific reference to Charlemagne and his wars against the pagans, setting a clear tone.[115] The Christian forces are magnificently equipped with glittering weapons.[116] They behave heroically both as individuals and as an army.[117] Where they are defeated it is against overwhelming odds and they are rewarded by going to Paradise.[118] Adhemar is a warrior bishop like Turpin in the *Roland*.[119] The Turks by contrast are barely human fiends who take delight in tormenting the Christians; they are like wild beasts; they are too cowardly to fight, preferring to use arrows and then flee.[120] There are detailed descriptions of single combat, of the carnage of battle and of reinforcements riding to the rescue.[121] At times these become formulaic (perhaps unsurprisingly – there are only so many ways to describe a battle). In Robert's hands the *chansons de geste* come to life, and the Crusades are invested with the myth of a legendary past.

This of course creates incongruities. The references to glittering weapons sit alongside a description of the army throwing away its weapons on a difficult mountain crossing.[122] Heroic Crusaders are portrayed as demoralised and slipping away by night.[123] There is a particularly acute clash of fiction and reality in the description of William of Melun:[124] he is described in conventional terms as the invincible warrior, who nevertheless succumbs to cowardice: as Robert comments, 'hoc non metu praeliorum, ut speramus, fecerat; sed tantam famis injuriam pati nunquam didicerat'.[125] Robert is a realist. But he is also a skilled craftsman capable of making his text function on a number of levels.

---

[115] I.1.

[116] See e.g. III.4, VII.9. Compare the description at *Guillaume* 1731: 'li soleiz raie, qui les armes esclargist' ('the sun shone, making the arms glitter').

[117] For example Godfrey at V.20 and Roger of Barneville at VI.8

[118] I.11. Compare, famously, *Roland* 2392–6: 'Deus li tramist sun angle Cherubin/E seint Michel de la Mer del Peril,/Ensembl'od els seint Gabriel i vint:/L'anme del cunte portent en pareis' ('God sent him [Roland] his angel Cherubin, and St Michael of the Dangerous Sea, and together with them came St Gabriel; they carry the soul of the Count to Paradise').

[119] VII.16.

[120] I.10, I.6, III.9. See Daniel 107–10: 'the hatred seems to be conventionalised, formalised, almost ritualised' (110).

[121] VII.11, IV.19, VII.15. For single combat compare Hugh's killing of a Saracen (VII.11) with virtually any chanson de geste: for example *Roland* 1265–8. For the carnage of battle compare e.g. *Raoul de Cambrai* ed. S. Kay (Cambridge, 1992) 3710–3. For epic motifs generally see J. Rychner, *La chanson de geste: essai sur l'art épique des jongleurs* (Geneva, 1955).

[122] III.28.

[123] VI.14.

[124] IV.12.

[125] 'One can only hope that it was not fear of battle but the fact that he had never before suffered so badly from hunger.'

There are few references to specific *chansons de geste*. The friendship of Godfrey and Hugh has overtones of Roland and Oliver, although this is not spelt out in detail. The most specific reference is to the *Pèlerinage de Charlemagne* where Godfrey, the hero and Advocate of the Holy Sepulchre, is described as following Charlemagne's route, a clear reference to his status.[126]

There are also a few references to poetry. Particularly striking is the evocation of the *alba* when Pirrus is waiting for Bohemond to enter Antioch.[127] An *alba* is a dawn song by a lover lamenting the arrival of dawn and the end of the night. Latin examples are rare; vernacular examples are found in Occitan in the twelfth century and in Old French from the thirteenth century.[128] This suggests that Robert must be drawing on a vernacular source: whether this constitutes a further link between him and Occitania we cannot say for certain. The implication at any rate is that Bohemond has been too busy overnight to take his responsibilities seriously now. The laments by Humberge for Walo and by Guy for Bohemond evoke the poetic form of the *planctus*.[129]

A more detailed analysis of allusions to classical authors awaits a future editor. In his prologue Robert quotes the *Ars Poetica* of Horace.[130] His description of Humberge meanwhile has overtones of Ovid's description of Niobe in the *Metamorphoses* and of phraseology in the same author's *Heroides*.[131] There are several reminiscences of Lucan's *Pharsalia*, which are pointed out in the notes: these are all shared with Gilo.[132]

Structure

No two chronicles of the Crusade follow the same structure. Robert imposes a tight and powerful structure on his account. The nine books fall very clearly into three sets of three. The first three books take the account from Urban's speech to arrival at Antioch. The middle three focus exclusively on events at Antioch, concluding with the Christians at their lowest point. The final three chronicle success, starting with the battle of Antioch and concluding with the battle of Ascalon. Each set of three has a Saracen anti-hero: Soliman in the first three, Kerbogha in the central

---

[126] I.5.

[127] V.12.

[128] See *Eos: an enquiry into the theme of lovers' meetings and partings at dawn in poetry*, ed. A. T. Hatto, (The Hague, 1965), in particular J. Lockwood, 'Classical, medieval and later Latin', 271–81 and B. Woledge, 'Old Provençal and Old French', 344–89. On Occitan connections see D. Rieger, `Zur Stellung des Tagelieds in der Trobadorlyrik', *ZRP* 87 (1971), 223–32.

[129] For references and discussion see note to translation.

[130] See note to translation of *Sermo Apologeticus* and discussion above. For discussion of the *Ars Poetica* as one of the most influential stylistic texts of the Middle Ages see P. Klopsch, *Einführung in die Dichtungslehren des lateinisches Mittelalters* (Darmstadt, 1980) 41–3.

[131] See note to translation for references and quotations.

[132] Lucan, *Pharsalia* ed./transl. J. D. Duff (Loeb, 1928); transl. R. Graves, *Lucan: Pharsalia: dramatic episodes of the Civil Wars* (Harmondsworth, 1956).

three and Clemens in the last three. Arrangement of books had symbolic importance:[133] Robert's, three times three, is evocative of the Trinity.

The story is framed to ensure that the aims of the Crusade remain central: it begins with Urban's preaching and ends with an encomium of Jerusalem regained; Urban's speech at the beginning is counterbalanced by Clemens' at the end. The heavenly music alluded to at the beginning becomes a principal theme at the end. Within the structure Robert cuts back on diversions such as the activities of Baldwin at Edessa in order to keep his narrative taut and dynamic.

Style

Robert was specifically given the objective by his abbot of improving the style of the *GF*. Unlike Guibert, who defiantly comments that those who do not understand his work have only themselves to blame and proves it by the elegant convolutions of his prose,[134] Robert placed a premium on clarity and simplicity: his aim is to explain and publicise the events of the Crusade to as wide an audience as possible.[135] This does not imply that his style is unsophisticated: far from it. But it is unobtrusive and does not become an end in itself.

The Latin is generally simple and paractactic in structure. There is abundant use of conjunctions and links – 'autem', 'igitur' and ablative absolutes – but these tend to be loosely used with little causative effect. As discussed above the text is shot through with biblical allusions and exegesis. With few exceptions Robert remains resolutely contemporary: the Turks are called Parthians on one occasion invoking classical Latin history.[136] For the most part Robert is clear not only that the Christians are fighting Saracens but also on the varying identities of the latter.

The stylistic devices used in the text play to Robert's strengths of vivid description and immediacy. There is abundant use of metaphor. Many metaphors evoke hunting;[137] wild beasts are also a common theme.[138] On a couple of occasions the slaughter on the battlefield is compared to a harvester,[139] and there are two horribly vivid comparisons with an abattoir.[140] Some of the metaphors become vignettes in themselves: the wind dispersing a pile of straw or blowing the branches off a tree, and bear-baiting.[141]

There is also consistent hyperbole. The description of the crush on the bridge at Antioch becomes a piece of *grand Guignol*, with corpses held up by living men.[142] Robert piles on the details of the slaughter in the streets at Antioch.[143] He states

---

[133] See Guénée, 179–84.

[134] GN 82.

[135] *Sermo Apologeticus*.

[136] VIII.3; Guénée 217–18. *GF* 77 has 'Turcis'.

[137] For example III.16, 19; VII.10; IX.4.

[138] VIII.7, IX.7.

[139] IV.7, IV.19.

[140] VII.14, IX.20.

[141] IV.20; VI.6.

[142] IV.19.

[143] VI.2.

that 100,000 knights and innumberable footsoldiers died in the battle of Antioch, almost certainly exaggerating massively.[144] Just occasionally he miscalculates and descends into bathos – for example when the victorious soldiers at Antioch are rewarded by the leftover meals of the Turks still warm in the pot.[145]

Robert uses various rhetorical devices to ornament his language. There is internal rhyme: 'omnes contristantur, nostrorumque funera lacrymantur'.[146] Emphasis is given by piling on details: 'nulli honor impenditur: pueri cum puellis, juvenes cum senibus, senes cum juvenibus, matres quoque cum filiabus interficiuntur'[147]. Alliteration is abundant: 'causasque consilii et prudentiae conferebant'.[148] There is elaborate language: 'ut primum lux matutina processit'.[149] He uses chiasmus: 'fortiter crescere et crescendo fortius insistere'.[150] None of this is particularly original or unusual, but it shows the extent to which Robert has taken care to ornament his text despite his protestations of simplicity.

Robert also has a fondness for word-play. A particularly striking example is the Emir Clemens, whom he characterises as 'Clemens, immo demens'. He is so delighted by his own cleverness that he returns to it twice and develops the conceit.[151] Another striking example is his extended play on the word 'fides' describing the example set by Pirrus.[152]

Prose and verse

Robert writes largely in prose, but his text contains some verses. The vast majority are hexameters; most of these are leonines although there is a sprinkling of other forms. I have commented above on the resemblance of some of these lines to Gilo, whose text is entirely in verse.

Latin historians wrote in both prose and verse.[153] Prosimetry was a recognised literary technique which combined the two. Used for satire in classical Latin by Petronius, it was used by Boethius and by Martianus Capella. Its first use for historiography was by Liutprand of Cremona.[154] It is used by a number of other

---

[144] VII.15.

[145] VII.15.

[146] VI.15: 'all were saddened and wept for the death of our men'.

[147] VI.2: 'Status made no difference: boys were killed alongside girls, the young alongside the old and the old alongside the young, and mothers too alongside their daughters.'

[148] V.1: 'conferred about the wisest and most prudent approach'.

[149] IV.22: 'when first light dawned'.

[150] IV.19: 'strongly growing and thereby growing stronger'.

[151] IX.13: 'Clementem, immo dementem'; IX.20: 'Clemens, nunc vero demens'; IX.21: 'Clemens, ut demens'.

[152] VI.1.

[153] For example, the *Carmen de Hastingae Proelio by Guy, Bishop of Amiens*, ed. C. Morton and H. Muntz (Oxford, 1972), is in Latin verse.

[154] See Epp, 358–60; P. Klopsch, 'Prosa und Vers in der mittellateinischer Literatur', *MLJ* 3 (1966), 9–24.

writers on the Crusade such as Guibert and Ralph of Caen.[155] Fulcher, for example, uses verse to highlight the role of some Crusaders, to emphasise some events and to create atmosphere.[156] Given the highly coloured nature of Robert's writing, it is difficult to see that his use of verse marks passages of heightened tone or emphasis other than in the lament of Humberge. It does, however, serve to underline his stylistic seriousness.

Storytelling

A good story, whether in a newspaper or a book, draws the reader in from the outset. It is populated by heroes and villains. It thrills with repeated cliffhangers, safe in the assurance that the heroes will win ultimately and the villains come to a sticky end. It is full of human interest. It is vivid and convincing. Often it has a rich mix of ingredients, comic and tragic, realistic and fantastic, with shifts of tone and register. By all these criteria Robert is a superb storyteller.

Robert's cast of characters is drawn in primary colours. He carefully limits the number of heroes so as not to diffuse interest: Godfrey and Hugh are unboundedly virtuous whilst Bohemond forms a flamboyant but ambivalent foil; the other leaders are softened into near-neutrality. They are opposed by three Saracen villains who are beaten in turn in the three great battles of the Crusade: Soliman at Dorylaeum, Kerbogha at Antioch; and Clemens at Ascalon. Each is caricatured in half-comic, half-menacing style: Kerbogha has the pomp and bombast of the typical Saracen leader[157] but is capable of flying into a rage the moment he is thwarted. Alexius is caricatured as an enemy of a different sort, the cowardly deceiver constantly scheming to undermine the heroes who consistently fails to meet his promises and ultimately loses all claim to land as a result. The supporting chorus consists of virtuous but frail Christians and of subhuman Turks gleefully tormenting them. Occasional heroes such as Roger of Barneville or Golfier of Las Tours are allowed a moment of individual glory.[158]

Robert several times uses a technique which might be described as mirroring: the Christians and the concepts of the Crusade are described as seen through Saracen eyes. Soliman in his speech describes their bravery in hyperbolic terms, casting them as superhuman and invincible.[159] Pirrus authenticates the existence of the supernatural white forces by his questions about them.[160] The speech of Kerbogha's mother sets out the preordained victory of the Christians and defeat of Kerbogha. The speech of Clemens underlines the magnitude of the victory at

---

[155] See Guénée 218–19: 'quand l'importance du sujet le réclamait, quand l'auteur voulait tirer d'un évènement quelque enseignement moral, ou simplement lorsqu'il jugeait bon de reposer son lecteur d'une trop lourde érudition, il lui arrivait d'insérer dans sa prose des vers' (218).

[156] Epp, 368–74.

[157] On Saracen arrogance see P. Bancourt, *Les Musulmans dans les chansons de geste* (Aix-en-Provence, 1982), 2 vols, vol.I 196–277.

[158] VI.8, VIII.6–7.

[159] III.17.

[160] V.8–9.

Ascalon and the power of God, contrasted with the failure of Mahommed to defend his people.[161] This technique allows Robert to underline the strength of the Christians by portraying them through the eyes of the Saracens, authenticating them by a different perspective.

Robert has a gift for building up suspense. The Franks hang back instead of storming into Antioch and Bohemond fails to appear: Pirrus becomes impatient and the enterprise hangs by a thread.[162] At the end of Book VI the Franks are deprived in turn of food, of help from the sailors and of potential help from the Emperor: when the situation is at its most desperate help comes almost literally from a *deus ex machina* in the form of visions.[163] Golfier is on the point of failing from exhaustion when there is unexpected success.[164] Throughout the text the Christians win, like all good comic-book heroes, in the teeth of overwhelming odds; but we know and they know that they will always win because God is supporting them.

Robert also has a gift for remarkably vivid vignettes which at their best evoke in just a few words the splendours and miseries of twelfth-century warfare. Examples are legion. The banners sway above the heads of the soldiers.[165] The bemused citizens of Antioch are awakened by the shouting, stumble out to see what is happening and never return.[166] Abandoned horses are left, reins trailing, whilst blood and dust fly through the air.[167] Dazed peasants wait with bowed heads to be slaughtered.[168]

Allied to this comes a taste for the lurid and violent. The appalling description of eviscerated Christians which Robert attributes to Urban II clearly made an impression on contemporaries: something similar is found in the later twelfth-century *Njalssaga*, and in the account given of Pope Urban's speech in the German *Magdeburger Aufruf*.[169] The dismemberment and decapitation of Roger of Barneville is described in detail.[170] Severed body parts float on a pool of blood in the Temple at Jerusalem.[171] There are repeated references to severed heads.[172] At times Robert himself seems shocked by the bloodshed he recounts: this is particularly evident at the massacre which accompanied the taking of Ma'arrat-an-Nu'man.[173] Descriptions of battle and violence were the stock in trade of the

---

[161] IX.21.
[162] V.12.
[163] VII.1.
[164] VIII.7.
[165] IV.15.
[166] VI.2.
[167] VII.14.
[168] IX.23.
[169] I.1; see note to translation for references.
[170] VI.8.
[171] IX.8; this passage is closely paralleled in Gilo.
[172] IV.3; IV.16; VI.9; VII.24, for example.
[173] VIII.7.

chanson de geste and hardly to be avoided in describing a military Crusade;[174] but they are unusually vivid and disturbing here.

Robert successfully manages a wide variety of tone. There is calculatedly heartrending pathos as in the description of Humberge's lament or the description of starving babies in one of the many famines. There is humour, as in the description of Soliman lying on the ground howling with terror and his sarcastic reception by the Arabs. Exaggeration goes hand in hand with flashes of pragmatic realism. He comments on the difficulties of keeping up morale without strong leadership.[175] He acknowledges the old truth that an army marches on its stomach.[176] His closing comment on the negotiations between the princes betrays a touch of world-weary cynicism honed, we may speculate, by bitter experience of such meetings.[177] There is also the occasional proverb.[178]

iv) Conclusion

Robert's chronicle seamlessly combines three perspectives: he writes as theologian, as historian and as storyteller. The three are interwoven. For example the historical Kerbogha was the focal point of resistance to the Christians at their most vulnerable and his defeat marked a turning point for the Crusade; whilst not losing this perspective Robert builds him simultaneously into a symbol of the diabolical Saracen opposition to the forces of good and a literary arch-villain. Other chroniclers may have brought more learning to their accounts (like Guibert), or more elegance (like Gilo). What Robert brings above all is an outstanding ability to tell a story based on and around the events of the Crusade. It is no coincidence that his popularity so far outstripped other chroniclers.

---

[174] See for example *Guillaume* 529–32: 'Tels set.c.homes trovent de lur terre/Entre lur pez trainant lur bowele;/Parmi lur buches issent fors lur cerveles/Et de lur escuz se covrent sur l'erbe' ('they found some seven hundred men from their lands dragging their bowels between their feet; their brains were coming out their mouths and they were covering themselves with their shields on the grass', Bennett's translation).
[175] I.6.
[176] II.19.
[177] VIII.8.
[178] IV.7, VII.22.

Chapter 5

Principles of translation

As the cliché about translations has it, 'quand elles sont belles elles ne sont pas fidèles; quand elles sont fidèles elles ne sont pas belles'. This translation aims to steer a middle course between fidelity and elegance.

I have used the version of the text in the *Recueil*, the only one readily available. I have made no attempt to edit the text and have worked on the basis of the variants given there (which give at best a partial picture of the manuscript tradition).

I have also followed closely the layout and structure of the *Recueil* text. I have split the text according to the chapters in the *Recueil* and translated the chapter headings. It is unlikely that either chapters or headings were inserted by Robert himself.[1] But this is outweighed by the advantages of a text which can readily be compared with the most easily available Latin text in print, and by the reasoning which led to their original insertion: the need for clear signposting through a long text. The headings for each of the nine books are mine, intended to make the thread of the narrative easier to follow.

For similar reasons I have translated the hexameters which appear at the opening to some chapters; they are distinguished from the rest of the text by italicisation. These appeared in the manuscript used by Bongars and he printed them in the margin. We do not know at what stage these entered the text: Kraft argues that they are not Robert's own because they tail off towards the end of the text,[2] which is not in fact the case. What is evident is that they were intended to summarise the events in the chapters they head; this suggests strongly that they were inserted by a later editor rather than being Robert's own. There is no discernible connection between them and Gilo's text.

I have standardised names of people on the forms used by Riley-Smith;[3] for Arabic names I have followed Runciman.[4] Names of places have been taken from the Gazetteer in Setton and Baldwin.[5] Chronology has been checked against Hagenmeyer's *Chronologie de la Première Croisade*.[6]

In general Robert's Latin is straightforward (which may be one of the reasons for his popularity). It becomes less so when he is in rhetorical mood or explaining theology; and occasionally I have found myself hard pushed to translate

---

[1] Kraft 16. III.1 refers to 'crucesignati', a term not used until much later. See M. Markowski, ' "Crucesignatus": its origins and early usage', *JMH* 10 (1984), 157–65.

[2] Kraft 16.

[3] J. Riley-Smith, *The First Crusaders, 1095-1131* (Cambridge, 1997).

[4] Runciman, *History*, vol.I.

[5] *A History of the Crusades*, ed. Setton and Baldwin (Madison, 1969–89), 6 vols.; vol.I: *The First Hundred Years,* ed. M. Baldwin, 1969: Gazetteer and note on maps, 626–66.

[6] H. Hagenmeyer, *Chronologie de la Première Croisade* (Paris, 1902).

comprehensibly for a modern audience. As translator I have adopted the following principles.

I have attempted to convey something of Robert's wordplay. Sometimes this falls neatly into English: 'arte, non Marte' can be reasonably rendered as 'the art of strategy rather than the art of war',[7] and the chiasmus in 'nostrorumque agmina fortiter crescere et crescendo fortius insistere' falls obediently into English as 'our battle columns strongly growing and thereby growing stronger'.[8] On other occasions it is impossible without sounding torturously stilted: Robert's favourite bit of wordplay 'Clementem, immo dementem' does not have the same ring when rendered as 'Clement, better described as the Demented'[9] whilst 'Clement the Dement' is fun but hardly recognisable English. Where necessary I have opted for clear English rather than reproducing the irreproducible.

Robert's style is paratactic, characterised by abundant and rather loose use of conjunctions, ablative absolutes and purpose clauses. I have treated these grammatical structures with a fairly free hand to avoid a stilted and awkward text. To a lesser extent and for the same reason I have changed the boundaries of some sentences. Robert's tenses tend to move seamlessly between past and present in a way which is distracting in modern English: again I have preserved this where it does not do too much violence to modern English. Although he refers to himself as 'nos' I have generally rendered this in the singular for the sake of clear English.

Robert's text is prosimetric and he makes (limited) use of verse. I have made no attempt to translate into verse; I have used prose broken to reflect the length of the lines and inset the passages so they are readily identifiable.

I have compared my translation against the early nineteenth-century version by François Guizot, which is elegant and readable although I disagree with a few points.[10]

I have chosen to render the frequent biblical quotations in the version of the King James translation. This is because many of the quotations from the Bible current in modern English use its phraseology; using it here is the best way of capturing its resonances for a modern audience. The quotations are italicised in the text. On occasion the Vulgate text used by Robert differs slightly from the King James version, and I have pointed this out in the notes.

Translations from other sources given in the notes are mine unless otherwise indicated.

---

[7] IV.1.

[8] IV.19.

[9] IX.13.

[10] See e.g. V.14: 'quem Boamundus in ipso portae introitu summisso capite salutavit, eique de collato beneficio gratias egit'. Guizot translates 'lorsque Boémond entra, il le salua à la porte, la tête baissée; celui-ci le remercia du service qu'il lui rendait', which confuses the issue of who was saluting whom. I take the Latin to suggest (backed up by the parallel passage in Gilo VII.115–16) that Bohemond made a point of stopping in the gateway and saluting Pirrus, who had just betrayed the city to him.

A word on some of the vocabulary may be helpful:

a.   'Franci': literally Franks. The difficulty here is that by the time of the First Crusade a term which had been clearly identified with the Franks of Charlemagne was beginning to take on more nationalistic overtones as a term for the French, although the dividing line is not clear.[11] Where the term describes the French in opposition to other national groupings, I have translated as 'French'. On all other occasions I have translated as 'Franks' to preserve the ambiguity inherent in the term.

b.   The term 'crusaders' ('crucesignati') was not used consistently in the twelfth century and certainly not this early.[12] Robert's terms shift, with the crusaders being described both as pilgrims and soldiers of God. I have followed his use of terms, and have where possible tried to avoid the terms 'Crusade' and 'crusaders' to reflect the fact that the concept was still fluid.

c.   'milites', 'equites' and 'pedites': it is tempting but misleading simply to translate these always as soldiers, knights and footsoldiers. Robert's use of the term 'miles' is fluid; in this he mirrors his contemporaries such as Fulcher.[13] 'Miles' can mean variously a soldier, a vassal, a Christian soldier or a knight: I have translated as appropriate to the circumstances.[14]

The notes aim merely to support the modern reader in understanding the text. They cover dates, names and places; biblical references; a few literary allusions, and points of interest or comparison with other texts where this might be helpful. They are not intended to provide a full supporting apparatus for the text.

---

[11] M. J. Bull, 'Overlapping and competing identities in the Frankish First Crusade', in *Le Concile de Clermont de 1095 et l'Appel à la Croisade: actes du Colloque à l'Université Internationale à Clermont-Ferrand (23–25 juin 1995)* (Rome, 1997), ed. A. Vauchez, 195–211.

[12] Markowski ('Crucesignatus').

[13] Epp, 251–63.

[14] P. van Luyn, 'Les "milites" dans la France du XIe siècle: examen des sources narratives', *MA* 26 (1971), 5–51.

TRANSLATION OF
ROBERT THE MONK'S
HISTORIA IHEROSOLIMITANA

Sermo apologeticus

A plea to all those who will read this history, or hear it read to them and think about it as they listen. I beg forgiveness for any element of clumsy composition you may find in it, because I was obliged to write it by my vow of obedience. A certain abbot called Bernard, distinguished by his knowledge of literature and his upright behaviour, showed me a history which set out this material. However he was not happy with it: partly because it did not include the beginning [of the Crusade] which was launched at the Council of Clermont; partly because it did not make the best of the sequence of wonderful events it contained and the composition was uncertain and unsophisticated in its style and expression. So he instructed me, since I had been present at the Council of Clermont, to add the beginning which was missing and to improve its style for future readers. I dictated and wrote it unaided all myself, being my own scribe. And so my hand obeyed my mind uninterruptedly, the pen obeyed my hand, and the page the pen, as is plain from the slightness of the poem and the unadorned nature of the style. As a result, if this work of mine irritates anybody with a better academic grounding, perhaps because the plain style I have chosen to use means I have simplified more than I should, let me tell him that I thought it more appropriate to clarify obscure things by simplifying than to cloud over the obvious by philosophising. If a text is monotonously well crafted it becomes monotonously unrewarding: because it is hard work to understand, the listener's attention wanders. My aim by contrast is to develop my text from this unvarnished beginning in the hope that anyone who hears it might try and emulate it, but if he should try to do so will find himself far off the mark.[1]

If anyone wants to know where this history was composed, for his information let it be known it was a cloister of a certain monastery of St-Rémi founded in the bishopric of Reims.[2] If there is any interest in the name of the author who composed it, he is called Robert.

---

[1] Horace, *Ars Poetica* 240–42: 'ex noto fictum carmen sequar, ut sibi quivis/speret idem, sudet multum frustraque laboret/ausus idem' ('my aim shall be a poem so moulded of common materials that all the world may hope as much for itself, may toil hard, and yet toil in vain if it attempts as much', Wickham's translation); *Q. Horati Flacci Opera*, ed. E. C. Wickham (Oxford, 1901), transl. *Horace for English readers*, E. C. Wickham (Oxford, 1903).

[2] The Abbey of St-Rémi is a large Benedictine foundation at the opposite end of Reims from the Cathedral. The Romanesque church is still extant although the monastery buildings have been extensively reconstructed.

Prologue

Amongst all the historians of the Old and the New Testament, the blessed Moses holds the first rank. It was he who, moved by the divine spirit, described the beginning of the world and the wonderful events of the First and Second Age and told us of the deeds of the Patriarchs, in the Hebraic alphabet which he himself had invented through God's revelation. Joshua,[1] Samuel and David followed his example: the first wrote the *Book of Joshua,* the other two wrote the *Books of Kings.* These precedents show how pleasing it is to God that an account should be written for the faithful of any miraculous deed he has brought to pass on earth which had been part of his plan from the beginning of time. And indeed since the creation of the world what more miraculous undertaking has there been (other than the mystery of the redeeming Cross) than what was achieved in our own time by this journey of our own people to Jerusalem? The more one thinks about it, the more overwhelming it becomes in the furthest recesses of the mind. For this was not the work of men: it was the work of God. And so it deserves to be publicised through a faithful account as much to those living now as for future generations, so that through it Christians' hope in God may be strengthened and more praise inspired in their minds. For what king or prince could subjugate so many towns and castles, fortified by nature, design or human ingenuity, if not *the blessed nation* of the Franks *whose God is the LORD; and the people whom he hath chosen for his own inheritance?*[2] So may the wisdom of God inspire us in what we offer up in praise of his name. And let everyone who may read or hear this be aware that our story will contain nothing frivolous, misleading or trivial – nothing but the truth.

---

[1] Ihesu Nave in Robert's text: Joshua was son of Nun, rendered as Nave by Origen.
[2] *Psalms* XXXIII.12.

Book I

The Council of Clermont and the Crusade of Peter the Hermit

November 1095–October 1096

Chapter I: the Council of Clermont in the Auvergne *q · ˅ ·*

You who read these words, listen to the delightful words of Pope Urban to improve your understanding.

In the year 1095 of our Lord's Incarnation a great Council was held in France; more precisely in the Auvergne, in the city known as Clermont. Pope Urban II attended this Council with the Bishops and Cardinals of Rome. (This Council was also very famous for the gathering of French and Germans, both bishops and princes). Having dealt with the ecclesiastical business on the agenda, the Pope came out into an open space of some size, none of the buildings being large enough to contain all those present. He embarked upon this speech to all, aiming to win them over with every rhetorical persuasion at his command, and said:[1]

'Frenchmen and men from across the mountains; men chosen by and beloved of God as is clear from your many achievements; men set apart from all other nations as much by geography as by the Catholic faith and by the honour of the Holy Church – it is to you that we address our sermon, to you that we appeal. We want you to know what sad cause has brought us to your land and what emergency of yours and of all the faithful it is that has brought us here. Disturbing news has emerged from Jerusalem and the city of Constantinople and is now constantly at the forefront of our mind: namely that the race of Persians, a foreign people and a people rejected by God, indeed *a generation that set not their heart aright, and whose spirit was not stedfast with God,*[2] has invaded the lands of those Christians, depopulated them by slaughter and plunder and arson, kidnapped some of the Christians and carried them off to their own lands and put others to a wretched death, and has either overthrown the churches of God or turned them over to the rituals of their own religion. They throw down the altars after soiling them with their own filth, circumcise Christians, and pour the resulting blood either on the

---

[1] I.1–4 are Robert's own. His version of the speech is one of the five we possess. He asserts he was at the Council of Clermont and there is no particular reason to disbelieve him; however his version of the speech does not necessarily command more confidence than any other. This point is discussed in more detail in the Introduction.

[2] *Psalms* LXXVIII.8. *authorial ~ anachronism*

altars or into the baptismal vessels. When they feel like inflicting a truly painful death on some they pierce their navels, pull out the end of their intestines, tie them to a pole and whip them around it until, all their bowels pulled out, they fall lifeless to the ground.[3] They shoot arrows at others tied to stakes; others again they attack having stretched out their necks, unsheathing their swords to see if they can manage to hack off their heads with one blow. And what can I say about the appalling treatment of women, which it is better to pass over in silence than to spell out in detail?[4] By now the Greek empire has been dismembered by them and an area which could not be crossed in two months' journey subjected to their ways. So to whom should the task fall of taking vengeance and wresting their conquests from them if not to you – you to whom God has given above other nations outstanding glory in arms, greatness of spirit, fitness of body and the strength to humiliate the *hairy scalp*[5] of those who resist you?

May the deeds of your ancestors move you and spur your souls to manly courage – the worth and greatness of Charlemagne, his son Louis and your other kings who destroyed the pagan kingdoms and brought them within the bounds of Christendom.[6] And most especially let the Holy Sepulchre of Our Lord the Redeemer move you – in the power as it is of foul races – and the holy places now abused and sacrilegiously defiled by their filthy practices. Oh most valiant soldiers and descendants of victorious ancestors, do not fall short of, but be inspired by, the courage of your forefathers. If affection for your children and parents and spouse holds you back, remember what Our Lord says in the Gospel: *he that loveth father or mother more than me is not worthy of me.*[7] *And everyone that hath forsaken houses, or brethren, or sisters, or father, or mother, or wife, or children, or lands, for my name's sake, shall receive an hundredfold, and shall inherit everlasting life.*[8] Do not be held back by any possession or concern for your family. For this land you inhabit, hemmed in on all sides by the sea and surrounded by mountain peaks, cannot support your sheer numbers: it is not overflowing with abundant riches and indeed provides scarcely enough food even for those who grow it. That

---

[3] Robert's account sails perilously close to bathos. This particular detail may reflect an epic theme: compare *Njalssaga* where Ulf Hreda kills Brodir in a similar way: 'Ulf Hreda slit open his belly and unwound his intestines from his stomach by leading him round and round an oak-tree; and Brodir did not die before they had all been pulled out of him' (*Njal's Saga*, transl. M. Magnusson and H. Palsson (Harmondsworth, 1960), 348). The same theme is picked up in the *Magdeburger Aufruf*. For further Saracen atrocities (though not this particular technique) see the letter of Alexius in the Appendix.

[4] See Emerson 94–5, 131–2, for similar catalogues of atrocities committed by the Antichrist.

[5] *Psalms* LXVIII.21.

[6] Robert evokes the legends of Charlemagne and the world of the *chanson de geste*, investing contemporary events with the glamour of the legendary Carolingian past. See Chapter Four for further discussion; see I.5 for reference to the apocryphal pilgrimage of Charlemagne. The reference here underlines both the status of the Crusaders as pilgrims and their links to a glorious past.

[7] *Gospel of Matthew*, X.37.

[8] *Gospel of Matthew*, XIX.29.

is why you fight and tear at each other, are constantly at war and wound and kill each other. So let all feuds between you cease, quarrels fall silent, battles end and the conflicts of all disagreement fall to rest. Set out on the road to the Holy Sepulchre, deliver that land from a wicked race and take it yourselves – the land which was given by God to the sons of Israel, as Scripture says *a land flowing with milk and honey.*[9]

Chapter II: in praise of the city of Jerusalem

Jerusalem, rejoice! Your praise is everlasting and comes from the heart.

Jerusalem is the navel of the Earth. It is a land more fruitful than any other, almost another Earthly Paradise. Our Redeemer dignified it with his arrival, adorned it with his words, consecrated it through his Passion, redeemed it by his death and glorified it with his burial. Yet this royal city at the centre of the world[10] is now held captive by her enemies and enslaved by those who know nothing of the ways of the people of God. So she begs and craves to be free, and prays endlessly for you to come to her aid. Indeed it is your help she particularly seeks because God has granted you outstanding glory in war above all other nations, as I said earlier. So seize on this road to obtain the remission of your sins, sure in the indestructible glory of the Heavenly Kingdom'.[11]

[handwritten margin note: common medieval concepts]

When Pope Urban had eloquently spoken these words and many other things of the same kind, all present were so moved that they united as one and shouted 'God wills it! God wills it!'[12] When the venerable Pope heard this, he raised his eyes to Heaven, thanked God and, gesturing with his hand for silence, said:

'Dearest brothers, today we have seen demonstrated what Our Lord says in his Gospel: *where two or three are gathered together in my name, there I am in the midst of them.*[13] Had the Lord God not been in your minds, you would not have spoken with one voice; certainly the voices were many but the thought behind them was as one. Let me tell you that God elicited this response from you after placing it in your hearts. So let that cry be a warcry for you in battle because it came from God. When you mass together to attack the enemy, this cry sent by God will be the cry of all – 'God wills it! God wills it!' We are not forcing or persuading the old, the simple-minded or those unsuited to battle to undertake this pilgrimage; neither should a woman set out under any circumstances without her husband, brother or other legitimate guarantor.[14] That is because such pilgrims are

---

[9] *Exodus* III.8.

[10] Guénée, 171 comments that Jerusalem came to be seen increasingly as the centre of the world from c. 1110. Robert is at pains to emphasise its centrality to the Crusade; his chronicle concludes at IX.24–6 as it begins, with praise of Jerusalem.

[11] Compare *I Peter* V.4: *a crown of glory that fadeth not away.*

[12] 'Deus vult!' See Lacroix, op. cit.

[13] *Gospel of Matthew* XVIII.20.

[14] The Patriarch's letter makes a similar stipulation: see Appendix.

more of a hindrance than a help, a burden rather than of any practical use. The richer shall help those with few resources, and take along with them at their own expense men equipped to fight. No priest or cleric irrespective of his rank shall be allowed on pilgrimage without the permission of his bishop, since it would be of little use to them if they were to go without such permission. Similarly a layman should set out on the pilgrimage only with the permission of his priest. Anyone who has a mind to undertake this holy pilgrimage, and enters into that bargain with God, and devotes himself as a living sacrifice, holy and acceptable,[15] shall wear the sign of the Cross on his forehead or his chest. And conversely anyone who seeks to turn back having taken the vow shall place the cross on his back between his shoulders. Such men will bring to pass through this double symbolism what God himself orders in the Gospel: *he that taketh not his cross, and followeth after me, is not worthy of me.'*[16]

Chapter III: how the Council was absolved of sin

As the Pope came to an end one of the Cardinals of Rome, Gregory, made his confession in front of all as they lay prostrate on the ground. In their turn all, beating their chests, begged absolution for the sins they had committed; after absolution they sought blessing; and, once they had received blessing, permission to return home. And, to make it quite clear to all believers that this pilgrimage had been set in train by God rather than men – as we have since established from many sources[17] – on the very day these speeches and deeds took place, the news announcing such an undertaking set the whole world astir so that even in the islands of the sea it was common knowledge that a pilgrimage to Jerusalem had been launched at the Council. The Christians gloried and exulted in the knowledge; to the Persians and Arabs it brought fear and trembling. The courage of the former grew; the latter were paralysed with fear. The heavenly trumpet rang out and made enemies to the name of Christ everywhere tremble. It is thus abundantly clear that this was the effect not of human utterance but of the spirit of the Lord which fills the earth.[18]

So all the lay returned home, whilst on the following day Pope Urban convened the College of Bishops. Once they were in session he sought their views on whom he should put at the head of such a large number of prospective pilgrims, because as yet they included no princes of any note.

---

[15] Compare *Romans* XII.1: *a living sacrifice, holy, acceptable unto God.*

[16] *Gospel of Matthew* X.38; see also *Gospel of Luke* XIV.27.

[17] One of Robert's rare references to sources. He does not say who, but the reference underlines the miraculous way in which the news spread.

[18] Compare Apocrypha, *Wisdom of Solomon* I.7: *the spirit of the Lord hath filled the world.*

Chapter IV: how the Bishop of Le Puy was given charge of the pilgrims

All unanimously chose the Bishop of Le Puy,[19] acclaiming him as the ideal choice for both spiritual and temporal reasons, highly capable in both fields and shrewd in his actions. He agreed, albeit unwillingly, to lead and organise the people of God like a second Moses, with the blessing of the Pope and the whole Council. How many of various ages and abilities and stations in life took crosses and committed themselves to pilgrimage to the Holy Sepulchre! The news of that revered Council spread throughout every country, and the story of its important decision reached the ears of kings and princes. It touched a chord, and more than 300,000[20] decided to go on pilgrimage and took action to carry out their vow insofar as God had given them the ability. And now the huge might of the Frankish race began to strain at its bounds and in spirit they were already ferociously attacking the Turks.

Chapter V: Peter the Hermit and Duke Godfrey[21]

The Duke set out first, and never came back.

At that time there was a man called Peter, a famous hermit, who was held in great esteem by the lay people, and in fact venerated above priests and abbots for his religious observance because he ate neither bread nor meat (though this did not stop him enjoying wine and all other kinds of food whilst seeking a reputation for abstinence in the midst of pleasures).[22] At that point he gathered round him a not insignificant force of knights and footsoldiers and set off via Hungary. He joined forces with a certain Godfrey, Duke of the Germans, who was the son of Count

---

[19] Adhemar of Monteil, Bishop of Le Puy 1087–98. He was the legate of Urban II on the First Crusade until his death in August 1098. He played a role as peacekeeper and spiritual authority on the Crusade (J. H. and L. L. Hill, 'Contemporary accounts and later reputation of Adhemar, Bishop of Le Puy', *MH* 9 (1955), 30–38); he was also heavily involved in the fighting and leadership of the crusade (J. A. Brundage, 'Adhemar of Puy: the bishop and his critics', *S* 34 (1959), 201–12). Both roles come out clearly in Robert's account.

[20] Here, as elsewhere, the numbers should probably be taken as indicating a very large amount rather than literally: Guénée, 179, 'des nombres énormes ... qui ne sont que des moyens rhétoriques de dire: beaucoup'.

[21] Borrowing from the *GF* starts here.

[22] Opinions, both medieval and modern, differ sharply over the role of Peter the Hermit. In some sources he rather than Pope Urban is credited with providing the impetus to the crusade through his pilgrimage to Jerusalem, vision of Christ and subsequent meeting with Urban. Riley-Smith describes him as a 'congenital boaster' (*First Crusaders*, 56). See H. Hagenmeyer, *Peter der Eremite* (Leipzig, 1879); F. Duncalf, 'The Peasants' Crusade', *AHR* 26 (1921), 440–53; E. O. Blake and C. Morris, 'A hermit goes to war: Peter and the Origins of the First Crusade', *SCH* 22 (1984), 79–107; J. Flori, 'Faut-il réhabiliter Pierre l'Ermite?', *CCM* 38 (1995), 35–54. Robert, perhaps understandably as a mainstream cleric, clearly has little time for him: his sideswipe is not in either of his sources.

Eustace of Boulogne but Duke of Germany by the virtue of office.[23] Godfrey was handsome, of lordly bearing, eloquent, of distinguished character, and so lenient with his soldiers as to give the impression of being a monk rather than a soldier.[24] However, when he realised that the enemy was at hand and battle imminent, his courage became abundantly evident and like a roaring lion he feared the attack of no man. What breastplate or shield could withstand the thrust of his sword? Godfrey, with his brothers Eustace and Baldwin[25] and a large band of horse and foot, journeyed through Hungary, doubtless following the same route as Charlemagne the incomparable king of the Franks once followed on his pilgrimage to Constantinople.[26]

Chapter VI: about those who were first to reach Constantinople and cross the Arm of St George

So Peter the Hermit, with his own followers and a large band of Germans, was the first to reach Constantinople, where he found a considerable force of Lombards and many others brought together from various places. The Emperor denied them all permission to enter the city because he was always suspicious about the strength of the Christian soldiers and more so the Franks.[27] He did, however, allow them to shop at a market which was in fact in the city, whilst forbidding them to cross the neighbouring inlet known as the Arm of St George[28] until the whole formidable army of the Franks should arrive. The reason was an infinite number of Turks, who were panting like wild beasts for their arrival; if the Christians fell into their clutches without the Frankish princes they would all – as events were subsequently to prove – be killed. The trouble is that any gathering of men which is not well ruled and which lacks firm leadership gets less effective by the day and further from safety.[29] Moreover, these men, lacking as they did a wise prince to lead them, were engaging in reprehensible activities: they were destroying the churches and

---

[23] Godfrey of Bouillon, Duke of Lower Lorraine. Son of Eustace II of Boulogne and Ida; he held the county of Verdun and fief of Bouillon, and was invested with the duchy of Lower Lorraine in 1087. As far as one can judge he did not play a particularly significant role during the battles of the Crusade, but achieved fame through becoming the first Advocate of the Holy Sepulchre. His posthumous career outshone his actual career: he acquired legendary status as the Chevalier au Cygne and finished as a member of the 'Nine Worthies' immortalised in the frescoes at La Manta in Saluzzo, Piedmont. This process can already be seen at work in Robert's account. See J. Andressohn, *The Ancestry and Life of Godfrey of Bouillon* (Indiana, 1947); H. Glaesener, 'Godefroid de Bouillon était-il un médiocre?', *RHE* 39 (1943), 309–41.

[24] Robert inserts praise of Godfrey into the *GF*'s text.

[25] Eustace III, Count of Boulogne; Baldwin, later to become ruler of the County of Edessa.

[26] See above for Charlemagne's apocryphal pilgrimage to Jerusalem.

[27] The Byzantine Emperor, Alexius. Robert consistently ascribes the worst possible motives to him, adding here to the *GF*.

[28] The Sea of Marmara and the Bosphorus.

[29] One of Robert's rare but shrewd observations on the difficulties of campaigning.

palaces in the city, carrying off their contents, stripping the lead from the roofs and selling it to the Greeks. This made the Emperor – who was called Alexius – furious, and he ordered them to cross the Arm of St George.

Chapter VII: how Rainald led them and how the Turks besieged the Christians

Once they had crossed, they chose a leader for themselves, placing a certain Rainald in charge.[30] Even though they had a prince, they still continued to plunder: they set on fire the houses they came across and stripped the churches of their riches and ornaments. So they reached Nicomedia[31] and entered Anatolia. After three days of wandering they left the city of Nicaea[32] behind them and found a certain castle known as Xerigordon empty of occupants. When they entered they found abundant supplies of wheat, meat, wine and all sorts of things necessary to sustain human life. The Turks, scared out of their wits by fear of the Franks, had put a considerable distance between themselves and that area. However, they had sent scouts, who reported back to them on the arrival of our men and the state they were in. Realising from the scouts that our men had come to plunder rather than settle, and destroy rather than take possession, they attacked them immediately and established a siege round the castle.[33] There were huge numbers of them forming a considerable multitude. In front of the castle gate was a well and next to it on the other side a spring. Rainald, the leader of the Christians, came out next to this and lay in wait for their arrival.

Chapter VIII: how the Turks boldly attacked our men, and the lack of water they suffered

The Turks did not hesitate in the slightest but rushed on him, and killed many who were with him whilst the others fled into the castle. The Turks then gradually cut off the water supply from our men, and subjected the Christians to excruciating torture through lack of it. It was then the feast of St Michael,[34] which all faithful souls should observe. The besieged men became so tormented by thirst that they cut open the veins of horses, cows, donkeys and other domestic animals and drank from them. Others dug down to damper earth, stuffed it into their mouths and quenched their burning thirst. Others again urinated into a jar or their hands and,

---

[30] Little is known about Rainald. Again Robert's distaste for Peter the Hermit's crusade is apparent.

[31] Modern Izmit.

[32] Modern Iznik.

[33] The reference to the scouts is not in *GF*.

[34] Michaelmas Day, 29 September.

amazing to relate, drank it. What more can I say? None of this brought relief to the living when death alone brought help to the dying.[35]

Chapter IX: the apostasy of Rainald, the leader

Rainald becomes an apostate although not even slightly wounded, and proves himself to be in the wrong in abjuring God.

Eventually their leader Rainald concluded a secret treaty with the Turks, preferring to hold onto this life rather than suffer such a martyr's death for Christ. So, drawing up his forces, he pretended to attack the enemy; but soon, as he came out, he changed direction towards them with many others. Alas! Alas! Cowardly soldier that he was, from the North and not from the South, how lukewarm and effeminate was his fight for the Heavenly King and Heavenly Kingdom when, not so much as touched by a light straw, he shrank from suffering martyrdom and renounced profession of the Christian faith despite being in good shape, on horseback and armed. It was only fitting that he deserved to lose God's grace and fall to the lot of he who chose to reside in the North.[36] Those who did remain, choosing not to change their allegiance to the Christian faith, suffered death.

Chapter X: the martyrdom of the Christians

So the Turks had a free hand in killing whom they wanted from all that vast multitude and taking others captive. They tied some to posts and shot arrows at them. They insulted the servants of God with every kind of mocking trick which took their fancy; the Christians preferred to die a glorious death rather than live unhappily with the Turks and renounce their faith. And God did indeed, as we believe, receive their souls into eternal Paradise because they refused to be turned away from belief in Him. And now, exulting in victory, the diabolical legion marched against Peter the Hermit, who was in a castle known as Civetot.[37] (This castle was above the city of Nicaea.)

---

[35] One of the set pieces found in similar form in most *GF* derivatives: compare GN 125, BB 19. Given that Christ is sometimes described in terms of a spring of living water, and that Rainald and Peter's Crusade was clearly not favoured by God, it is tempting to wonder whether the thirst portrayed is symbolic of the lack of divine support.

[36] See *Isaiah* XIV.13: the prophet addresses Lucifer, saying *thou hast said in thine heart, I will ascend into heaven, I will exalt my throne above the stars of God: I will sit also upon the mount of the congregation, in the sides of the north.* See also *Daniel* XI.5 for the King of the South.

[37] The port of Cibotos, some twenty miles west of Nicomedia and north of Nicaea; a fortified Byzantine camp the other side of the Sea of Marmara from Constantinople.

Chapter XI: how Walter fought the Turks and was killed

Walter's death was dearly sold and deserves to be described ...

As the Turks marched to the castle they came upon Walter, the captain and standard-bearer of Peter's army.[38] Despite his record as a famous soldier with a string of military successes, he was unable to withstand their combined might and sold his death dearly for a high price of Turkish blood, flinging himself on them like a starving bear on its prey and striking down and killing those who crossed his path.[39] Similarly the armed men with him sold for a high price whilst still alive their inevitable deaths; as long as their arms lasted them their enemies were unable to celebrate victory. But sheer numbers defeated their courage rather than courage defeating numbers even though their bravery reduced the number of their opponents six-fold. Eventually their weapons – though not their bravery – gave out, and they ended their lives with an exemplary death in battle, for God, and angelic spirits took their souls up to Heaven.[40] It was then that the Turks first realised, as they turned over the bodies of their own men, that it was Franks they had been fighting.

Chapter XII: The story of the priest who was martyred by the Turks while he was singing Mass

... and so does the death of this priest

Having done this, some of the Turks ran to the Christian camps and there found one priest celebrating Mass. They cut his head off in front of the altar. What a fortunate martyrdom for that fortunate priest, who was given the body of Our Lord Jesus Christ as a guide up to Heaven! The Turks continued in the same way, killing or dragging away all they came upon. Peter the Hermit himself had slipped away and returned to Constantinople.

Chapter XIII: the second Turkish siege of the Christians

A large body of Christians had stayed in the castle we talked of above, Civetot, and those who had escaped alive from the camps or from the battlefield had flooded back into it. The Turks followed them and piled wood around the castle to burn them alive. The besieged Christians, keen to save their lives, set fire to the piles

---

[38] Walter of Poissy in the Ile de France, nicknamed 'sans aveir' (penniless). Four other members of his family also went on crusade (Riley-Smith, *First Crusaders*, 93)

[39] Robert adds praise of Walter to the *GF*, reflecting his interest in crusaders from the Ile de France.

[40] Like Roland: *Roland* 2389–96.

and with God's help and a favourable wind burnt several of the enemy. The Turks nevertheless overcame them by brute force and amused themselves by inflicting various tortures on them, killing some and selling others into captivity. Those who managed to escape by luck or judgement returned to the Arm of St George and thence Constantinople, on the orders of the infinitely wicked Emperor. He and his Greeks were delighted by the Turkish victory, and cunningly bought up all the arms from our men so as to render them defenceless.[41]

Romans?

So, having described these events, let us bring this part of the story to a close and, taking our pen back in time, focus on how the noble race of Franks came on Crusade and which princes came with them.

Here ends the first book.

---

[41] Again Robert disparages the Byzantines.

Book II

The journey to Constantinople and negotiations there

October 1096–April 1097

Chapter I: about the Count of Normandy, the Count of Flanders and Hugh the Great[1]

The armies come together in their thousands; if you were to see their lords assembling such a powerful army, you would rightly praise the Holy Sepulchre for whose sake they have rejected their own country.

Meanwhile, during the course of these events, God inspired two counts with one name, one bloodline, equal power, matched in strength and arms and spirit and of equal rank as counts, from remote parts of the west towards the North – the Count of Normandy[2] and the Count of Flanders,[3] and along with them Hugh of Vermandois, brother of King Philip I of France who at this time sat on the French throne.[4] Hugh was a credit to the royal blood from which he sprang because of the

---

[1] Robert continues to follow the *GF* as his source, but alters the order to improve narrative flow: *GF* has Bohemond setting out twice over (5, 7–8).

[2] Robert, Count of Normandy: one of the main princes on the Crusade. He was the eldest son of William the Conqueror and Matilda of Flanders, born in 1054. On William's death he inherited Maine and the Duchy of Normandy. In 1106 he was defeated by his younger brother, Henry I of England, at the battle of Tinchebrai and spent the rest of his life as Henry's captive. His role on Crusade does not seem to have been particularly outstanding, although William of Malmesbury attributes to him the killing of Kerbogha at the battle of Antioch (702–3), echoed in the *Antioche* (8749–67): this suggests a certain amount of posthumous legend-building. See C. W. David, *Robert Curthose, Duke of Normandy* (Cambridge, Massachusetts, 1920). Interestingly Robert always refers to him as 'comes' and never 'dux'; so does Fulcher of Chartres (Epp, 265, who suggests this may reflect a less than favourable view of him at the court of Chartres).

[3] Robert II, Count of Flanders, was the son and heir of Robert the Friesian and another of the main leaders of the Crusade. See M. M. Knappen, 'Robert II of Flanders in the First Crusade', in *The Crusades and other historical essays presented to Dana C. Munro by his former students*, ed. C. J. Paetow (New York, 1928), 79–100.

[4] Hugh of Vermandois was the brother of King Philip I of France, younger son of Henry I and Anne of Kiev. Despite the praise Robert lavishes on him, his Crusading career seems to have been less than impressive. He was to die on the Crusade of 1101. His reputation grew posthumously, with his nickname of 'maisné' (younger son) becoming deformed to 'Magnus' (OV, V.34, n.9; GN 131.) For discussion of his role on Crusade see Bull,

integrity of his conduct, his refined bearing and his courage. Stephen of Blois accompanied him, starting well but ending in ignominy.[5] And how many nobles and less well-known counts came with them, both from France itself as well as from Britain and Brittany!

Chapter II: about the Bishop of Le Puy and the Count of St Gilles

From the South came the forces of Adhemar, Bishop of Le Puy, and Raymond IV of St Gilles.[6] The latter, immensely rich and loaded with all good things of this earth, sold all he owned and set out to liberate the Holy Sepulchre. So now we see demonstrated in actual fact what God promised through the mouth of the Prophet Isaiah: *Fear not, for I am with thee: I will bring thy seed* from the north, *and gather thee from the west; I will say to the north, Give up; and to the south, Keep not back: bring my sons from far, and my daughters from the ends of the earth.*[7] Now we see the sons and daughters of God making for Jerusalem from the ends of the earth, and neither the South nor the North wind dare to stand in the way of their children. In very truth God now rises above the West, resting as he does in the spirit of the Westerners. The West prepares to illuminate the East, rousing new stars to dispel the blindness which oppressed it. And no matter how much the terrible glint of arms glittered from innumerable columns, the splendour of their courage would still outdo it if it were visible. They march out to fight with one mind – not to flee but to die, or win. They do not see death as loss of life; winning is the evidence of divine help. Thus the princes described above left their homes in a relatively short space of time but, having crossed their lands, crossed the Alps at various times by various routes. They continued through Italy and under divine

---

'Capetian Monarchy'. Philip I ruled 1060–1108: Robert's description of Philip I, 'qui ipso tempore Franciam suo subjugabat imperio', led Marquardt, 45–6 to argue that the text must postdate 1108.

[5] Stephen Count of Blois and Chartres; husband of Adela, daughter of William the Conqueror, and father of King Stephen of England. Although he began the Crusade as one of the key leaders, he fatally misjudged events at Antioch, leaving the siege and returning to Constantinople where his report convinced the Emperor there was no point sending any help. The chroniclers of the Crusade concentrate on his perceived cowardice at the siege of Antioch; his later death on the crusade of 1101 did little to rehabilitate him. See J. A. Brundage, 'An Errant Crusader: Stephen of Blois', *T* 16 (1960), 380–95. Wolf, 214 suggests he was deliberately blackened by Bohemondian propaganda. Robert is better disposed to him than is the *GF*: see VI.15 compared to *GF* 63.

[6] Raymond IV, Count of St Gilles. He was the second son of Almodis de la Marche and Pons of Toulouse; by 1095 his estates extended widely over Occitania. Urban II's preaching of the Crusade began in Occitania, and Raymond was closely involved in its organisation. The tensions between him and Bohemond ran throughout the Crusade, and came near to wrecking it after the taking of Antioch: he became the de facto leader once Bohemond had effectively withdrawn to Antioch. After the fall of Jerusalem he remained in the Holy Land as ruler of Tripoli until his death in 1105. See J. H. and L. L. Hill, *Raymond IV, Count of Toulouse* (New York, 1962).

[7] *Isaiah* XLIII.5–6; Robert changes a reference to the east into a reference to the north.

protection had an untroubled journey to Rome. What a glorious host for Christ, too big to be housed in the open spaces and homes within the walls of such a spacious city! As a result many of the princes set up camp outside the city. They remained there several days and visited the holy sites on the usual pilgrims' route, recommending themselves to the merits and prayers of the Holy Apostles and others. Then, having been blessed by the Pope, they left the city and led their forces into Apulia.[8]

Chapter III: about Bohemond, Duke of Apulia[9]

Rumour goes round the world and reaches Bohemond. He does not reject such a heavyweight force; on the contrary he is alight with enthusiasm to take such a vow.

As they made their way, the news of such an army reached the ears of a certain prince of that area, Bohemond,[10] who at the time was busy besieging Amalfi on the coast near Scafati.[11] On hearing the news he sent to inquire which princes were in charge of such a large army, what arms it carried, the order of march and whether it intended to plunder or to buy supplies. His scouts told him about the princes: Hugh of Vermandois, brother of Philip King of France, was the standard-bearer and leader of the massive army;[12] Robert Count of Normandy, Robert Count of Flanders, Stephen Count of Blois, Raymond Count of St Gilles and the Bishop of Le Puy were its leaders and rulers. The army moreover was marching in such a disciplined and pious way that none could be found who had suffered from its passing. The arms of the knights were just such as befitted an army of God engaged on such a venture – what human eye could bear the glitter of their

---

[8] Robert emphasises their status as pilgrims and their endorsement by the Pope; this is not in the *GF*.

[9] The heading is wrong: the Duke of Apulia was Roger Borsa, as Robert goes on to make clear. See J. J. Norwich, *The Normans in Sicily*, (Harmondsworth, 1992) 195–6

[10] Bohemond was the eldest son of Robert Guiscard by his first wife Alberada of Buonalbergo. On Robert's death in 1085 the succession passed to his half-brother Roger Borsa. A series of wars between the two assured Bohemond substantial territories in southern Italy. He seized on the First Crusade as an opportunity for further gains and became arguably its dominant figure. Initially his career in the Holy Land was successful, with the taking and holding of Antioch. However, he was held captive by the Turks for three years (1100–03); in 1108 he was defeated by the Byzantine emperor and forced to swear an oath of fealty. He died in 1111. Shrewd and unscrupulous, he fascinated his contemporaries: see for example the detailed description in AC 422. See R. B. Yewdale, *Bohemond I, Prince of Antioch* (Princeton, 1924).

[11] Probably the modern Ponte di Scafati. For discussion see 188–90 in E. Jamison, 'Some Notes on the *Anonymi Gesta Francorum* with special reference to the Norman contingent from Southern Italy and Sicily in the First Crusade', in *Studies in French language and medieval literature presented to Professor Mildred K. Pope* (Manchester, 1939), 183–208.

[12] An addition to the *GF* by Robert.

breastplates, helmets, shields or lances in brilliant sunshine? The footsoldiers likewise were armed with all kinds of weapons sufficient to terrify the whole of the Orient if it approached them. Yet despite being protected by all those weapons and armour, they still bought their provisions like unarmed pilgrims.[13] When the shrewd and immensely wealthy Bohemond heard this, he spoke thus in front of all:

'Let us all as we ought give thanks to God, who holds all hearts in his power and inclines them as he will. For who could have brought together so many princes and such a multitude of people if God were not present in their minds?'

Asking what symbol of pilgrimage they wore, he was told that they bore the Holy Cross either on their forehead or their right shoulders. When they were training for battle across fields and turning their lances in mock fight on each other, all shouted with one voice 'God wills it! God wills it!' This was their warcry. When Bohemond, a sharp and intelligent man, heard this further information, he praised God more and more, realising that this could not be the work of men alone.

Chapter IV: how Bohemond took the cross and ordered his men to take it

Alight with religious fervour, he immediately ordered two precious cloaks to be brought, and having them cut into strips ordered crosses to be made of them.[14] Then he said to all, footsoldiers as well as knights:

'If anyone follows the Lord, let him join me. At present you are my soldiers; now, men, be soldiers of God. Take the road to the Holy Sepulchre and take my possessions as yours. After all, are we not French? Didn't our parents come from France and take this land for themselves by force of arms?[15] For shame! Are our relatives and brothers to head for martyrdom – indeed for Paradise – without us? If this divine force marches to war without us, both we and our children will be labelled as spinelessly lacking in courage for ever afterwards.'

When the brave soldier finished what he had to say, all those present shouted with acclamation, saying: 'We will come with you and vow ourselves irrevocably to pilgrimage to the Holy Sepulchre!' Then Bohemond, intelligent and sharp as ever, ordered crosses to be brought which he had had prepared earlier, and once they were brought said: 'If you want to match your words with your actions, let each of you take one of these crosses; accepting a cross shall be taken as a promise to set out on pilgrimage.' At that point so many surged forward to take crosses that there were not enough for all those wanting them.[16]

---

[13] Robert again emphasises the status of the crusaders as pilgrims.

[14] See *Gospel of Matthew* V.40; *Psalms* XXI.19; *Gospel of Mark* XV.24.

[15] Bohemond's comments serve as praise of the French: see discussion in Chapter Four. But they also serve as an implicit reminder that he had recently married Philip I's daughter and therefore regarded himself as French for the purposes of recruiting a Crusade.

[16] Robert adds details to *GF* 7 such as Bohemond preparing crosses earlier and not having enough.

Chapter V: how the Apulians eagerly received crosses

The people of Calabria and Apulia join the army; but the Duke of Apulia refused to become its commander- in- chief.

When the nobles of Apulia, Calabria and Sicily heard that Bohemond had taken the cross, they all flooded to him and promised to go to the Holy Sepulchre – the lowly and the powerful, young and old, servants and masters – to the point where the Duke of Apulia became very worried at what he could see and hear because he could picture himself being left with nothing but small children and women in his dukedom. (This was the brother of Bohemond; both were sons of Robert Guiscard.)[17] While Bohemond was preparing supplies needed for the pilgrimage, the French arrived at the seaports and took ship, some at Brindisi, others at Bari and others again at Otranto.[18] Hugh of Vermandois and William Fitzmarquis[19] took ship at the port of Bari and sailed to Durazzo.[20]

Chapter VI: how Hugh the Great was taken prisoner

When the Duke of Durazzo learnt of their arrival, he hatched a wicked plan:[21] he ordered them to be arrested immediately and taken to Constantinople as prisoners. This was because the crafty Emperor had decreed that all Crusaders should be taken captive and brought to him in Constantinople; he wanted all of them to take an oath of fidelity to him, doubtless to ensure that whatever they conquered by force of arms would fall to him.

Chapter VII: about Hugh and Godfrey[22]

However, when the prisoners reached the city, a very pleasant surprise awaited them because they found Duke Godfrey there with a large army. Anyone who saw Hugh of Vermandois and Duke Godfrey embracing and kissing each other might have wept for joy. Hugh rejoiced at his capture because it had led to him being brought to Duke Godfrey; the Duke rejoiced to embrace his dear friend, his relative and a noble man of surpassing generosity. They congratulated each other on being able to renew the bonds of longstanding familiarity distinguished on both sides by a high degree of virtue. The tricks of the Emperor first came to light in the treatment of these two men, as the following page will reveal.

---

[17] Roger Borsa, Bohemond's half-brother. There was little love lost between the two.
[18] Robert drops the list of Norman crusaders given at *GF* 7–8.
[19] Tancred's brother, son of Odobonus Marchisus and Emma; see Jamison 195–97.
[20] Classical Dyrrachium, now Durres in Albania.
[21] John Comnenus, nephew of Alexius.
[22] Robert adds the meeting of Hugh and Godfrey to the *GF*.

Chapter VIII: how Duke Godfrey was the first to reach Constantinople

The Duke was the first to reach the royal city.

Duke Godfrey reached Constantinople before all the French princes because he had travelled straight across Hungary. That meant he arrived two days before Christmas; he intended to camp outside the city, but the crafty Emperor asked him inside the walls. (He hoped the Duke would stay there safely until the French armies might arrive.) When he started sending his men on some days to buy supplies, the cunning emperor instructed his Turcopoles and Petchenegs[23] to set an ambush, attack and kill them.

Chapter IX: the open treachery of the Emperor and the number of his men killed by Baldwin, brother of the Duke

However, Baldwin (the Duke's brother)[24] found out about this wicked strategem. He hid and thwarted their ambush, attacking them with considerable courage and a sharp assault whilst they were pursuing his men with a view to killing them. With God's help he overcame them, killed several of them and presented the captives to his brother the Duke. When the Emperor heard of this he was furious, realising that the French had discovered his cunning plans. The Duke realised that the Emperor's anger was directed at him and his companions, so he left the outskirts and erected his camp outside the city. At sunset, when night was starting to cover the earth, the Emperor's forces had the presumption to attack the Duke; but with the help of divine grace the band was only just able to escape at the cost of suffering considerable damage. The two sides rushed upon each other, but one was stronger than the other. The Duke and his men, like a roaring lion, swiftly dispersed them and killed seven, pursuing the remainder right up to the gates of the city. He then returned to his camp and from then on remained there quietly.

---

[23] Petchenegs were Turkish tribesmen from beyond the Danube used as auxiliaries by the Byzantines, largely as policemen and frontier guards: Runciman, *History*, vol.I, 104.

[24] Baldwin of Boulogne, brother of Duke Godfrey, later to become the first king of Jerusalem (1100–18). His role on the First Crusade was a restricted one: he turned aside to the County of Edessa and became its ruler after some dubious manoeuvres: see Runciman, *History*, vol.I, 197–212.

Chapter X: how the Emperor and the Duke concluded a peace, and the numbers of Frankish armies which reached Constantinople

The Franks arrive at the city at the same time because of the threat of death to their countrymen.

The Emperor now sought peace with him through a large number of ambassadors and gained it; in return he allowed him and his men to buy what they could in the city. Meanwhile the French began to arrive in the royal city: the Bishop of Le Puy and the Count of St Gilles as well as the Count of Normandy , the Count of Flanders and Stephen Count of Blois.

Chapter XI: Bohemond crosses Bulgaria with his men

Whilst all this was going on Bohemond of Apulia, as we described, having prepared at his own expense all that was needed for such a major expedition, took ship and had a smooth journey to the region of Bulgaria. He was accompanied by very noble princes: Tancred, his nephew[25] and son of the Marquis, Prince Richard[26] [of the Principate] and all the greatest lords of that land. They found such abundance of food in Bulgaria that *their corn and their wine increased.*[27] From there they descended into the valley of Andronopolis,[28] and waited there until all had made the crossing.

Chapter XII: how Bohemond laid an obligation on his men not to take anything by force

At that stage Bohemond sensibly made it very clear to his army that nobody should extort anything from anyone by violence but that each should buy what he needed. At length, once all had made the crossing, they entered a part of the country overflowing to bursting point with good things. They progressed from village to village, castle to castle, city to city and came to Kastoria,[29] where they celebrated

---

[25] Tancred was Bohemond's nephew. Although not yet twenty at the start of the Crusade, he played a significant role throughout. He became Prince of Galilee, and successfully acted as regent of Antioch during Bohemond's captivity. See R. L. Nicholson, *Tancred: a history of his life and career* (Chicago, 1940). He is the hero of Ralph of Caen's account.

[26] Richard of the Principate, count of Salerno. Jamison ('Some notes', 197–8) describes him as son of William of Salerno, Guiscard's brother; Richard's brother Robert was the Count and he also had a brother known as Rainulf or Rainald. He is often found in Tancred's company on the crusade (*GF* 13, BB 25, AA 349–50).

[27] *Psalms* IV.7.

[28] Adrianople, now Edirne.

[29] Taken by Robert Guiscard in 1082; subsequently retaken by Alexius. Classical Celetrum.

Christmas and rested for several days. When they asked the natives to trade provisions with them they were unable to get them to do so because all fled at the sight of them, thinking our men had come to plunder and depopulate the whole area. So our men were positively forced by lack of food to steal and plunder sheep, cows, rams, pigs and whatever could be eaten.[30]

Chapter XIII: the castle of heretics

They left Kastoria and came to Pelagonia, which contained a particular castle of heretics. This they attacked from all sides, took straight away amidst blaring trumpets and flying arrows and weapons, stripped it of all its goods and burnt it along with its inhabitants. That reflected no discredit on them because the detestable preaching of the heretics was creeping like canker and had already infected the surrounding regions with its depraved dogmas just as its perverted aim had been to turn them aside from the true faith.[31]

Chapter XIV: the soldiers of the Emperor killed by Bohemond

The Emperor's army attacks our men; Bohemond being allied to our men, the mad Emperor of Constantinople raves in fury.

They then came to the River Vardar; many crossed over that same day whilst others did not, deciding not to cross as the sun set.[32] The following day very early, as dawn began to glow, the Emperor's army came upon those who had not crossed and began preparations to kill them all or chain them up and take them prisoner. Our men put up stout resistance and the noise reached the ears of Bohemond and Tancred. Tancred, unable to bear for longer than necessary the idea of his men being harmed, flew to his horse, galloped back to the river and flung himself into it complete with horse and armour. Two thousand knights followed. Riding immediately to the fray they found Turcopoles and Petchenegs fighting their men; they galloped up to them straight away as if beside themselves with rage, killed many, took a large number prisoner and chained them up, and led them to Bohemond loaded with bonds. When he saw them Bohemond offered thanks to God and, beaming all over his face, said to them through an interpreter:

'You fools. Why do you want to kill soldiers who belong to me and to God? We are companions and servants and pilgrim soldiers of the Holy Sepulchre. We have no intention of harming any of you, and no plans to wrest anything from your Emperor.'

---

[30] Even by Robert's standards this is a rather disingenuous justification.

[31] Robert adds this explanation to the facts given by *GF*. The heretics were probably Paulicians or Bogomils, who detested the sign of the cross: see M. Lambert, *Medieval Heresy* (London, 1977), 23. Robert is clear that heretics deserve no mercy.

[32] Robert drops *GF* 9's reference to the Count of Russignolo.

They replied: 'We are soldiers in the pay of the Emperor, and we want him to pay our wages: so we go where he pleases, do what he says and obey him more than we do God. However, we recognise full well that *we ought to obey God rather than men.*[33] Our Emperor is more frightened of your armies than of storms in heaven, because his view is that you are more interested in taking his kingdom from him than in pilgrimage; that is why he constantly plots against you. But please deign to take pity on us for the sake of God, whose pilgrims and soldiers you are.'

At this the renowned Bohemond, moved by the spirit of pity, granted them their lives and allowed them to depart unharmed. Whilst he continued his march with no problems, the French army had reached Constantinople and waited for his arrival, having heard that he was not far off. Meanwhile, when the Emperor saw the forces of God gathering in camps on all sides and how the army he had sent against Bohemond had been scattered, he boiled with rage and, becoming anxious, began to mull over plans for treachery.[34]

Chapter XV: the Emperor's deceit[35]

In the mean time he put up a good pretence. He sent an embassy to Bohemond under guise of congratulating him on his arrival who were to receive him graciously in the Emperor's own cities and castles and bring him to the Emperor with all honours. Our men, nevertheless, had worked out that he was not doing all this out of friendly motives but out of secret machinations of his heart.[36] The natives, under orders from the Emperor, flocked to bring necessary supplies and sold them at a reasonable price. On arriving at the city known as Susa,[37] Bohemond sent his army to it and made his way to Constantinople with a few companions to negotiate with the Emperor. Tancred remained behind in charge as leader of the army. He decided against remaining any longer at Susa because the food he was obliged to eat was unfamiliar,[38] and led them out into a valley overflowing with more than enough good things eminently suited to the nourishment of the body. Meanwhile the greatest part of the French army came to meet Bohemond as he arrived at the city, and welcomed him to a man like a mother welcoming her only son.

---

[33] *Acts* V.29.

[34] Again Robert adds criticism of the Byzantine Emperor.

[35] Robert drops some of the details given by *GF* 10.

[36] Robert puts the worst possible interpretation on Alexius' actions.

[37] Classical Hadrumetum; Rusa at *GF* 10.

[38] Something seems to have gone amiss here: one struggles to imagine Tancred refusing the local delicacies like a fussy tourist. *GF* 11 talks of Tancred 'vidensque peregrinos cibos emere, ait intra se quod exiret extra viam' ('when he saw that the pilgrims were buying food he had the idea of turning aside from the road', Hill's translation): Robert's wording, 'quia extranei erant cibi quos sibi oportebat emere', may be a misreading of his source, taking 'peregrinos' as meaning 'alien'.

Chapter XVI: Bohemond's speech to the Franks

Bohemond's speech does not praise the things of this world; neither does it give enough credit to the army of other Christians.[39]

When Bohemond saw so many counts, dukes and nobles coming to meet him, he raised his hands to heaven and wept copious tears of joy. Having kissed many of them and scarcely able to hold back his sobs enough to speak, he began to speak these words in a voice choked with emotion:[40]

'O soldiers of the Lord and tireless pilgrims to the Holy Sepulchre, who was it that led you to these foreign lands if not He who led the sons of Israel from Egypt dry-shod across the Red Sea?[41] Who else influenced you to leave behind your possessions and the home where you were born? You have given up your relatives and neighbours, your wives and your children – more than that, you have renounced all fleshly pleasures. Now you are born again through confession and penitence, as you show daily through your hard labours. Happy are you who weary yourselves with such work, who will see Paradise before you see your homes again! What an order of soldiers, three and four times blessed! Until now you were stained with the blood of killing; now you are crowned with heavenly laurels like the martyrs through the sweat of the saints. Until now you have stood out as an incitement of God's anger; but now you are the reconciliation of his grace and the rampart of his faith. So with all this in mind, undefeated soldiers as you are, now that we start for the first time to fight for God, let us not glory in our arms or our strength but in God who is more powerful than all, because *the battle is the Lord's* and *he is the governor among the nations.*[42]

With these words and many others of the same kind, Bohemond brought his audience round to his way of thinking and was well received by everybody. Then they all accompanied him to the city and led him to his lodging, which the Emperor had ordered to be prepared outside the walls.

---

[39] A rather cryptic heading.

[40] We do not know whether Bohemond, the arch-manipulator, really did this. But epic heroes routinely indulge in such displays of emotion: compare *Roland* 2907–8, 'Cent milie Franc en unt si grant dulur/N'en i ad cel ki durement ne plurt' ('100,000 Franks were so grieved/that every single one was in floods of tears').

[41] For comparison of the Crusaders to the Israelites in *Exodus* and others in the Old Testament see Introduction, Chapter Four.

[42] *I Samuel* XVII.47; *Psalms* XXII.28. The speech sets out clearly the Divine justification for the crusade and the promise of reward for martyrdom. It is interesting that this should be put in the mouth of Bohemond, something which occurs later in the text at IV.10 and V.8–9.

Chapter XVII: the sheer number of Franks terrifies the King of the Greeks

As he saw the camp of the Lord grow and increase from one day to the next, the crafty Emperor – lacking in courage, devoid of sense and short on wisdom – began to get extremely angry. He had no idea what to do or where to turn, or where he should flee if it became necessary. He was terrified in case such a large army with so many soldiers might turn upon him. (For a deceitful mind is always on edge and worried about falling prey into the same traps it sets for others.) This, however, our men had no intention of doing, as they had no desire to fight against Christians. So he ordered Bohemond to be summoned to his presence and held discussions with him and with his own Greeks along these lines. He asked our men that the leaders of the army should do homage to him; he would then personally ensure that supplies of all kinds could be brought and sold to them throughout the wastelands which they were about to enter, and would make himself and the help of his men available in all military operations; he would also make himself personally responsible for supplying everyone with everything they needed in the way of arms and clothes; and he would no longer harm any pilgrim to the Holy Sepulchre or allow one to be harmed.[43] When this plan was revealed, it found favour with just about all since many were suffering from a lack of supplies.

Chapter XVIII: the oath the Franks swore to the Emperor

The King's oath does not last long: those with little self-respect swear and perjure themselves.

So they did homage to him in the terms of this oath, on condition that it should last as long as the Emperor should hold to his own oath and promise.[44] The Count of St Gilles, though, refused point-blank when asked to do homage: if he had been taken at his word, the whole city along with its inhabitants and Emperor would have been destroyed. But there was no justification for sacking such a royal city and so many churches consecrated to God, nor for burning so many holy relics or taking them from their resting-places. At length the Count of St Gilles, brought round by the arguments of the others, agreed and promised fidelity to him with these words:

'I swear to the Emperor Alexius that he shall never through me or my men suffer loss of life or territory, or anything which he currently possesses whether justly or unjustly.'[45] He swore this oath to the Emperor, who accepted it.

---

[43] The terms proposed by the Emperor are identical with those recorded in *GF* 12. Unlike the account in the *GF* there is not a separate oath for Bohemond.

[44] This comment applies only to Bohemond in *GF* 12. Robert is keen to downplay any suggestion that Bohemond had a particular agreement with the Emperor as this would have risked undercutting his legitimacy as ruler of Antioch.

[45] Hill and Hill, 24, n.10 translate the version in RA as 'life and possessions'. See J. H. and L. L. Hill, 'The convention of Alexius Comnenus and Raymond of St Gilles', *AHR* 58 (1953), 322–7; they argue that 'honor' should be translated as land or territory, reflecting a

Chapter XIX: the oath the Emperor swore to the Franks

The Emperor then likewise took an oath, saying:

'I, the Emperor Alexius, swear to Hugh the Great and Duke Godfrey and the other French princes here present, that I shall never during my lifetime injure any pilgrim to the Holy Sepulchre or permit them to be injured; and that I shall join with them in military affairs, and as far as it is in my power I shall have enough supplies brought for them.'[46]

Nobody should be surprised that so many and such noble Frenchmen did homage as if under compulsion because – thinking it through rationally – it becomes clear that they in fact had no alternative. After all they were about to enter a deserted and trackless land, one completely without goods of any kind; and they knew that those not getting their daily ration cannot cope with a day's work. The agreement on homage was made on account of necessity of this kind; but the Emperor did not forget his underhand plans. The agreement reached in the homage would have sufficed if the Emperor's assertion could have been trusted. But whatever he might have promised, he went back on it in what he said, and chose to incur the fault of perjury rather than fail to get the French out of his territory.[47]

But to avoid seeming to have gone through the royal city and said nothing of it, I shall talk a little about it, because that does not seem irrelevant to our story.

---

form of oath common in the South of France at the time. See *Glossarium mediae et infimae latinitatis*, C. Du Cange (Paris, 1840–8), 6 vols., vol.IV 228–9 for examples. Compare English terminology: 'the lands which formed a lord's endowment were known collectively as his "honour"' (F. Stenton, *Anglo-Saxon England*, third edition (Oxford, 1971), 627). *GF* 13 is quite clear that Raymond did not swear fidelity to the Emperor.

[46] This repeats the terms offered by the Emperor at II.17, the justification for the crusaders accepting them and the statement from II.18 that their oath was valid only as long as the Emperor observed his oath. Robert leaves the reader in no doubt as to who agreed what with whom. The reference in *GF* 13 to Tancred and Richard of the Principate avoiding taking the oath is dropped. The exact text of what was sworn is not clear: see F. L. Ganshof, 'Recherches sur le lien juridique qui unissait les chefs de la première Croisade à l'empereur byzantin', *Mélanges offerts à M. Paul E. Martin* (Geneva, 1961), 49–63.

[47] See Lilie, 18–28, 39–60 for detailed discussion of the Emperor's oath. In essence he would have sworn to help the Crusaders in return for all conquests as far as Jerusalem, the Crusaders becoming full vassals. The (wrong) advice of Stephen of Blois that the Crusade was defeated meant that there was little point in sending help. This allowed Bohemond to argue – with some justification, I think –that by retreating at Philomelium the Emperor had violated his oath, thereby legitimising Bohemond's own apparent betrayal of his oath and refusal to surrender Antioch. Robert states this case clearly, and backs it up by vitriolic criticism of the Byzantines though (unlike the *GF*) softer criticism of Stephen of Blois.

Chapter XX: about the city of Constantinople

This was the vision, completely clear, of Constantine.

We read in a history somewhere that the Roman Emperor Constantine, asleep one night in the city known as Byzantium, saw a vision which appeared to him as follows.[48] A certain old woman, without clothes and bound round with a kind of belt, came to him and sought help from his riches; she demanded clothes to wear, a covering to shield her, and a gift of food to eat; she promised him that he would shortly become king, and would without doubt give her what she asked. And thus the vision disappeared. Constantine the omnipotent, excited by the dream and turning over in his mind what the vision might mean, then realised through divine inspiration that it was the very city in which he found himself seeking help and begging to be put in better state. And so he built it up from its foundations and called it Constantinople after himself. He made it equal to Rome in the height of its walls and the noble structure of the buildings, making it sublime in equal glory and earthly distinction: just as Rome is the capital of the West, thus Constantinople should be the capital of the Orient. It is located between the Adriatic Sea and the sea which is now known as the Arm of St George, above which the walls of the city are located. This city is richer than all others through its fertile land and all the trade of mercantile riches. Let none doubt that it was founded on divine will – God saw what was to come, which we now see come to pass. For if such a city had not been founded, where would the Christianity of the East have found a refuge? The most sacred relics of the holy prophets, the Apostles and the innumerable holy martyrs now have a home there, brought from the domain of the pagans. Asia and Africa were once Christian possessions; they are now subject to the filthy rituals of

---

[48] This is Robert's addition. A more elaborate version of the story is found in WM I.622–5, where Constantine is advised both by his mother and by Pope Silvester on the meaning of the vision, and builds the city by following the trail traced by his spear. WM explicitly says that he found the story in St Aldhelm's *De Virginitate (Aldhelmi Opera* ed. Ehwald, *MGH AA* 15 (1919), 209–323, prose version, 259–60); Aldhelm in turn derived it from the *Gesta Silvestri.*

the Gentiles.[49] For that reason the royal city of Constantinople was set up such that, as we said above, it might form a royal and unshakably safe home for the holy relics. And thus it should indeed be equal to Rome in the dignity of what it protects and the excellence of its royal dignity, except that Rome is elevated by the presence of the Pope and is thus head and chief of all Christendom.[50]

So let that suffice for now, and the second book finish here.

---

[49] The themes of the riches of Constantinople and its status as a refuge for relics recur in the apocryphal letter of Alexius: see Appendix.

[50] For the primacy of Rome over Constantinople see e.g. I. S. Robinson, *Authority and Resistance in the Investiture Context: the polemical literature of the late Eleventh Century* (Manchester, 1978) 20–21, 26.

Book III

Nicaea, Dorylaeum and the arrival at Antioch

May 1097–October 1097

Chapter I: the crusaders[1] reach Nicomedia and then Nicaea

Now they cross the sea but reach a trackless desert.

Once the French princes had reached agreement with the Emperor, he ordered ships to be brought to the port so that the whole army could be ferried across without major delay. So Duke Godfrey and Tancred crossed first, reached Nicomedia and kicked their heels there for three days. The Duke then realised that there was no practicable route for those waiting to cross down which such a large army could be led. He sent ahead 4000 men with axes, ploughshares and other tools useful for carving out a route. The land was indeed impassable, blocked everywhere by mountain passes, deep valleys and uneven ground. The men therefore built a road over which they sweated blood as far as the city of Nicaea, passable by those on foot, on horseback and every mode of transport; and they erected wooden crosses on the bends as a symbol so that everyone should know this was a road of pilgrimage. The whole multitude travelled along it except for Bohemond, who remained with the emperor to make arrangements with him about making available the promised supplies. Yet the Emperor procrastinated interminably on fulfilling his promise – so much so that, before he delivered on it, the poorer pilgrims suffered enormous torture from their hunger.[2] The main body of the army arrived at the city of Nicaea on 6 May; before the supplies were brought for sale one loaf was being sold for 20 or 30 denarii. But once Bohemond arrived with supplies, all shortage evaporated and there was an abundance of all good things.

---

[1] The text uses the word 'crucesignati', not found until much later than Robert's text: see discussion in Chapter Five. This is good evidence that the headings were added later and are not Robert's own.

[2] Compare *GF* 14: again Robert adds criticism of Alexius, bolstering his case that Alexius was an oathbreaker.

Chapter II: the siege of the city of Nicaea[3]

You too, Nicaea, will give them ample trophies of victory when they ravage you then take you.

On Ascension Day they dug in for a siege around Nicaea and positioned catapults, rams and other siege machines of that kind which generally defeat the inhabitants. The following princes stationed the strongest section of their army on the eastern side because it seemed harder to take and better defended: the Bishop of Le Puy, Count Raymond, Hugh the Great, the Count of Normandy, the Count of Flanders and Count Stephen of Blois. Duke Godfrey was at the north side; Bohemond on the west. Nobody was stationed to the south because there an enormous lake protected the city; the citizens went out on it in their ships and ferried in wood, grass and other supplies. When the princes discovered this, an embassy set off hotfoot to the Emperor to ask him to have ships brought to Civetot, where there was a port, and oxen with them to drag the ships to the lake. This was no sooner said than done and carried out in accordance with the wishes of the princes.[4] Why go into detail? The supporters of Christ deployed their forces around the city and attacked valiantly; the Turks, fighting for their lives, put up strong resistance. They fired poisoned arrows so that even those lightly wounded met a horrible death.

Chapter III: the city is attacked and siege machines constructed round it

In tumult the noise of tumult spreads through the city.

Our men, completely without fear of death in order to gain life, nevertheless erected tall siege machines around the walls from which they could look down onto those below them on the walls. Wooden towers faced stone towers. Now the enemy is attacked at close quarters with lances and swords:

> And now stakes, torches and stones are hurled into the city:
> The enemy is terrified, now fearing death
> The noise of battle and shouting rang through the city.[5]

---

[3] Until this point Robert follows the *GF* with a few additions. It is here that Gilo's text begins, with Robert showing extensive parallels. His description of events at Nicaea in III.2–6 is similar to Gilo's text, IV.20–145, with a few details added from *GF*.

[4] The embassy to the Emperor is inserted from *GF* 16: for once Robert forgets to criticise Alexius.

[5] These are the first hexameters in Robert's text, and coincide with the start of Gilo's text and of Robert's parallels with it. The wording is close to Gilo: Gilo IV.59, 'magnus erat turbe clamor trepidantibus in urbe' ('the shouting of the terrified crowd in the city grew loud', Grocock and Siberry's translation); 'unde fragor turbe clamorque sonabat in urbe'.

Mothers were fleeing on all sides with their sons and daughters, hair flying, seeking hiding places because they no longer had any prospect of escape. The enemy was preparing to surrender, defeated, when they saw 60,000 Turks approaching in the distance. That was because those in the city had sent messengers out to them, telling them to come to the south gate and help them.[6] Meanwhile our men had been besieging that gate in force, with the Bishop of Le Puy and the Count of St Gilles guarding it. The Turks came down from the mountains and were terrified when they saw our columns from far off; it was only because they were confident in their large numbers that they did not immediately seek protection in flight, swinging their horses round. They made three columns with the intention that the first should break through to the above-mentioned gate, and the [other] two would fight as necessary to be able to follow more freely in its footsteps.[7] The Turks drew themselves up in this order. Our men, one step ahead of them, thwarted this strategy under God's inspiration: the Bishop of Le Puy and the army of Count Raymond, as soon as they saw the Turks, rode away from the city and towards them very swiftly, no more frightened of all that multitude than dogs of a fleeing hare.[8] How many thousands of chosen soldiers followed them, more enthusiastic about tearing Turkish souls from Turkish bodies than any starving man to a wedding feast!

Chapter IV: how the Turks intending to enter the city were killed

Now the Turks flee, and are reduced to fear by everything.

When the Turks saw the incomparable splendour of so many weapons (indeed the sun made them glitter with its flaming rays), the swift attacks of neighing horses, and so many spears flung towards them, they turned tail and sought to return to the mountains in a way that was not exactly slow or unenthusiastic. But any who had come down from the mountain were unable to regain it:

> And some were terribly tortured by a miserable death.
> With God's help, our forces thus rejoice
> In such trophies [of victory], and return to the city.

There they climbed up again onto their machines, and lobbed the severed heads of slaughtered Turks from their throwing-machines and catapults into the city to strike more fear into their enemies.[9]

---

[6] A detail in neither Gilo or the *GF*: Robert adds a motive.

[7] It is less than clear what is going on here. The corresponding passage at Gilo IV.128–31 suggests that the first column would break into the city to strengthen the defence whilst the remainder would attack the Christian troops besieging the gate.

[8] This is mentioned neither in Gilo nor in the *GF*.

[9] Another detail neither in Gilo nor *GF*. Robert, as will become apparent, has something of an obsession with severed heads.

> Without delay, at that very moment arrived
> The ships brought from Constantinople.

However,[10] they did not put them onto the lake that day but waited for night, filling them with Turcopoles belonging to the Emperor, well trained and experienced in dealing with ships.

Chapter V: about the ships sent to the lake by night

The enemies are trapped and scatter in overwhelming fear, unsure where to turn for safety. The captives, reprieved from slaughter, are sent alive by the Franks to Constantinople.

As dawn rose the following day and those in the city saw the ships, they were terrified out of their wits and, losing the will to resist, fell to the ground as if already dead. All howled, daughters with mothers, young men with young girls, the old with the young. Grief and misery were everywhere, because there was no hope of escape. Inside there was sadness and paralysis; outside joy and exultation. Even so the citizens came up with a plan of escape. Through the Turcopoles they sent a message to the Emperor to say that they would surrender the city to him if they were allowed to leave safe and sound with their belongings. When this was put to the Emperor he was delighted. But it led him to think up a cunning plan which was to lead to iniquitous results. He ordered the city to be surrendered to his troops, complete safeguard to be afforded to the Turks, and that they should be brought to him in Constantinople. He did this (as events later made plain) so that when the right time came he should find them readier to harm the Franks. And so the city was surrendered and the Turks brought to Constantinople. However, the Emperor was not completely blind to his huge gain: he ordered alms to be given to the poor of the army.

Chapter VI: how many weeks the siege lasted

The siege of Nicaea lasted seven weeks and three days; and the town was overcome not by any human force but with the help of God. For it is protected by very thick walls and high towers, so that it is the chief place to which no other is equal in Anatolia. Long ago, in the time of Constantine, 318 bishops met [in Council] there; they discussed our faith because of the malice of the heretics which was then prevalent; and all agreed unanimously on the articles of faith now held by our Catholic Church. And so it was highly appropriate that it should be wrested from the enemies of the Holy Faith, reconciled to God and returned to our Holy

---

[10] Robert here returns to *GF* 16–17 until the end of Chapter V.

Mother Church like a limb being restored.[11] And this new restoration was provided and arranged by God because it was consecrated by the martyrdom of the many who were killed there. It was thus, as we have explained, that the city of Nicaea was liberated and all the fetters of the devil cast off.

> Having accomplished these things, our men soon
> Strike their tents, and prepare to depart, thus leaving the city behind
> And sending off the Byzantine ambassadors.

Chapter VII: the army splits[12]

So after they had left the city behind, they marched for two days as one army. They came to a particular bridge; here they rested for two days at ease whilst they restored their horses and animals with lush grass. As they were about to enter a deserted land without water, they agreed amongst themselves that they should divide and split the army into two parts: there was no way that one land or region would support so many men, horses or animals.[13] So one section, the larger, was entrusted to Hugh of Vermandois; the other followed Bohemond.[14] In the first with Hugh were the Bishop of Le Puy, Count Raymond, Duke Godfrey and Robert Count of Flanders. In the second with Bohemond were Tancred, Robert Count of Normandy and many other princes whose names we do not know.

Chapter VIII: how one part came upon 3,000 Turks in a sudden attack

They rode through Anatolia with no trouble, starting to feel almost safe. Then after the third day, at the third hour of the fourth day,[15] those with Bohemond saw 300,000 Turks coming towards them and shrieking heaven knows what barbarisms in loud voices. Their numbers were so large that some of our men began to be unsure whether they should put up a fight or flee to a safe distance. At that point Bohemond, perceptive as ever, and the Count of Normandy, ever the brave soldier, realising that some of their men were wavering, ordered all the mounted soldiers to descend and pitch camp. At the spot there was a certain river with a swift current,

---

[11] Gilo has a similar reference to the Council of Nicaea (AD 325), although in his text it comes before the battle of Nicaea (IV.14–19). The defeat of heresy then corresponds to the defeat of the pagan Turks now.

[12] Again Robert's description of Dorylaeum follows the structure and many of the details of Gilo IV.151–344.

[13] The split is in *GF* 18 although the chronology is different.

[14] Robert reverts to following Gilo's source. IV.157–8 likewise puts Hugh and Bohemond in charge of the two contingents.

[15] 1 July 1097. *GF* 16 puts this on the third day; Robert follows Gilo IV.161 in putting it on the fourth day.

And they pitched their tents along its banks.

Bohemond, thinking quickly, immediately sent a swift soldier:

Who was tasked with riding swiftly and summoning our men
To hurry to the battle which was imminent.

Chapter IX: about the wonderful battle fought against 300,000

Here battle is joined, bringing diverse fortunes.

Before the tents were erected, 150 Turks[16] rode up to our men on swifter horses, and bending their bows shot poisoned arrows towards them. Our men spurred forward, met them and attacked and killed them all. That was because the Turkish tactic is to turn and flee after shooting their arrows and whilst fleeing to inflict serious wounds on those following them. But this time there was no room to flee because the mass of the enemy was so great that even the summits of the mountains were covered with them. So our men slaughtered them to left and right, the lie of the land meaning their bows and arrows were of no use to them. After a while the Franks, having broken their lances against the bodies of the infidels, started in with their swords. How many bodies fell with their heads cut off and how many could be seen there with some of their limbs slashed, because the rear columns of the army were pushing the front columns onto the swords of their killers!

Whilst the fight takes its course and the vanguard is killed
Another part of the Turkish army which had crossed the river
Immediately attacked the tents of the Christians.

They turned them upside down, slaughtered mothers with their children and all they found unprepared to fight and without arms. The noise of the dying reached Bohemond's ears, and he realised immediately what was happening. He entrusted the battle to the Count of Normandy; and ran to the tents with a few companions.

When the Turks saw them, they soon turned tail.

Seeing many lying there dead he began to lament, and implored God to be a refuge for the living and the dead. He returned swiftly to the battle, but left soldiers in the tents to protect and guard them.

---

[16] Gilo IV.174–5 puts the number at 150,000. Robert seems to have misread his source (although ironically his number is likely to be nearer the truth). None of the variants listed by the *Recueil* insert an 'M'.

Chapter X: how our men became tired and weak

*The effort and the heat, thirst, a terrible enemy and arms bore down on our men,
and as a result they started to turn tail.*

Before Bohemond could get back to the battlefield, our men had become so
exhausted by thirst, exertion and the summer heat that if the women had not
brought water to them from the river flowing nearby many would have died in
battle that day.[17] In fact they were already running away from the Turkish assault,
and if the Count of Normandy had not swung his horse round, brandishing his
golden standard in his right hand, and bellowed the warcry 'God wills it! God wills
it!'

This day would have been a disastrous one for our soldiers.[18]

However, once they had seen Bohemond and the Count of Normandy turn
back, they regained their courage and decided to die rather than flee further. The
Turks were attacking with such ferocity, one pushing another on, that there was no
safe place anywhere to afford a breathing space. They surrounded our men so
effectively that they could find no empty space except around the tents. Many of
ours died at that point, shot down by Turkish arrows. Not one of our men was
spared from action and none was without a job to do. The soldiers and those who
could fight, fought; the priests and clergy wept and prayed; and the women,
lamenting, dragged the bodies of the dead back to the tents.[19]

Chapter XI: the sudden arrival of Hugh and Duke Godfrey

Godfrey and Hugh come to the rescue.

Whilst our men were beleaguered in this way, covered by the shadow of a cloud of
flying arrows,

Duke Godfrey flew to the rescue with Hugh.[20].

When with 40,000 chosen soldiers they came to the mountain, they saw the
tents of their comrades surrounded on all sides by Turkish forces, their allies

---

[17] Referred to in Gilo but emphasised more here and in the *GF*.

[18] Compare Gilo IV.220, 'lux ea plena malis nostris foret exitialis' ('that day, full of
misfortune, would have been deadly for our men', Grocock and Siberry's translation).

[19] Robert omits the description given in Gilo I.241–53 of a cutting-out expedition to the
mountains by 1000 Saracens.

[20] The description by Gilo of Godfrey's heroism (IV.260–65) is surprisingly absent from
Robert.

fighting as best they could and the women in the tents shouting and lamenting wildly. Their courage took fire and, like an eagle swooping on its prey,

> Spurred on by the sound of its eaglets hungry for food
> They drive into the thick of the opposition, burning with anger.

How great was the clash of arms, how loud the splintering sound of lances meeting; what a noise from the dying and how joyful the voice of the Franks as they fought, all shouting their warcry at the tops of their voices! Their voices echoed, bouncing off the sides of the valleys, the summits of the mountains and the clefts in the rock. It is a bad day for those they meet first: living men become mere corpses whom neither breastplate nor shield can protect and whom neither arrow nor taut bow can help. They howl, they groan, they beat the earth with their heels as they die, or tear the grass with their teeth as they sprawl prone. When these sounds suddenly reached those far off the one side rejoiced, the other side was stricken. The Franks recognise the warcry of their own soldiers; the Turks by contrast the pitiful groans of their own men dying. The hand of the infidels slackens, stupefied; conversely the exhausted hand of the Christians finds a new burst of energy.

Chapter XII: the arrival of the Bishop of Le Puy and of Count Raymond

Never before was there a battle of such great forces: fear gained the upper hand on one side and receded on the other.

Meanwhile, when the Turks who were busy fighting our men looked up at the mountains, they saw the Bishop of Le Puy and Count Raymond with the remainder of the knights and footsoldiers in the army riding down to attack them. They were struck rigid with terror by the numbers of soldiers, thinking that either soldiers were raining down on them from heaven or that they had come out of the mountains themselves. So battle is renewed and several thousand Turks killed with fresh impetus.

> What should the Turkish people do now, reviled by everyone,
> If not retreat back whence they came and stay there?
> Those who were at the tail end start to find themselves at the head
> And just as the head follows the tail, one flees following another in flight.[21]

---

[21] A further passage from Gilo, a battle and an attack by 1,000 Christians on the mountains (IV.276–321), is absent from Robert.

Chapter XIII: how our men regained their courage, and the great massacre of the Turks

Now the Saracens flee, the Arabs and the Agareni with the Publicani, Medes, Persians and Agulani.

Our men, virtually confined to their tents up to this point, found fresh reserves of courage and revenge themselves on the enemy for their wounds and serious injuries:

> Those who were attacking them now flee by every possible route
> And do not care whether they are coming or going;
> But the military might of Christ[22] inflicts a terrible death on them:
> The earth is crimson with blood, every fold of the mountain is red,
> And the river is swollen with flowing blood.
> So many dead bodies were strewn over the battlefield
> That horses struggled to find somewhere to put their feet.

The battle lasted from the third hour until dusk that day; and it was a source of wonder as to where such a large force could have been assembled from. Those recognised as being in the know said that Persians, Publicani, Medes, Syrians, Candei,[23] Saracens, Agulani, Arabs and Turks were all there and covered the face of the earth like locusts and grasshoppers, *and that without number.*[24]

Chapter XIV: battle and victory: how the Christians gave thanks and rejoiced

Night brought an end and that was what saved them; for, if darkness had not concealed them, few indeed would have survived from such a great multitude.[25]

> Great is the glory of God, for such a great victory as this.
> He destroyed the evil enemy and glorified his own soldiers.

And so our soldiers, forced by the coming of night, returned to their tents with the priests and clergy chanting the following hymn to God:

---

[22] Robert uses the term 'miles Christi'. There is no obvious leader to be referred to at this point unless we assume that Robert has pasted rather clumsily from his source.

[23] Publicani are dualist heretics, the Paulicians: see Lambert, 23. The Candei are rendered in some manuscripts as Chaldeans. The Agulani have provoked debate: Iorga (*Narrateurs* 76) suggests that they are Turkish mercenaries, deriving the name from *oghlou* (son); Jamison ('Some notes' 185–6) derives the word from Agareni, the sons of Hagar, and links it with the Aigolant in the *Chanson d'Aspremont*, ed. L. Brandin, (Paris, 1923–4, reprinted 1970). *GF* 49 has a fantastic description of them repeated in its derivatives.

[24] *Psalms* CV.34.

[25] The details given at Gilo IV.323–30 are omitted.

'Thou art glorious in Thy saints, O Lord, and wonderful in majesty; *fearful in praises, doing wonders.*[26] *Thy right hand, O Lord, hath dashed in pieces the enemy,*[27] *and in the greatness of thine excellency thou hast overthrown them that rose up against thee.*[28] *The enemy said, I will pursue, I will overtake, I will divide the spoil; my lust shall be satisfied upon them; I will draw my sword, my hand shall destroy them.*[29] But Thou, Lord, wast with us as a strong warrior, and *Thou in thy mercy hast led forth the people which thou hast redeemed.* Now we realise, God, that Thou art *guiding us in Thy strength unto Thy holy habitation,*[30] Thy Holy Sepulchre.'

After this they fell silent and, now safe from the enemy, slept well that night.

Chapter XV: the burial of the dead and the desecration of the Turkish graves

The corpses of the Turks are despoiled on the battlefield; the corpses of our men are buried amidst praise of God.

The next day, when the sun rose and made the world beautiful with its flaming rays, all hurried to the battlefield, where they found many of their own dead; indeed had it not been for the crosses they wore they would have had a great deal of trouble picking them out. Those better able to make informed judgements revered them as Christian martyrs and buried them with as much honour as could be managed. The priests and clerics sang the funeral service. Mothers wept bitterly for their sons, friends for their friends. Once this was done, they hastened to despoil the corpses of the enemy. Who could possibly describe the rich pickings of clothes and the sheer amount of gold and silver they found? What a huge number of horses, male and female mules, camels and donkeys our men acquired! Those who were poor suddenly found themselves rich with the help of God;[31] before they were half naked, now they were dressed in silken garments. Missiles and arrows are picked up and empty quivers filled. The wounded were cared for and given to the doctors to look after:

And thus our people stayed there the whole day.[32]

---

[26] *Exodus* XV.11.

[27] *Exodus* XV.6.

[28] *Exodus* XV.7.

[29] *Exodus* XV.9.

[30] *Exodus* XV.13.

[31] A commonplace of crusading rhetoric; see e.g. *Canso d'Antioca* 426 'tal .m. n'i iran paupre; tuih en venran manen', ('so many thousands will depart for battle in poverty; all will return rich men'); FC III.37.6–7 'qui enim illic erant inopes, hic facit eos Deus locupletes' ('God made rich those who used to be poor'). The apocryphal letter of Alexius lays heavy stress on the riches of Constantinople as a motive for Crusade: see Appendix.

[32] Gilo passes straight to arrival at Antioch, and the remainder of Book III follows the *GF*; the exegesis here is Robert's own.

If anyone thinks about this sequence of events worthy of high praise, he will be able to discern clearly the wonders of God at work. For *He hath filled* his own *with good things* and those not his own *he hath sent empty away;*[33] *he hath put down the mighty from their seats, and exalted them of low degree,*[34] casting down the powerful and glorifying the humble. This is what he promised to his beloved Jerusalem through the Prophet Isaiah: *I will make thee an eternal excellency, a joy of many generations. Thou shalt also suck the milk of the Gentiles, and shalt suck the breast of kings: and thou shalt know that I the Lord am thy Saviour and thy Redeemer, the mighty one of Jacob.*[35] The pride of the centuries is the nobility of famous men; the breast of kings, those burying the treasures of their wealth in the ground. That nobility feeds off the breast of kings, whilst it derives earthly power from them. And that creates joy and gladness not only in the present generation but in the generations of centuries to come.

Chapter XVI: they pursue the fugitives on the third day, and the Arabs come to Soliman's aid

Soliman was terrified with enormous terror.[36]

On the following day, 3 July,[37] they struck their tents first thing in the morning and hurried to follow in the tracks of the fleeing Turks. However the latter fled before them like timid doves frightened by the appearance of a hawk. After four days of dodging in retreat hither and thither, their leader Soliman happened across 10,000 Arabs coming to their rescue.[38] (He was by the way the son of Soliman the Elder, who wrested the whole of Anatolia from the Emperor.[39]) After he had fled from Nicaea, he had brought his forces together into one and led it towards the Christians to avenge his injuries. When he saw them and the Arabs saw him, he collapsed from his horse to the ground overwhelmed by grief and began to howl loudly, proclaiming himself miserable and unfortunate. To this the Arabs, ignorant of the facts, said:

'Why are you fleeing like this more shamelessly than any man? You really are degenerate – your father never fled from battle. Get your courage back and get back onto the battlefield, because we are coming to help you.'

---

[33] *Gospel of Luke* I.53.

[34] *Gospel of Luke* I.52.

[35] *Isaiah* LX.15–16.

[36] The Latin is equally clumsy: I have reflected it.

[37] Hagenmeyer (*Chronologie*) suggests 4 July 1097.

[38] Soliman is the first of Robert's three Saracen leaders; the other two are Kerbogha at Antioch and Clemens at Ascalon. All three are portrayed as bombastic figures of fun although there is real menace in the portrayal of Kerbogha.

[39] Kilij Arslan I ibn-Sulaiman, Sultan of Rum who ruled 1092–1107, son of Suleiman ibn-Kutulmish; referred to in Western sources as Suleiman the Young.

At these words Soliman, his voice broken with sighs, said:

Chapter XVII: Soliman's speech

'You are totally insane. You have never come up against Frankish valour or experienced their courage. Their strength is not human: it comes from heaven – or the Devil. They trust not in their own powers but in the power of God. We had crushed them to the point where we were already getting bonds of rope and reeds ready to put round their necks when suddenly innumerable forces with no fear of death and unconcerned by enemies burst out of the mountains and fearlessly thrust into the middle of our columns. Who could bear to look at the terrifying splendour of their arms? Their lances glittered like shining stars; their helmets and breastplates were like the brilliant light of growing dawn; the sound of their arms was more terrible than the roar of thunder. When they get ready to attack they come forward in disciplined ranks, lances erect towards the sky, silent as if they were dumb. But when they reach their enemies, then they rush forward to attack, slackening the reins, as if they were lions raging with the hunger of starvation and thirsting for the blood of animals. Then they shout and grind their teeth and fill the air with their shouts, and, strangers to all pity, take no prisoners but kill everyone. What more can I say of such a cruel race? There is no people strong enough to resist them or to find anywhere safe from them because they are assisted by either divine or diabolical help. All other races are terrified by our bows and fear our weapons; but these, once armoured, fear an arrow about as much as a straw; a missile frightens them as much as a wooden stick. Alas! Alas! There were 360,000 of us, and yet we were all killed by them or fled in disorder. Today is the fourth day after we began to run away from them, but we are trembling with fear no less than we were on the first day. And so if you want to show any common sense, abandon Anatolia as fast as you can, and take the greatest care not to let anyof them catch sight of you.'[40]

Chapter XVIII: how the Arabs flee

The Arabs acted deceitfully as they retreated. After plenty, our men found hunger.

When the Arabs heard all this, they immediately took to their heels with Soliman. The Christians tracked them skilfully, but they never stayed in one place for long. As their flight brought them to various Christian cities or castles, they put on happy expressions as if they had been the winners, saying:

---

[40] Soliman's speech is a good example of the mirroring technique Robert often uses to depict Christians through Saracen eyes. To the diabolical Saracens the Christians are themselves devils; they grind their teeth and slaughter pitilessly, much as do the Saracens depicted by Christians.

'Open your doors to us happily and gladly, because we have killed all the Franks for you. They were coming to plunder you and your lands; there is not one left who is not either dead or safe in our chains (Soliman our leader, by the way, is travelling by another route and taking the captives with him).'

Those who believed them opened up and suffered serious damage for their credulity, for the Turks took their possessions, burned their houses and either butchered them or took them away trussed in bonds. The point of this was to ensure that the Franks following them could find nothing left so that they would cease to pursue them for want of provisions. It was a clever tactic, because it helped them greatly and damaged our whole army. For our men found this land to be empty of water and provisions alike. They tore off nearly ripe ears of corn and hulled them by rubbing them in their hands, appeasing their hunger as far as they could with such food. The greater part of the horses died there, and many who used to be distinguished as knights became footsoldiers. They rode cows and oxen, and native rams and dogs of considerable strength and height. So they crossed that region as quickly as they could and came to Lycaonia, a province fertile with all necessaries, and thence to Iconium.[41]

Chapter XIX: about Iconium

This city received our men and restored them when they entered.

Iconium is a city very rich in the things of this earth, which the Apostle Paul talks of in his letters.[42] Indeed those who had wandered in the solitude of the waterless desert found the way to the hospitality of a city and at the behest of God were filled with the good things of the earth. When they decided to leave the city they carried water with them in containers and skins on the advice of the inhabitants, because they would find none on the following day. In fact on the evening of the second day they came to a river and stayed there for two days. On the second day the scouts who went ahead of the army came to the city called Heraclea,[43] where an enormous number of Turks was gathered. However, when they saw the Frankish standards fluttering in the distance, they bolted immediately like a fawn sprung from a trap or a doe shot by arrows.[44] So praising God our men entered the city unimpeded and stayed there for four days.

---

[41] Modern Konya.

[42] II *Timothy* III.11. Robert again evokes a parallel with the Exodus.

[43] Modern Ereghli.

[44] Robert departs here from *GF* 24 which says there was a fight.

Chapter XX: about Baldwin and Tancred, who split off from the others and took Tarsus

This army, splitting off, seeks out a city known as Tarsus.

They all left on the fifth day. At that point Count Baldwin (brother of Duke Godfrey) and Tancred split off from the others with their forces and turned aside to the city of Tarsus.[45] There were plenty of Turks in it; they marched out to give battle but were unable to resist for long. Incapable of withstanding the swift attacks, agile manoeuvres and heavy blows inflicted by our men, they retreated inside the protection of the city walls leaving many of their men dead. Our men set up camp outside the walls and posted sentinels. The Christians in the city came to the camp at dead of night, exclaiming aloud with joy, and said: 'Come on and get yourselves out of bed, you undefeated Frankish soldiers, because the Turks are all fleeing from the city and no longer dare to fight you!' Our men, though, decided not to follow them because it was the middle of the night, a time not exactly suited to pursuit. Once day broke our men entered the city and the citizens received them very enthusiastically.

Chapter XXI: the argument between Baldwin and Tancred

A dispute then arose between Count Baldwin and Tancred as to which of them should rule the city or whether they should do so jointly. Tancred refused because he wanted it all for himself; but eventually he ceded to Baldwin, whose army was the stronger.

Chapter XXII: Adana and Mamistra

The fierce race of Franks subdues the land of the Armenians.

In a short space of time two further cities were surrendered to them: one was known as Adana, the other as Mamistra.[46] Several castles were also handed over. By this point they were making excellent progress, since the Turks were no longer riding freely abroad but had shut themselves away behind powerful defences. The greater part of the Franks entered the region of Armenia, desperately keen to drench the earth with Turkish blood. The whole region fell quiet when it saw them;[47] the Armenians came out to meet them rejoicing and received them into their cities and castles. They did come to one particular castle which was so well

---

[45] Modern Darsous. Robert abridges the longer account given in *GF* 24–5.

[46] Both Armenian cities. The latter was the classical Mopsuestia.

[47] Compare *I Maccabees* I.3: *the earth was quiet before him* (referring to Alexander the Great).

protected by its site that it feared no arms or siege machines. They decided against lingering there given that the whole of the rest of the region was submitting to them and well disposed to accept their rule.

Chapter XXIII: about a particular soldier who received Armenia to rule as his own from the princes

The soldier gains what he seeks and is granted land.

There was a particular soldier in the army who was strong and energetic, a native of that region.[48] He asked all the princes whether he might have it to guard faithfully for God, the Holy Sepulchre and for them, thus protecting his life and his honour. The princes unanimously agreed to this because they knew him to be trustworthy and a strong, capable fighter.

Chapter XXIV: Caesarea in Cappadocia

Continuing their successful march they came to Caesarea[49] in Cappadocia. (Cappadocia is a region forming a gateway to Syria which stretches out to its northern territory.) The inhabitants of the city surrendered spontaneously and received the Christians well.[50] Leaving Cappadocia behind them and continuing their good progress, they came to a city which was very attractive and fairly rich, which the Turks had recently besieged and attacked for three days but not been able to capture.[51] When they arrived the citizens came out in short order to greet them with great delight and received them hospitably.

Chapter XXV: Peter of Aups

Land is granted to this man along with Caesarea.

Another soldier, Peter of Aups,[52] sought this city and was granted it almost immediately by unanimous agreement of the princes. The same night some gossip came to Bohemond and told him that as many as 20,000 Turks were nearby in ignorance as yet of the Frankish presence. Bohemond, believing these lies, chose a select band of soldiers to come with him and rode out to the place where the Turks

---

[48] Symeon, a local Armenian lord (*GF* 25;see Runciman, *History*, vol.I, 191).

[49] Modern Kayseri.

[50] Not according to *GF* 25.

[51] Comana/Placentia, now abandoned; Baldwin and Setton vol. I, 297.

[52] An Occitan knight in the service of the Emperor: *GF* 25–6, BB 38–9; AC 148, 166, 173, 348, 406, 434 for details of his career in the Byzantine court.

were supposed to be hiding. But the result of his expedition was as empty as his original information.

Chapter XXVI: about Coxon

Here hunger is a thing of the past and happy abundance takes its place.

Moving forward, they came to a city known as Coxon full of all things needed for human sustenance.[53] When they arrived they were received most hospitably by the Christians in the city, and rested there for three days. There every man satisfied his needs: the tired found rest, the hungry were fed, the thirsty drank, the naked found clothes.[54] Indeed God provided a resting place of this kind for them so that they would be better equipped to deal with the terrible torments of hunger to come. At that point Count Raymond was informed that that the Turks, terrified, had fled from Antioch and left the city virtually unprotected. He therefore decided to send 500 soldiers there to take the citadel before anyone else could find out about the situation.[55] However, when they reached the valley near Antioch, they discovered that not only was it untrue that the Turks had left the city but that on the contrary they were preparing to defend it with every possible effort.

Chapter XXVII: how the castle of Publicani was violently taken

Here a castle of Publicani falls to our men.

They continued their journey to a castle of Publicani and took it. They changed their route and arrived without problems in the valley of Rugia, where they found many Turks and Saracens and, defeating them in battle, put them to the sword.[56] When the Armenians who lived there saw this, they were delighted that the Christians had so bravely defeated and killed the Turks and pagans, and immediately surrendered themselves and their land to them. Thus they gained the city of Roussa[57] and placed many castles under their rule.

---

[53] Modern Goksun.

[54] Compare *Gospel of Matthew* XXV.35–40.

[55] Perhaps surprisingly, given the interest in the Occitans he shows elsewhere, Robert omits the names of the soldiers on this expedition given by *GF* 26.

[56] Compare *Judith* XV 5–6.

[57] Probably modern Keshan.

Chapter XXVIII: a difficult route

The fortunes of this world are as changeable as the moon: if something starts well it turns bad and prosperity fails. That is true in many undertakings such as these battles.

The whole of the remaining army set out and suffered greatly during a difficult passage over some mountains where the routes through were suitable only for beasts and reptiles; the paths were wide enough to put one foot down, with sheer drops and thorny undergrowth and thick scrub pressing in on both sides; the valley floors seemed far down in the abyss, the summits of the mountains up in the stars. The soldiers and arms-bearers made their way along this rough path with the weapons hanging round their necks, all reduced to marching on foot because none of them could ride along it. Many would have sold their breastplates, helmets and shields all too willingly if they could have found a buyer; and many, staggering with exhaustion, flung them away to make it possible at least to go on as they were. The pack animals were unable to go on with their burdens, and in many places men were carrying the burdens of the pack animals. Nobody could stand still or sit down because those behind were pushing on those in front. None was able to help his companion except for the last one pushing the man in front of him, whilst the one in front was barely able to turn round to the one behind.[58] At length they came to the end of such a harsh road – or non-road – and came to the city known as Marash. The inhabitants greeted them with honour and rejoicing. There they found an abundance of temporal supplies and were offered a recovery from their misery and scarcity. The vanguard of the army waited for the rearguard, but a whole day elapsed before the tail caught up with the head.

Chapter XXIX: the site and nobility of the city of Antioch

Nobody can describe how praiseworthy was Antioch or to what it can be compared. Its towers and walls are higher than those of lofty cities.

They reassembled and rested for a day. On the following day they arrived in the valley where Antioch is situated, the royal city founded by King Antiochus and named after him.[59] It is the metropolis and the capital of the whole land of Syria, originally distinguished in the worship of the Catholic faith through St Peter, the Prince of the Apostles; it was the city where he established his episcopal see and

---

[58] The description of crossing the mountains is from *GF* 27, but typically Robert adds much vivid detail. It is tempting to speculate that he had experienced similar journeys.

[59] Inaccurate: it was founded by Alexander's general Seleucus. Antiochus IV Epiphanes, King of Syria 175–63 BC, was notorious for forbidding Judaism and converting the Temple in Jerusalem to a temple of Zeus: as such he is 'the most widely discussed type of Antichrist in the Middle Ages' (Emerson, 28).

ordained the apostles Paul and Barnabas.[60] Now, so that God might show mortal eyes that no strength or power comes except through him,[61] he wanted to regain it firstly through the meekness of a sermon in the mouths of his preachers, then to regain it through the grandeur of the power of warriors' arms. And so our men, hastening to the city and strengthened by God, came to the Iron Bridge.[62] There they found a large number of Turks eager to cross the bridge and help those who were in the city. However, it is not for men to determine their own paths;[63] it is for Him to Whom all things are subject. Our men rushed on them as one without delay and spared none, putting a large number of them to the sword; others fled in confusion, preserving their earthly lives. Thus the Christians were victorious and gained a great deal of booty: beasts of burden, donkeys and camels loaded with wine, wheat and oil and other things needed by those under siege.[64] They then set up camp on the riverbank, not far from the city walls. The following day they organised themselves to march to the city, loaded with all their spoil; led by God they arrived and set up camp around it in three sections (for on one side the mountains prevent access and ensure that no military ploys can be used). The siege was set up around Antioch on Wednesday 21 October.

Praise and future glory be to Our Lord Jesus Christ, who is always to be marvelled at for the goodness of his deeds.

---

[60] *Acts* XI and XIII.

[61] Compare *Romans* XIII.1: *there is no power but of God.*

[62] Variously known as the Pons Ferreus, Pons Fernae, Pons Pharphareus or Pharpharicus; it spanned the Orontes, also known as the Farfar. AA 362 gives elaborate details on its fortifications, including two iron towers which justified its name.

[63] *Psalm* XXXVII.23: *the steps of a good man are ordained by the LORD*; Jeremiah X.23: *the way of man is not in himself; it is not in the man that walketh to direct his steps.*

[64] *GF* 28 gives Bohemond a role here not reflected by Robert.

Book IV

The siege of Antioch

October 1097–February 1098

Chapter I: the siege of Antioch[1]

The city of Antioch is eminently defensible not only because of its natural site but also by virtue of very high walls, towers stretching up tall and numerous defensive devices built on top of the wall. The princes therefore decided to attack it not by force but by cunning – the art of strategy rather than the art of war – using machines and not outright combat. So they started by throwing a bridge across the river to make it easier to cross every time they needed to do so.[2] They then found in the environs of the city a considerable amount of rich produce, abundant grapes, pits full of wheat and barley and other foodstuffs and trees laden with fruit of various kinds. The Armenians in the city also slipped in amongst them, coming to visit them during the day with the agreement of the Turks but leaving their wives and children behind in the city. All this was simply a cunning strategem on their part; even though they were Christians they reported back to the Turks in the city on what our men were saying and doing.[3] The Christians were busy building siege machines designed to attack, wooden towers, catapults, sickles, rams, sapping machines, moles, missiles, stakes and things to throw, and whatever else ingenious minds could devise.[4] But what use were they against an impregnable city, particularly given that it was full of defenders who could have fought alongside our men on the battlefield if they had not been enemies of the name of Christ?[5]

> The rising star of morning had preceded the beams of dawn
> So that dawn itself might shake out its shining dew
> And the sun make the world gorgeous with its flaming light.
> The lords rise hastily, their troops with them,
> And seize their arms and run to the walls.
> Right arms fought a hard battle inside and out:
> Those inside defend, whilst our men throw darts

---

[1] Gilo's text resumes with the arrival at Antioch, and so do the parallels with Robert.

[2] Compare Gilo V.12.

[3] The bridge, food and Armenians are in *GF* 28–9. The remainder of the chapter is largely parallel to Gilo V.14–31; the shooting of the woman and building of the castle are from *GF* 29–30, the latter also occurring at Gilo V.118–21.

[4] Robert's wording is close to Gilo's at V.14–17.

[5] A frequent epic sentiment: compare, famously, *Roland* 899, 'Fust chrestïens, asez oüst barnét' ('if he [the Emir of Balaguer] were a Christian, he would be a true knight').

And weapons, sticks, and indeed stones and stakes.
The effort was immense, but in vain.
So they retreated, unable to overthrow
The towers and walls, susceptible to no force.
Seeing that their efforts were in vain, our men
Stop fighting, but carry on the siege.

The Turks, supremely confident in the strong defences of their city, opened the gates at night and made sorties to shoot arrows at our camps. In the process they shot a woman in front of Bohemond's tent. More effective sentinels were therefore posted throughout the camp, who were also charged with watching the exit gates. The princes and lord of the army decided to have a castle built for themselves to ensure that they would be safer in the event of the enemies of God gaining the upper hand, since they were swarming in from all sides like bees to hives. That was done. In the mean time provisions were starting to become scarce. It was therefore decided to go out foraging and send armed men and a number of soldiers to guard those who went. However, out of those who went out to plunder,

Some ended up as plunder themselves and others were killed.[6]

Chapter II: the castle of Harim and how our men were killed

The castle of Harim prepares a fatal attack.

The reason for that was a castle up in the mountains not far from our camp, known as Harim.[7] It was full of infidel Turks who ambushed our men, wounded many and killed several, took large numbers captive and forced the remainder to return to camp much mistreated. When the army of God heard how badly things had turned out, it was upset; it then hit upon a good plan. As before a thousand soldiers were sent into a prearranged valley, followed by Bohemond and the Count of Flanders with handpicked soldiers; the first soldiers were under instructions to retreat back to those in the valley if the Turks pursued them. That was what happened almost immediately: the Turks, seeing them from a distance, slackened their reins and spurred their horses on, pursuing them and making them flee. Just as planned, our men fled back to the safety of their own forces and were protected by divine help. Meanwhile the Turks, realising that they were too close to our forces who were ready to fight, initially hesitated and would have been delighted to give ground had it been of any help.

---

[6] This hexameter recurs in identical form in the same context at Gilo V.38.
[7] Robert renders this as 'Areth'.

Chapter III: the fight between the Christians and the Turks[8]

When they realised that the Christians had a smaller force than them, they fought – albeit with some nervousness – trusting in their large numbers. But what use is it fighting those who receive divine help? For God is *strong and mighty, the Lord mighty in battle.*[9] Two of our men died, whilst countless numbers of the innumerable Turks were killed, pushed back by the hand of God. The Christians led a large number of prisoners back to the camp and cut their heads off in front of those watching from the walls of the famous city. To add to their grief and terror, they lobbed the severed heads into the city from their catapults. From then on our men had less difficulty going to the Armenian towns and settlements to search for food, and the Armenians and other natives brought food to sell to our men.

Chapter IV: Christmas Day[10]

It came round to the Holy Day of Christmas, which God has raised to a most important one for all his faithful: having brought about the birth of all creatures, he chose to be born for men alone. So the Christians celebrated as much as one can celebrate a festival in tents. Even so there was a lot more enjoyment in the camps than inside the walls of the famous city – I say famous not on account of the foul occupation of the pagans but because of its position in the whole human condition and its reconciliation to God, especially that of St Peter, Prince of the Apostles.

Chapter V: the poor winter weather and the demoralisation of the besiegers

Bad weather and lack of bread began to weigh upon them.

With the celebration over, they debated what they should do: food was short in the camps, and the bitter winter cold prevented food being brought to them to buy.[11] Moreover, those in the city attacked our men increasingly hard the more they knew they were suffering from hunger. The harshness of the weather, the shortage of food caused by miserable indigence and the closing in of the enemy all weighed on them. As you would expect in a large group, there was no lack of discontented muttering; indeed it was only to be expected that human fragility should start muttering under the weight of so much suffering. *Hail, snow* and ice, and *stormy wind*[12] made life extremely unpleasant for those who were not sheltered under any

---

[8] The fight is similar to Gilo V.34–62, although the beheading and reference to Harim are in *GF* 29; lobbing the heads from catapults is, predictably, Robert's own contribution.

[9] *Psalms* XXIV.8.

[10] The reference to Christmas is in *GF* 30 although, as so often, Robert embroiders.

[11] Compare Gilo V.63–4.

[12] *Psalms* CXLVIII.8.

roof; it was hardly surprising that those outside the tents were almost at the end of their tether when the tents themselves were awash.[13]

Chapter VI: how Bohemond and the Count of Flanders arranged to go foraging[14]

The Medes, Arabs and Persians deploy their own forces with the Saracens and Agulani (or Agareni).[15]

So, as we said above, they debated what they should do and decided to proceed as follows. Bohemond and the Count of Flanders offered their services to help deal with the situation; all agreed and willingly went along with the plan. They chose 30,000 knights and soldiers,[16] and marched into the land of the Saracens. Oh God, who oversees all things, how swiftly do you help those labouring under dangers and difficulties, such that what Solomon wrote in the *Book of Proverbs* comes to pass: *the wealth of the sinner is laid up for the just!*[17] Persians and Arabs and Medes had come together from Jerusalem, Damascus, Aleppo and other regions, an enormous number of people who had decided to come to Antioch and defend it against the Christians. But events had been ordained differently in Heaven, completely reversing their plans. For when they heard that some of the Christians had entered their territory they danced with joy, convinced that they were as good as imprisoned in Turkish chains. So they divided into two columns with the aim of surrounding our men so that they were unable to find anywhere to flee. That was a stupid thing to do: stupidity is a distinguishing characteristic of infidels.[18] When the two armies saw each other they rushed together immediately; one trusted in its size, the other in the omnipotence of God, and the outcome of the battle was very different for each.

Chapter VII: the Christians are victorious and the Turks flee[19]

The armed soldiers cut down all those they met in their attack like the harvester cutting the harvest with a scythe. But when they wanted to wheel round to attack them again, relaxing their reins for the turn, they found only fugitives remaining to

---

[13] Compare Gilo's wording at V.90: 'castra natabant' ('the camps were swimming').

[14] Robert combines material similar to Gilo V.104–112 with *GF* 31.

[15] See III.13 for the mysterious Agulani

[16] Gilo V.104 agrees on 30,000; *GF* 30 says 20,000.

[17] *Proverbs* XIII.22.

[18] Compare *Proverbs* XIV.33: *wisdom resteth in the heart of him that hath understanding: but that which is in the midst of fools is made known.*

[19] Chapters VII and VIII do not show much similarity with either Gilo or the *GF*. But Robert's imagination is quite strong enough to generate these kind of generic details unaided.

be attacked. Those who fell into the hands of our footsoldiers fell to headlong slaughter. (Those who know something about war are well aware that footsoldiers kill more effectively than cavalry.) The second column, which had split from the first to surround our men, heard the voices of soldiers fighting and the clash of armour on armour and, slackening their reins, raced to the rescue. However, once they saw the desperate case of their comrades and looked round at the fugitives, they were struck down with sheer terror and joined in the rout. So what else could our men do other than pursue? For, as the old proverb has it, 'If someone flees he will not be short of pursuers'; by now all our men were in hot pursuit, with those who had arrived as footsoldiers were being turned into cavalry. To cut a long story short, those who managed to escape were pleased and happy; those who were caught met a truly horrible end.

Chapter VIII: how an abundance of supplies was found there and the joy that occasioned in the camps

Here those tortured by terrible hunger are abundantly fed.

What numbers of donkeys and camels and beasts of burden laden with wheat, wine and other foodstuffs were captured, welcome to the hungry army of God! What rejoicing and triumphant spiritual joy there was in the camps that day, receiving such gifts from the supreme Provider! It was a matter for wonder and joy that God had restored his faithful followers through offerings brought from far off by their enemies. He *filled the hungry with good things*[20] plundered from their enemies. Just so did He once act for the people of Israel when they wanted to cross the lands of pagan kings who refused to allow them to travel the main road.[21] In exactly the same way all who drew swords on them perished by the sword;[22] and their lands and property were given over to them. And today God metes out the same treatment to the enemies of his people, so that they may believe that what is written of them comes to pass. May God, who should be blessed, be blessed for all because without him we can achieve nothing.[23]

Chapter IX: how those in the city attacked and killed our men[24]

Meanwhile in the absence of those glorious princes, the inhabitants of the city suddenly made a sortie and attacked our men inside the camps, killing many of them. On that day the Bishop of Le Puy lost his steward, who used to bear the

---

[20] *Gospel of Luke* I.53.

[21] *Numbers* XXI.21–31.

[22] Cf. *Gospel of Matthew* XXVI.52.

[23] Cf. *Gospel of John* XV.5, *without me ye can do nothing.*

[24] Robert picks up borrowing from the *GF* again at 32.

standard for his column.[25] Had it not been for the river between the camps and the city they would have suffered worse and more frequent insults from the enemy.

Chapter X: Bohemond's exhortation to those planning to flee

Here the spirits of our men began to waver; the eloquent Bohemond strengthens their resolve.

Several of our men, suffering from the vicissitudes of war and particularly from acute shortage and hunger, were working up plans to leave; they found it too much to bear the famine, and thus plotted to seek a way out of the siege. Bohemond, who had a gift for fluent and winning speeches, spoke to them thus:[26]

'You men have been distinguished up to now as outstanding soldiers. God has upheld you through the many dangers of various battles and given you victory. You have an impressive track record. So why are you now muttering against God simply because you are suffering from the pangs of famine? When he stretches out his hand to you, you exult; now he withdraws it, you despair. It seems as if you love not the giver but the gifts; not the one who is generous but the results of their generosity. When he is generous God is treated as your friend; when he ceases to give, you seem to consider him unworthy and irrelevant. Yet to what race has God granted the privilege of fighting so many battles, beating so many terrible enemies, enriching themselves with so much spoil from races and being crowned with the palms of so many triumphs? Here we are having beaten so many enemies and taken their spoils as your own – so what is it that saps your confidence when we are daily victors? He who fights for you is not far away; he often sends trials upon his faithful so that he can discover whether they love him. Right now he is testing you through the deprivations of famine and the incessant attacks of your enemies. If they had inflicted as many injuries on us as we have on them, if they had killed as many of us as we had slaughtered of them, any of us who remained alive would have every right to complain – but not one would be able to complain because not one would remain alive. So do not lose confidence, but keep your courage up. Whether you live in him or die for him you will be blessed.'

He restored strength to their faltering hearts with these and other such words, and brought manly courage to effeminate spirits.

---

[25] Heraclius according to RA 82, who has him still alive at the battle of Antioch.

[26] Again the theology of the Crusade is expounded by Bohemond. Compare II.16.

Chapter XI: the full blast of winter and the lack of food in the camps

A nut was in such demand that it fetched one nummus; it passes belief and is quite unheard of that an egg should fetch twelve.

A few days later winter took a ferocious grip and abundance of food vanished. Those who usually sold food were completely prevented by snow and ice from coming. The scouts for the army were infiltrating Saracen lands but were unable to find anything more because every single person in the whole region had either fled far off or was hiding in caves or quarry diggings. When the Armenians and Syrians saw our men plunged into such dire straits of hunger, they made their way by routes they knew, carefully searching for anything they might be able to bring to our men. But what they found did not go far with so many and could not support such large numbers. So an ass-load of wheat was sold for six pounds, an egg for twelve denarii and one single nut for one. Why give a whole list of items when things of little value were sold for huge prices?[27] The result was that many died of hunger because they had nothing they could eat. Considerable uncertainty began to grow in their minds, their courage failed and they lost faith in any favourable outcome. And it was hardly surprising if the courage of the poor and weak wavered given that those who could be seen as it were as the pillars of the army were completely weakened.

Chapter XII: the flight of Peter the Hermit and William the Carpenter

Fearing for his life the Hermit fled. The desertion of the leaders damaged the morale of many.

In fact Peter the Hermit and William the Carpenter[28] fled, escaping by night, and left the sacred company of God's faithful. Let us say a word about who William was since I mentioned Peter above. William came from royal stock and previously had a reputation as viscount of a particular royal castle at Melun. He acquired the name of 'Carpenter' because nobody wanted to take him on in battle – there was no breastplate, helmet or shield which could withstand the shattering impact of his lance or sword. So that made it all the more astonishing – and therefore worrying – that such a lack of morale should overtake such an exceptional man, making him flee so shamefully from the camp of his distinguished comrades. One can only

---

[27] Such lists of prices are something of a topos in the literature: compare *GF* 33 here, GN 176.

[28] William of Melun near Paris. He fought in Spain in 1087 (Riley-Smith, *First Crusaders*, 43). Robert gives more details than the *GF*, and is at some pains to stress William's previous heroism and exonerate his conduct here: more evidence of his interest in crusaders from the Ile de France. He goes to some lengths to explain the nickname of 'Carpentarius'.

hope that it was not fear of battle but the fact that he had never before experienced such suffering from hunger. When Tancred, a brave soldier whose determination remained unshaken, learnt of the desertion he was extremely concerned: he followed and overtook them, forced them to return in disgrace and took them to Bohemond's bivouac. There is no need to spell out the shame William suffered as being the first one to desert before anyone else. Many who knew him were sorry; others who did not know his reputation insulted him. Eventually, after being comprehensively insulted, he was pardoned because of deference to Hugh of Vermandois (whose relative he was)[29] and because he had invariably fought bravely in the battles which had already taken place; he took an oath in the presence of all that he would not leave again. But he did not hold to it for long because, as soon as he could, he left in secret. God allowed this suffering from hunger to come about so that he might test his people and strike terror of himself into all nations. He oppressed his own people with hunger whilst he ravaged their neighbours with the sword; 1,000 fell on one side, 10,000 were felled by Christian right arms on the other.[30] So one should never despair of such a God: whatever he does, *all things work together for good to them that love God.*[31] It was to ensure that they did not get complacent from so many victories that he made them suffer serious pangs of hunger. In the whole army it was impossible to find 1,000 horses in a condition to fight, and by this God wanted to make them realise that they should trust not in their horses[32] but in Him through Whom they were victorious how and when He wanted.

Chapter XIII: the treachery of a certain soldier known as Taticius

There was a certain soldier in the army called Taticius,[33] rich and well known amongst his own people and a figure of note in Byzantium, though he hid this under a cloak of lightweight banter. He came to the princes and said:

'Why are we stagnating here? Why do we not go out and look for what we need? If you agree I will go to Byzantium and will bring back to you abundant supplies for purchase in fulfilment of what the Emperor promised. I will have ships laden with all manner of merchandise - wheat, wine, oil, barley, meat, flour and cheese – brought to you by sea, and horses, male and female mules by land. To ensure that you can trust me to deliver, I shall leave here my tents and all my goods

---

[29] A detail added by Robert to *GF* 34.

[30] Cf. *Psalms* XCI.7: *a thousand shall fall at thy side, and ten thousand at thy right hand.*

[31] *Romans* VIII.28.

[32] Cf. *Psalms* CXLVII.10: *he delighteth not in the strength of the horse.*

[33] Taticius was a eunuch in the service of the Emperor, Grand Primicerius for some of his career (AC 141). The Emperor entrusted him with a variety of missions and sent him as representative with the Christian army. As such he became the lightning-conductor for growing (and not necessarily justified) resentment, and it is difficult to find a chronicler who has a good word to say for him. AC returns the compliment, suggesting that Bohemond orchestrated his departure by means of mysterious death threats (AC 343).

except those I carry with me. And if you still do not trust me, I shall swear to return to you swiftly.'

The princes believed his lying words, but accepted his oath; he did not keep his oath and did not fulfil his promise. (I am making a point of telling you about these two soldiers to give you an understanding of how bad the shortage was in the camps, compelling even the rich to flee and to perjure themselves.)[34] Since things had reached this pass and all human hope had vanished, the greater part of the whole army sought permission to go home from the princes, and, weeping, they agreed unanimously. For what was the point in keeping them there when they could do nothing for them?

Chapter XIV: a messenger in the camps announces that the Turks are close at hand

God[35] helps them in their desperation.

At this point, when despair reigned in the camps and nobody knew what to do, divine mercy as ever came to their rescue. A messenger arrived and told them that innumerable thousands of Turks were close, and were going to assemble in a castle near to them known as Harim, which we mentioned above. They were coming secretly and quietly so that they could catch them unawares in their camps. The news spread to all and restored vigour to those whom it had caught napping in a stupor of laziness. Men who had been unable to walk leapt to their feet and jumped. Spirits which had fainted from lack of food revived. Raising their hands to Heaven, they praised God and applauded as if they had already won the battle, preferring to die an honest death on the battlefield than the lingering tortures of hunger. The leaders of the army decided that one part would remain in the camps and guard them; the other would march out to do battle with the approaching Turks. So they left the camps by night and set up ambushes, awaiting the arrival of the first enemies and lay between the river and the lake. Early in the morning, just as dawn brought the first light to the world, they sent scouts to reconnoitre the enemy armies and report back to them. The scouts reported that they had never seen so many thousands together, and that two columns had split off from the main crowd and were approaching from the river on very swift horses. Then our men, drawn up on a slope, made the sign of the Cross with their arms and, stretching their hands up to Heaven, committed themselves to God and begged his aid.

---

[34] Robert returns to Gilo's source from this point to the end of Chapter XV: see V.145–98.

[35] The literal wording is 'a spring of piety': the 'fons vivus' is a frequent synonym for divine power.

Chapter XV: how battle was joined and victory gained

Battle is joined: the enemy flees, routed on all sides. This race cannot enjoy the prize of victory without God.

Soon our men clashed with the oncoming enemy and, landing heavy blows, knocked to the ground all those they encountered. Other Turks scattered and rode round the battlefield, raining down poisoned arrows. They grind their teeth and bark like dogs, believing that terrifies their enemies.[36] Our men laughed at this; protected by their shields, breastplates and helmets they despised these volleys. However, when the main Turkish force approached, they attacked our men so fiercely that they started to give way. Bohemond, keeping guard in the rear, saw this and threw himself and his column into the midst of the battle; rallying his allies, he turned the course of battle against the enemies. When they saw the banners of our men swaying above their heads and our men, roaring like lions, running through their midst and slashing all around them, they were frightened and lost their nerve, and turning their horses fell back to the Iron Bridge as fast as they could. What should the Franks do other than engage hand to hand with the sword? The road was strewn with the bodies of the dying; the air was full of groaning voices; the earth, soaked crimson with the blood of the dying, was pitted by the hooves of trampling horses. On the approach to the bridge the road narrowed and the bridge could not take all of them; many were forced into the river and those in the water were caught up and dragged under by its swift eddies. Why dwell on details? More perished than escaped; more were killed than remained alive. Those who escaped fled to their castle, which we named above; but they did not remain in it for long; having stripped it of everything they left it empty and fled.

Chapter XVI: the violent capture of Harim[37]

So our men took the city and posted guards to secure it and the bridge, The Armenians and Syrians followed those who had fled and, lying in wait in places which would slow their progress, killed many and took some prisoner. And thus the sons of the Devil jumped from the frying pan into the fire and received the end they deserved. Our men returned to the castle rejoicing greatly, bringing with them horses, male and female mules, a great deal of plunder, and many other things which the starving allies desperately needed. They likewise brought the heads of many of the dead, which they placed in front of the gate of the city where the

---

[36] Compare *Canso d'Antioca* 321, which describes the Agulani as barking like dogs. The reference goes back to St Augustine. See '"Canum nomine gentiles designantur". Zum Heidentum aus mittelalterliches Bibellexika', G. Dickerhof, *Secundam regulam vivere*, ed. G. Melville, P. Norbert Backmund, O. Praem (Windberg, 1978), 41–71.

[37] Robert reverts to following *GF* 37–8 briefly.

ambassadors of the Emir of Babylon[38] were lodged. Their companions in the camp, who had fought all day against those who had sallied out from the city and who had had the upper hand, received them with unbounded delight. The double joy of twin victories made for a happy time, and restored to happiness those who had been almost overcome by the misery of famine. Now the Armenians and Syrians brought provisions to the camp and congratulated our men on their fortunate victory. But the citizens crept out and hid amongst the rocks on the mountains,[39] ambushing those who brought provisions and killing whomever they could catch. That worried the lords greatly, and they debated how to deal with this crisis.

Chapter XVII: the castle built on the bridge

They constructed a castle in front of the city gate on the bridge next to the mosque;[40] this controlled the enemies most effectively, none daring to go out across the bridge once it was built. There were not enough men in the camp to complete the work, so Bohemond and the Count of St Gilles went to the port of St Simeon with the aim of hiring workers and bringing them back.

Chapter XVIII: the great battle fought before Antioch[41]

The number of ours they killed amounted to one thousand.

When they did, they ran into an ambush set by the Turks, who had left the city by night. They attacked our men suddenly and so fiercely that those on horseback fled into the mountains without the least shadow of resistance, whilst those on foot – who could not run away – suffered an atrocious death, more glorious by the fact of its being so horrible. Those who died there numbered nearly 1,000. However their killers did not rejoice for long. When the news of this slaughter reached the camps, all the princes and lords were deeply upset. They leapt onto their horses and, ordering their columns, swept out to revenge the death of their men. They found the enemy still on the battlefield, busy cutting off the heads of the dead. Trusting in their weight of numbers and completely unconcerned, the Turks gathered to fight. However, they were defeated in short order by our men brimming with determination and strength once the footsoldiers had joined the cavalry.

---

[38] More severed heads: clearly a crude way of intimidating the ambassadors. They are mentioned here for the first time. Robert probably means Al-Afdal, vizier of the boy Caliph al-Mustali. The Fatimids of Egypt were enemies of the Turks and tolerant towards Christians (Runciman, *History*, vol.I, 229).

[39] Robert returns to Gilo's source for the remainder of the chapter and Chapter XVII.

[40] See Runciman, *History*, vol I, 228 and *GF* 42, PT 78. This was a crucial strategic point, dominating as it did the only exit from Antioch to cross the Orontes.

[41] This chapter and Chapter XIX show some similarities to Gilo V.307–33 but are not close to either his text or the *GF*.

Chapter XIX: the fighting of this battle and how our men were victorious

Here one of our men put 1,000 to flight; there two together [put] 10,000 [to flight].

When the Turks saw those they had driven to flee to the mountains running back towards them, and our battle columns strongly growing and thereby growing stronger, they turned tail and fled towards the bridge. But the narrowness of the path made it extremely difficult for them, so that they could neither escape nor turn around. There was no way of going backwards because the enemy was pushing them on; turning to right or left was impossible because of the narrow path; the packed crowd of fugitives made it impossible to go forward. So by divine will they found themselves in a situation where neither fight nor flight were possible. Poisoned arrows were no use to the Turks, nor was the speed of their horses of any help. The footsoldiers were responsible for more of the carnage than those on horseback, going through systematically cutting off heads like the harvester with his scythe in meadow grass or corn. Other swords and other types of weapon could be satiated with the blood of Turks; because these were of Frankish manufacture they could not be blunted and could not tire of blood. Our men fought ferociously and their opponents suffered; our men struck and the enemy died. No matter how much tireless hands slashed they did not come to the end of what was there to slash. The dead remained standing upright amongst the living because, supported by the thick crowd of living people they could not fall down dead;[42] the enemy were so desperate with fear that they crushed each other to death. So great was their terror that those behind trampled those in front to get away.

Chapter XX: in praise of Duke Godfrey

Duke Godfrey and his trusty sword, fury, the battlefield, the sword and strong arms all come into play in battle. Here the Duke is ablaze with tremendous fury at his opponent. He strikes; the opponent falls cut in two. Here the strength of the Franks was fully displayed.

Duke Godfrey, outstanding ornament of chivalry, saw that they were not going to be able to strike anyone except in the back and flew on his swift horse to cut them off at the entry to the bridge. What tongue could explain how much damage the Duke inflicted unaided on the bodies of the wicked pagans? They began to flee, throwing their arms to the ground; they feared the Duke's sword like death but could not avoid it. He sliced through their necks with his arms bare and sword

---

[42] Compare Gilo V.331: 'sustenantes erecta cadavera vivos' ('the living holding the dead upright', Grocock and Siberry's translation). Lucan employs the same topos (*Pharsalia*, ed./transl. J. D. Duff (Loeb, 1928); transl. R. Graves, *Pharsalia: dramatic episodes of the Civil Wars* (Harmondsworth, 1956), IV.787, 'compressum turba stetit omne cadaver' ('no corpse had even space to fall', Graves' translation).

unsheathed; they unwillingly offered him their naked bodies, hardly resisting. The site, fury, his sword and his strong hand all fought them; all this fell upon the limbs of the wretches. One of them, bolder than the rest, unusually heavily built and of greater strength rather like another Goliath, saw the Duke savaging his men mercilessly; he urged his horse towards him with bloodstained spurs, and lifting his sword high he sliced through the whole shield of the Duke, which he held above his head. If the Duke had not parried the blow with the boss of the shield and twisted over to the other side, he would have paid the debt of death; as it was God looked after his soldier and defended him under a protective shield. The Duke, ablaze with furious anger, prepared to return the blow and thus aimed for his neck. He raised the sword and plunged it into the left side of his shoulder-blades with such force that it split the chest down the middle, slashed through the spine and vital organs and, slippery with blood, came out unbroken above the right leg. As a result the whole of the head and the right side slipped down into the water, whilst the part remaining on the horse was carried back into the city.[43] All those inside rushed together to see this horrible sight, and were struck with amazement, panic and fear, overcome with terror; here there were screams like those of a woman in labour, there voices raised in misery, because he had been one of their emirs. Then they all unsheathed their swords, drew their bows and prepared arrows in their quivers ready to shoot the Duke and intending, if possible, to extinguish such a shining light of Christendom. God thwarted this wicked desire because the Duke retreated, no longer able to cope with the hailstorm of missiles and arrows. How praiseworthy is the right arm of the unconquered Duke, and how strong his courageous heart! Let us praise his sword too, which resisted unbroken and offered unswerving support as a companion to his right arm as he brandished it. What heart could tell, what voice describe, what hand write, what page be worthy to tell of the deeds of the other princes, who equalled him in all the encounters of battle? The Duke's victory shone more than the others because the part of the body cut in two which remained bore witness to his achievements. The limbs of the dead were hacked just as a gust in a storm splinters the limbs of elderly trees. In this battle one man pursued 1,000 and two put to flight 10,000.[44] In their rapid flight they flung themselves headlong into the river, and as they surfaced clung to the wooden columns of the bridge; but our men up above plunged lances down into them and killed them.

---

[43] Godfrey's exploit is mentioned in several chronicles: PT 75, AA 385, RC 646, BB 50. Orderic Vitalis imaginatively describes the Turk being sliced 'quasi tenerum porrum' ('like a tender leek', V.84–5). Robert's account is close to that of Gilo, V.355–69, although as ever spiced up with lurid detail. The exploit is not mentioned in *GF*. A classic epic topos: compare *Roland* 1367–78.

[44] Cf. *Deuteronomy* XXXII.30: *how should one chase a thousand, and two put ten thousand to flight.*

Chapter XXI: how many thousands of Turks were killed on the bridge

Now the Turks were weeping, walking with heads bowed.

The blood spilled turned the river to crimson, and filled all those watching with total horror. The piles of bodies in the river stopped the current and forced it to flow back the other way. What was so surprising about that? Five thousand were killed on the bridge, and all ended up in the river.[45] And who could count how many were forced into the river by the ferocity of the sword? The son of Cassianus the great ruler of Antioch[46] was killed in this fight, and along with him twelve emirs of the King of Babylon, whom he had sent with his armies to help the King of Antioch.[47] (Those they call emirs are in fact kings, who rule the provinces out in the regions. The definition of a province is an area with a metropolitan, twelve consuls and a king.) Troops had come from as many provinces as there were emirs killed in the battle; the numbers of prisoners were calculated at 7,000.[48] Nobody could possibly remember the full total of clothes, arms and ornaments. That was how the Turks were gloriously defeated by the Franks; their jabbering voices, the grinding of their teeth and the noise of their daily insults were no longer heard. Now they walked round instead with heads bowed, and some lost all confidence and fled, sneaking secretly out of the city. The fall of night brought things to an end and our men returned victorious to their camps; the Turks regrouped inside the city, bolting the gates behind them.

Chapter XXII: how the burial places of the Turks were shamefully destroyed by the Christians[49]

The following day, when first light dawned, the Turks left the city and collected up the bodies of the dead – as many as they could find – and took them for burial. When the younger soldiers of the army heard this, they gathered together and ran to the cemetery. The Turks had buried the bodies with great honours; the Christians disinterred them in shame. They had been buried beyond the bridge by the mosque, in front of the city gate; many had been wrapped in cloaks and buried with gold bezants, arms, bows and arrows and many other things, as is their custom at funerals. Our custom is to rob the graves with delight.[50] Having dug up all the bodies, they cut the heads off so that they could find out how many had been killed

---

[45] Gilo V.383 gives the same number.

[46] Yaghi-Sian, Governor of Antioch.

[47] The death of Cassianus' son is also at Gilo V.381–2; the twelve emirs from *GF* 41. Cassianus' son is resurrected at VI.9 as envoy to Kerbogha, a slip by Robert in combining his sources. Ambassadors from the King of Babylon appear at V.1–2.

[48] Gilo V.393–4 has the same number of horses.

[49] *GF* 42.

[50] It is hard to tell whether there is implicit criticism of the Christians here: if so, a rare example in Robert. More severed heads.

at the river bank; they carried the severed heads back to the camps, and left the headless bodies lying unburied for the wild animals and birds. The Turks looked on from the high walls and lofty towers, weeping bitterly, tearing their cheeks and pulling out their hair. They started to beg the help of Mahommed, their master; but Mahommed could not bring back those Christ had decided to destroy through his soldiers.

Book V

Events leading to the fall of Antioch

February 1098–June 1098

Chapter I: the ambassadors from Babylon[1]

The Prince of Babylon sent those ambassadors, who arrived and said the following.

Whilst troubles came thick and fast, a herald appeared and announced that envoys from the Prince of Babylon would arrive the following day; he sought an oath from the leaders of the armies that they should be able to come unmolested. They agreed willingly and bound themselves solemnly to receive them. They decorated their tents with various ornaments; fixing poles in the ground they attached their shields to them so that they could train at the sport of the quintain, a mounted exercise. There were dice, games of chess, swift horse races where they turned by sharply reining in, and practice attacks; and they made a show of brandishing their spears at each other. All these activities were designed to show that those indulging in them had no grounds for fear. That was what the younger soldiers did; those who were older and more experienced sat together and conferred about the wisest and most prudent approach.[2] When the envoys from the Emir of Babylon drew near, they were amazed to see so many men disporting themselves so happily, because the news had reached Babylon that they were tortured by hunger and prostrate with fear. So they were brought before the princes and explained their mission as follows:

'Our master, the most mighty Emir of Babylon, sends greetings and friendship[3] to you, the princes of the Franks, provided you consent to obey him. A massive

---

[1] V.1–2 are not paralleled elsewhere. There is a passing reference to the envoys at *GF* 42; they are also mentioned in RA 58 and by Anselm of Ribemont (*Kreuzzugsbriefe*, 160). The Charleville poet, Gilo's continuator, has a long but different account at V.296–481: the editors suggest that as he wrote after 1118 he may have drawn on Robert's account (Introduction, xxiv). The arguments set out clearly the twin justification for the Crusade: safeguarding the routes of pilgrimage to the Sepulchre and regaining land which by rights belonged to the Christians. The Emir himself appears in book IX.

[2] The description is reminiscent of the *chansons de geste*: compare the description of Charlemagne's court at the beginning of the *Roland* when the envoys from Blancandrin arrive (110–13).

[3] A phrase straight out of the *chanson de geste*. Compare *Canso d'Antioca* 232, 'Senhor, lo reis vos manda salutz e amistas' ('my lords, the king sends you his greetings and signs of friendship').

council has gathered because of you in the palace of the King of Persia and our master;[4] it has debated for seven days over what they should do about this situation. They are amazed that you should seek the Sepulchre of your Lord as armed men, exterminating their people from long-held lands – indeed, butchering them at swordpoint, something pilgrims should not do. So if you agree to complete the journey carrying staff and scrip, they will ease your passage with every honour and plenty of provisions; those on foot will be mounted; the poor will no longer suffer from hunger on the whole of the journey there or back. If you decide to stay at the Holy Sepulchre for a month, there will be no lack of supplies; you will be free to visit the whole of Jerusalem and venerate the Temple and the Sepulchre with what honour you please. But if you spurn this offer and place your trust in the greatness of your courage and your arms, we regard it as the height of rashness that any human power should take on the Babylonians and the King of Persia. Now tell us what appeals to you from these proposals and explain publicly what you cannot accept.'

Chapter II: the princes' response

The words of the Franks are full of a proud sense of what is right.

The princes replied to this with one accord, saying:

'Nobody with any sense should be surprised at us coming to the Sepulchre of Our Lord as armed men and removing your people from these territories. Any of our people who came here with staff and scrip were insulted with abominable behaviour, suffered the ignominy of poor treatment and in extreme cases were killed. The land may have belonged to those people for a long time but it is not theirs; it belonged to our people originally and your people attacked and maliciously took it away from them, which means that it cannot be yours no matter how long you have had it: for it is set out by divine decree that what was unjustly removed from the fathers shall be restored by divine mercy to the sons. Neither should your people take any pride in having overcome the effeminate Greek race because, by the order of divine power, the payback will be exercised by Frankish swords on your necks. And let those who do not already know be aware that it is not down to men to overturn kingdoms but to Him through Whom kings reign.[5] These people say they want to tolerate us with good humour if we are willing to cross their lands with scrip and staff. Let their concession be flung back in their faces because, whether they want it or not, our shortages will be met and dispelled by their treasures. Since God has granted us Jerusalem, who can resist? No human strength can inspire us with terror because when we die we are born; when we lose our earthly lives we gain eternal life. So go and tell those who sent you that we will not lay down the arms we took up at home until we have captured Jerusalem. We

---

[4] The Sultan of Persia.

[5] Cf. *Proverbs* VIII.15: *by me princes reign.*

place our trust in Him who *teacheth my hands to war, so that a bow of steel is broken by mine arms*;[6] the road will be opened by our swords, all wrongdoing will be eradicated and Jerusalem captured. It will be ours not by virtue of human toleration but through the justice of divine decree. It is by God's countenance that Jerusalem will be judged ours.'[7]

The envoys could see no further grounds for negotiation and were appalled by these words. They entered Antioch with the agreement of our men.

Chapter III: the castle built on the mountain

They went on to construct two castles in a short space of time: both were designed for a specific purpose.

After these events they began to build the castle we mentioned above on the third day after the battle, erecting it at the end of the bridge near the mosque, where the cemetery was outside the town gate. They destroyed all the stone tombs of the dead and fortified the castle with them.[8] Once the castle was complete it was assigned to the famous Count Raymond of St Gilles. It trapped those who were in the city most effectively so that they were no longer able to come out through that part of it. In contrast our men could now go safely where they wished. Then the lords chose the best men and the swiftest horses; they crossed the river not far from the city and found an enormous booty, stallions and mares, male and female mules, donkeys and camels, and 5,000 animals. They led the whole herd of good-quality animals back to the camps, to the great joy of the Christians. This turn of fate weakened the citizens of Antioch badly, because the abundance of provisions which strengthened our men weakened them by its loss.

Chapter IV: another castle repaired on the other side of the river[9]

There was an old castle where the booty was taken, in ruins because of its age and lack of maintenance, with a flourishing monastery next to it. To put a further check on the movements of the enemy, the lords decided to rebuild it and protect it with strong fortifications. That was done in short order and there was a search for someone to guard it. Whilst the discussion about guarding it went back and forth, with much hot air being talked, Tancred – a famous prince and outstanding young man, typically bold in word and deed – leapt into the middle and said:

---

[6] *Psalms* XVIII.34.

[7] Cf. *Psalms* XVII.2: *let my sentence come forth from thy presence.* The twin justification for the Crusade is again clearly set out: to protect pilgrims and to liberate Jerusalem.

[8] *GF* 42; the remainder of the chapter parallels Gilo V.394–405.

[9] *GF* 43.

'I will guard the castle provided I receive a fitting reward for my guardianship.' They all agreed on a price and gave him 400 marks of silver. Tancred entered the castle and protected it more than other fortifications with his formations of footsoldiers and strong force of knights. It was lucky that, with God's help, he did hold it, because on the same day a large number of Armenians and Syrians came to the city and brought abundant supplies to its inhabitants. Tancred set an ambush and intercepted them all; he did not want to kill them since they were Christians, but brought them to his castle with their bundles. He let them go on condition that they would promise him, on their Christian faith, to bring him supplies at a reasonable price until Antioch should fall. The Armenians did this assiduously as they had promised.

Chapter V: the terms conceded in hope of achieving peace[10]

Tancred obstructed the roads and paths very effectively for those who were in the city, so that none dared to come out. At length they sought a truce, saying that they would use the time to discuss amongst themselves on what legal basis and under what conditions they would surrender themselves and the city to the Christians. The princes took them at their word: terms were drawn up and a time agreed, and they gave mutual promises to observe the truce. The gates of the city were opened, and each side was permitted to go and visit the other. So the Franks walked freely round the walls and stood on the ramparts with the citizens, whilst the citizens were delighted to visit the camps.

Chapter VI: the death of Walo

Walo is killed and his death violates the truce.

Time passed, and on the last day of the truce a certain Walo,[11] a Christian soldier well known in the army and recognised as one of the best, dropped his guard too far with the infidels. He was strolling that day amongst the bushes and feasting his eyes on the pleasant valley[12] when he was attacked, unarmed, by armed dogs and

---

[10] The truce and the death of Walo are found in detail only here and in Gilo V.415–60.

[11] Walo II of Chaumont-en-Vexin, seneschal and constable of Philip I of France. He is not referred to in GF but appears in AA 316, 332, 363, 422; his death is referred to by Anselm of Ribemont (*Kreuzzugsbriefe*, 159). His wife was Humberge of Le Puiset (Riley-Smith, *First Crusaders*, 249); Riley-Smith, 107, believes she accompanied her husband on Crusade. Her brother Everard III of Le Puiset viscount of Chartres is well attested on Crusade (Riley-Smith, *First Crusaders*, 205); the Le Puiset family sent more than one Crusader to the East (Riley-Smith, 170). See J. L. LaMonte, 'The Lords of Le Puiset on the Crusades', *S* 17 (1942), 100–118.

[12] Both Robert and Gilo (V.426) use the term 'tempe'. Tempe was a valley in Thessaly whose name was used metonymically for any pleasant valley; cf. Statius *Thebaid* X.119, *P. Papini Stati Thebaidos. Liber decimus*, ed. R. D. Williams (Leiden, 1972). Gilo makes much

cut to pieces with horrible suffering. Alas! The truce was broken by the death of Walo, the solemnly given oath broken, and the gates of the city once more blocked; the treacherous Gentiles scuttled back to the shelter of their walls and towers. There was immense mourning in the camps, with men and women lamenting the death of Walo and sobbing bitterly.

Chapter VII: the desperate grief of his wife

His wife moved everyone to tears, tearing herself in a way well beyond what most wives would do; she could not speak or shout because she was choked by sobs and enormous sighs, which moved others to grief. (She was born of noble blood and, as fleshly frailty goes, outstandingly beautiful.) She stood as motionless as a marble column so that you might more than once have thought her dead had it not been for the heat of life beating in her breast and the pulsing of the vein beneath the hairless part of the face between the eyebrows. Once she could breathe, she writhed on the floor forgetting all female modesty, tore her cheeks with her nails and ripped at her golden hair. The other married women ran to her to prevent her harming herself in this way and kept a watchful eye on her. When she was able to speak she burst out:

> 'King of Heaven, three in one, have compassion on Walo
> Give him eternal life, you who are the One God.
> Did Walo deserve to die without striking a blow?
> You, sprung from a Virgin mother, cleanse Walo of his sins,
> Whom you lifted out of the changing fortunes of war
> And now have allowed to be martyred.

Alas! He wanted so desperately to see Your Sepulchre, and in comparison held all he had in little regard including himself! What unlucky chance was it that found him separated from his sword which always hung at his side? How happy I should have been if I could at least have closed his eyes at his last breath, washed his wounds with my tears and wipe them dry with my hands and clothes, and put his sweet body in the tomb!'[13]

---

use of classical allusions. Such allusions as I have identified in Robert's text are mostly in passages close to Gilo's text.

[13] Humberge's lament follows in a well established literary tradition, the *planctus*, found both in Latin and the vernacular. See S. Aston, 'The Provençal planh: lament for a prince', *Mélanges de philologie romane dédiées à Jean Boutière*, ed. I. Cluzel, F. Pirot (Liège, 1971) vol.I, 23–30; see also C. Cohen, 'Les éléments constitutifs de quelques *planctus* des Xe et XIe siècles', *CCM* 1 (1958), 83–86. Gilo V.423–60 is alone in having a similar lament at this point: for resemblances between that and Ovid's *Heroides* see C. W. Grocock, 'Ovid the Crusader', *Ovid Renewed*, ed. C. Martindale (Cambridge, 1988), 55–69. Robert's version is reminiscent of Ovid's description of Niobe in *Metamorphoses* VI.303-12 ed. D. E. Hill (Warminster, 1985–2000) 4 vols.

Her brother Everard[14] broke into these laments and, as far as he could, calmed the violence of her grief.

We should not forget to report what happened before the death of this man, whilst the truce was still unbroken and observed in line with the agreement.[15]

Chapter VIII: about Bohemond, and Pirrus who betrayed Antioch to him[16]

This Saracen was a prince of Antioch; he freely handed over the city to the eloquent Bohemond. The names of the Saints from Heaven bearing standards.

There was a certain Turkish emir in the royal city with whom Bohemond had a large number of private discussions during the truce.[17] Amongst other things he asked one day where he had put the camp of the innumerable army of shining white soldiers who came to their help in every battle. He said that the Turks could never withstand their onslaught; as soon as they saw them, fear took hold; the white soldiers attacked the Turks like a whirlwind whilst the Christians wounded them; they rushed on the Turks whilst the Christians killed them. Bohemond asked:

'Do you think that to be a different army from our army which you see here?'

The Turk replied: 'By Mahommed my teacher, I swear that if they were here this whole plain would not be large enough to hold them. They all have white horses of astonishing speed, and clothes, shields and banners of the same colour. Perhaps they are hiding so that we do not realise your full strength. But by your faith in Jesus, where on earth are their camps?'

Bohemond realised in a flash of inspiration from God that this vision came from God, and that the Turk was asking him not to lead him into temptation but in good faith. He replied:

'Although you do not follow our law, I can see that you are well disposed towards us and approaching things in a good spirit. So I shall explain to you some of the mystery of our faith. If you had any understanding of what lies beneath the surface you should thank the Creator of all for showing you the army of shining white soldiers; and be aware that they live not on earth but in the heavenly mansions of the King of Heaven. These are the ones who suffered martyrdom for

---

[14] Everard III of Le Puiset in the Ile de France.

[15] An awkward join as Robert returns to *GF* 44.

[16] The treachery of Pirrus is in most sources; the long discussions are Robert's own. As at II.16 and IV.10, the theology of the Crusade is explained by Bohemond. Another good example of Robert's mirroring technique: the power of the divine help received by the Christians is validated and magnified by being seen through Saracen eyes.

[17] Pirrus in the *GF*; Firruz in Ibn al-Athir (*Extraits de la chronique intitulée Kamel-altevarykh par Ibn-Alatyr, RHC Or.*, vol.I, 187–744, 192; Zarrad in Kemal ad-Din (*Chronique d'Alep, RHC Or.*, vol.III, 571–732, 581–2), who adds that he was a cuirasse-maker punished by Yaghi-Sian for hoarding. Some sources describe him as an Armenian (AC 342–3, RC 651–2; RA 64).

the faith of Christ and fought against unbelievers across the earth. Their particular standard bearers are St George, St Demetrius and St Maurice,[18] who whilst they were on earth bore arms and died in the faith of Christ. Every time we need it they come to help us by order of Lord Jesus Christ, and defeat our enemies. To show you that I am telling the truth, make enquiries today, tomorrow and the next day as to whether their camps can be found anywhere in this whole region. If they can, we will blush under your gaze, shown up as liars. And even though you will have been unable to find them anywhere in the region, you will see them here tomorrow if we find it necessary. How could they get here so quickly if not from the heavenly regions in which they dwell?'

To this Pirrus replied (that was his name): 'So if they do come from the sky, where do they find all those white horses, shields and standards?'

Bohemond answered: 'You are asking me about weighty issues beyond my understanding. If you do want to know the answer I shall send for my chaplain, who can reply to your questions on these matters.'

Chapter IX: how the chaplain replied to Pirrus' questions

A question to which few hearts know the answer.

The chaplain responded:

'When the all-powerful Creator decides to send his angels or the spirits of the righteous to earth, they assume bodies of air so that they can appear to us, because they cannot be seen in their essential spiritual form. So now they appear bearing arms to show that they are coming to help warriors in battle. But if they appeared as pilgrims or priests covered with white stoles, they would foretell not war but peace. Once they have finished the task they came to do, they return to the heavens from whence they came, and return their bodies – which they assumed to make themselves visible – to the same material from which they came. You should not wonder that the omnipotent creator of all things changes the material he made into whatever form he chooses since he created the essence of all things from nothing.'

---

[18] These saints were to appear amongst various combinations at the battle of Antioch aiding the Christians. *GF* 69 and BB 77 refer to saints George, Mercurius and Demetrius. PT 112 refers to saints George, Demetrius and Theodore. The Patriarch's letter to the West (*Kreuzzugsbriefe*, 146–9, 147) has saints George, Theodore, Demetrius and Blaise. RA has none at all. St George was a local saint possibly martyred at Lydda with a major church at Ramleh. St Demetrius was a military martyr of the fourth century killed at Sirmium in the Balkans. St Maurice was an officer in the Theban legion composed of Christians from Egypt; he and his comrades refused to sacrifice to the Roman gods to ensure victory and the entire legion was put to death at Agaunum in the Savoy. For references see the *Oxford Dictionary of the Christian Church*, ed. F. L. Cross and E. A. Livingstone, second edition (Oxford, 1974). Robert emphasises their role more than *GF*, referring to them here and at VII.18 as well as during the battle, and supplies the explanation of how they take shape.

To this Pirrus replied: 'You describe wonderful and credible things stemming from him whom you say is the Creator, things which we had never heard of before.'

Bohemond interrupted, saying: 'Oh Pirrus, surely the things the Lord Jesus Christ (in whom we believe) achieves through us must seem truly miraculous to you? The fewer we are, the stronger we become; whereas you become weaker as your numbers grow. Whose power do you attribute this to: man's or God's? Man belongs not to himself but to his Creator, from whom he derives his being and his powers. You can work out from that that, although one Creator brought both us and you into being, he gave a much greater amount of his strength to us than to you. So we are certain that, relying on his strength, we will take not only Antioch but the whole of Anatolia and Syria and Jerusalem itself, because that is what Jesus the all-powerful son of God promised us.'

Pirrus thought long and hard about these and other similar things Bohemond said, and Bohemond exercised a powerful attraction over him.

Chapter X: the plan which led to the capture of Antioch

After the diabolically inspired events described above over the death of Walo, Pirrus was no longer able to talk freely with his friend Bohemond, but sent the following message to him secretly:

'I have realised that you are a noble man and a faithful Christian. I commend myself and my household to your faith. I shall do what you encouraged me to do for you.[19] I shall hand over to you the three towers I guard in Antioch, and open one of the gates to you and your men.[20] To show that I am not joking and that you need have no doubts on my word, I am sending my son to you: he is my only son whom I love uniquely,[21] yet I am entrusting him – and myself – to your faith.'

When he saw and heard this, Bohemond was alight with unsurpassed joy, and enormous gratitude to the Lord welled up in him: he wept copiously and raised his hands to Heaven in thanks to God.[22] Without delay he called the princes together and spoke to them thus:

'Famous princes and warriors that you are, you know how many reverses we have suffered in this siege, how much we have suffered and will continue to suffer as long as it is God's will. If God were to decide to surrender this city to someone by means of some stratagem, tell me whether your decision would be to concede it to him.'

At this they exclaimed with one voice: 'We will possess it together, since we have all suffered privation together!'

---

[19] Bohemond has in fact done no such thing: a slip by Robert, poetic licence or lost source material?

[20] This is the only resemblance to *GF* 44: the rest is Robert's own.

[21] Cf. *Gospel of John* III.16: *God so loved the world, that he gave his only begotten son.*

[22] An edifying reaction rather the reverse of *GF* 44, which describes Bohemond 'gavisus serenaque mente' ('coolly, looking pleased with himself', Hill's translation).

Bohemond replied with a thin smile: 'I feel sorry for any city ruled by so many masters! Do not take that view, brothers; let it be the possession of whoever can take it.' Seeing that he was getting nowhere, he returned to his camps although he kept there the messengers who had come with Pirrus.

Chapter XI: what the princes decided about who should get Antioch once it was handed over

Here the lords of the army discuss who should possess the city. At length it is given to Bohemond against Raymond's will.

The princes, unsettled by Bohemond, held council. 'We are not acting sensibly in going against the advice of Bohemond, an extremely shrewd man. If it had been possible to take the city from the time we first arrived, we would have gained considerably from it. None of us left our homeland because we wanted to take the city of Antioch: let the one to whom God decides to give it keep it. We all have but one goal: the liberation of the Holy Sepulchre.'[23] All agreed. Bohemond was called, and was given a free hand with Antioch by all provided he could take it. Wasting no time, he sent men he could trust to his friend under cover of night to tell him what to do and when. Pirrus sent back to say that the Frankish army should be moved off the following day as if they were going plundering in the Saracen lands. When twilight came, they should return to their camps near the city, 'where', he said, 'I shall stay awake in the towers I am responsible for and keep my ears open. Come up to the wall well armed and fear nothing.'

Bohemond put some of his allies in the picture: Hugh of Vermandois, Duke Godfrey, the Bishop of Le Puy and Count Raymond of St Gilles. He told them: 'This very night Antioch will be handed over to us, if God so wills it', and told them of the message [sent by Pirrus]. They were delighted when they heard this news and gave thanks to the Lord. The following day the leaders assembled huge detachments of cavalry and as many battalions of footsoldiers; they marched out and crossed the mountains as if on their way to plunder in the lands of the Saracens. At nightfall they returned in absolute silence and, full of hope, prepared themselves. Bohemond himself made his way to the place designated by his friend with his own soldiers, and remained well back from the walls with a few of them whilst sending the rest up to the walls with a ladder long enough to reach the battlements.

---

[23] Robert abbreviates the account of *GF* 45, dropping the justification afforded by the arrival of the Saracens and the description of the herald Mala Corona.

Chapter XII: how Fulcher was the first to climb the ladder

A man known as Fulcher of Chartres, famous for his prowess with the sword, was the first to climb up and scaled the top of the walls.

Once the ladder was up, nobody from all that great multitude dared to go up it. They all hung back until eventually one soldier, Fulcher of Chartres,[24] bolder than the rest said:

'I will go up the ladder first in the name of Jesus Christ, ready to brave whatever God may please to send me, whether martyrdom or whether to gain the prize of victory!'

He went up; others followed; and they came to the top of the wall in short order. Pirrus was standing there waiting for them, furious at the delay. Failing to see Bohemond, he asked where he was. They said he was nearby. But Pirrus was bitterly upset by his absence, saying:

'What is that lazy man up to? Why is he hanging back and delaying? Send someone to tell him to come immediately; send someone to tell him that the light of dawn is approaching and that swelling birdsong foretells the approach of first light. Choose a messenger to tell that to Bohemond!'[25]

When Bohemond heard of this he came running; but he found the ladder broken when he got to it.

Chapter XIII: how Fulcher killed the brothers of Pirrus

Meanwhile Fulcher, who had gone up the ladder with 60 young armed men, had gone on from the towers held by Pirrus to take three others in combat, and had killed in the process two brothers of Pirrus.[26]

---

[24] Fulcher is not mentioned in the *GF*. However he and his brother Bartholomew Boel were prominent on the Crusade: both are referred to by RA 64, and RC 654–5 mentions him; he is mentioned several times by AA (357, 442, 446), who suggests that he was in the army of Peter the Hermit (281, 283, 286, 288). Gilo (VII.62) agrees that he was first into Antioch, as does RA 64. His father was Fulcher fitz-Gerard, canon of Notre Dame de Chartres (Riley-Smith, *First Crusaders,* 47). Again a link to the Ile de France.

[25] Gilo has a similar reference to dawn at VII.62: 'Iamque recedebat nox et matuta rubebat' ('and now night was fading and morning reddening the sky', Grocock and Siberry's translation). Robert elaborates by borrowing the themes of the lyric *alba* form. An *alba* is a song describing the parting of lovers at dawn. Robert employs the standard motifs of hanging back and being unwilling to leave, the messenger or night watchman, and the first light of dawn and song of the birds. For examples see the anonymous 'En un vergier sotz fuella d'albespi' and Guiraut de Borneil's 'Reis glorios, verais lums et clartz' (respectively 26 and 28 in F. R. Hamlin, P. T. Ricketts, J. Hathaway, *Introduction à l'étude de l'ancien Provençal* (Geneva, 1967)); for further discussion and references see Introduction, Chapter Four. Pirrus is clearly implying that Bohemond is putting pleasure before business. The detail of Bohemond's late arrival is in *GF* 46: the petulance of Pirrus is Robert's own.

[26] Also referred to in Gilo VII.104, who says Fulcher's brother Boel killed them.

Chapter XIV: how Pirrus opened the gates of the city

Then a celestial comet shone with joyful appearance.

Even though Pirrus knew this, he did not go back on his promise; on the contrary, when he heard that the ladder was broken, he opened the gates to Bohemond and the whole multitude of the Franks. Although heartrending groans and deep sighs racked his chest, no injury could divert him from delivering what he had promised. Bohemond bent his head and greeted him in the middle of the gateway, thanking him for what he had done.[27] When he realised why Pirrus was grieving, he was concerned and left him a faithful bodyguard of his own soldiers to protect him and his possessions. It is worth remembering that on that night a comet blazed amongst the other stars in the heavens, giving off rays of light and foretelling a change in the kingdom; the sky glowed fiery red from north to east. It was with these portents shining prominently in the heavens and as dawn began to bring light to the earth that the army of God entered Antioch, in the strength of Him who *hath broken the gates of brass and cut the bars of iron in sunder,*[28] to whom with the Father and the Holy Spirit every kingdom and empire is subject, whose power remains for ever and ever.[29] Amen.

---

[27] A vivid vignette also found in Gilo VII.111–6. The comet which follows is in Gilo VII.64–7. Robert surprisingly omits Gilo's praise of Godfrey at VII.141–50.

[28] *Psalms* CVII.16. See also *Isaiah* XLV.2: *I will break in pieces the gates of brass, and cut in sunder the bars of iron.*

[29] Cf. *Revelations* V.13: *power be unto him ... for ever and ever.*

Book VI

The Christians besieged in Antioch

June 1098

Chapter I: how the infidel kept his promise

Take note, all you faithful, of how Pirrus kept faith; bear it in mind so that if ever you promise on oath for your faith you keep your promise with no excuses.[1] No thought of the deaths of his brothers, no power of grief and no prompting of sorrow could suffice to shake his promise, and he regarded the delivery of his promise as more important than the death of two of his brothers under violent circumstances. We might refer to the ancient riddle of Samson here and adduce this to it. Samson said: *out of the eater came forth meat, and out of the strong came forth sweetness.*[2] Now here faith came out of a man outside the faith, and true brotherly love out of a stranger. But to avoid seeming to get too caught up in an elaborate digression, let us return to the story we were telling.

Chapter II: the date on which Antioch was taken

Divine vengeance wished to avenge itself thus on the race of dogs, and was content.

It was on 2 June[3] that the Christians entered the city of Antioch, and delivered it from its invaders at the point of the sword. Fulcher and the companions who had climbed the wall with him stormed towers everywhere, plunged their darts and swords into careless sentries asleep on their watch, and flung them from the top of the towers to the ground. Those who were asleep in the houses were woken by the noise of shouting, went out to find out what was happening and never returned because they stumbled on swords ready and waiting to kill them. Those who were Christians chanted *Kyrie Eleison* and other songs praising God to make it clear to our men that they were not Turks but Christians. The squares in the city were strewn with the bodies of the dying; none of them resisted, all sought to hide or take refuge in flight. Status made no difference: boys were killed alongside girls, the young alongside the old and the old alongside the young, and mothers too alongside their daughters. Those who could get away went out through the gates,

---

[1] An elaborate piece of wordplay on the word 'fides'.

[2] *Judges* XIV.14.

[3] 3 June according to Hagenmeyer, based on *GF* 48.

but that did not help them escape death: they fell into the hands of those coming from the camps.

Chapter III: the death of king Cassianus

Cassianus dies and his belt is taken as a prize.

Cassianus, king and ruler of the city, managed to flee among the rest and escaped disguised in squalid rags, fleeing to Tancred's domain.[4] He was unlucky enough to be recognised by the Armenians, and they cut his head off on the spot; they took it to the princes along with his belt, which they valued at 60 bezants.[5] The majority fled to the citadel which dominates the city; it is so well protected by its position and the lie of the land that it has no need to fear the use of any machine of war. At that point a mountain backs onto the city, whose summit stretches so far towards the stars that those looking up at it can barely see to the top; the whole region can be seen from it. It was here that a large number of Turks fled, having no other place to seek refuge.

Chapter IV: the battle between the Christians and the infidels[6]

There was a tower very close to this citadel, which Bohemond had already taken with his followers, and he prepared to attack the citadel using the tower as a base. The Turks, recovering their strength, rained down arrows and darts like hail since they were higher up than the tower. That made it completely impossible for our men to fight them or do anything other than protect themselves with shields and defend themselves with their weapons. They were caught in a narrow place and the enemy was attacking them from above; the only room the fighters had was the width of the wall. Then as the Turks rushed to attack the tower one man was forced forward by another; there was no way of retreating and no way of escaping to right or left. The more the Turkish attack put pressure on our men, they responded with lances, darts and swords and flung the injured down to the ground. They knocked flat those who were mining the tower from beneath, such that a corpse was responsible for the death of a living man, whilst those who were alive were like dead bodies.[7]

---

[4] Yaghi-Siyan, the Turcoman Governor of Antioch; nominally a vassal of Ridwan of Aleppo but by this time a vassal of Duqaq of Damascus (Runciman, *History*, vol.I, 213).

[5] Robert here follows *GF* 48.

[6] Chapters IV–VI are parallel to Gilo VII.167–202. The wounding of Bohemond is only in these two sources.

[7] Compare Lucan II.206, 'peraguntque cadavera partem/caedis: viva graves elidunt corpora trunci' ('the dead took a hand in the massacre by tumbling on those still alive and

Chapter V: Bohemond is wounded

Bohemond retreated wounded and ceased fighting.

In that fight Bohemond was badly wounded in the thigh, and already was reduced to limping.[8] Blood began to pour profusely from the wound, and the heart of the most noble prince began to lose its normal strength. He retreated to another tower and left the battle unwillingly and reluctantly. Seeing his wound, the courage of the others began to waver, all of them worrying that their leader was about to meet a sad end.

They leave the battle, and relinquish the tower to the Turks.

Chapter VI: about the soldier who flung himself down on the Turks, laden with weapons, since he could not escape with his life

This man dies so that the enemy may meet their end in death.

Just one man was left behind on the very top of the tower, and the whole army of our men joined in lamenting his spectacular end.[9] When he saw himself left alone, still unbowed, he began to defend himself on every side like a bear amongst mastiffs; he tore stones and mortar from the walls and flung them down onto those who were attacking him. Eventually, weighed down by 1,000 arrows, he realised that he was not going to escape with his life. So he hastened his death, jumping with shield and arms down into where he could see the thickest press of enemies and thus harming his killers. No earthly tongue can tell all the damage the hand of the Franks did that day. If the protection afforded by the citadel had not been so strong, the Lord might have considerably alleviated that day the calamities awaiting his people. But it was His will that the city of Antioch should be difficult to take so that, once gained, it should be valued the more. (For things we gain are quickly disregarded, whilst we treasure more things we have desired for longer.) Night brought an end and a relief from the labours of the day; it took away the need to fight but did not allow the exhausted men to sleep – for where the enemy is inside the walls, there can be no possibility of sleep. The following day, a Friday, some dragged the mutilated corpses outside the walls whilst others fought those in the citadel from the towers with missiles and arrows.

---

smothering them', Graves' translation). Gilo VII.174 has a different slant, with the living trampling the dead.

[8] Robert goes out of his way to emphasise that the wound was in the thigh: another literary motif? Compare *Guigemar* 97–132 where the hero's wound in the thigh can be cured only by a woman's selfless love: *Marie de France: Lais*, ed. A. Ewert (Oxford 1947); *Guigemar*, 3–25.

[9] A rather pointed contrast.

Chapter VII:[10] Kerbogha's arrival at Antioch

Standing on the wall they see in the distance the shadow of whirling dust, and have little idea what it is. Our youth fear the arrival of these men.

Meanwhile, those who were standing on the towers and the walls were looking at an enormous cloud of dust swirling in the distance.[11] There were various views as to what it was. Some said it was the Emperor of Constantinople coming to their help; others said, accurately, that it was the battalions of the Persians. The first arrivals grouped together when they came in sight of the city of Antioch, waiting for the main body of the army which was behind them. It was Kerbogha , the general of the Persian King's army, who had for some considerable time been assembling an army made up of various races.[12] There were Persians and Medes, Arabs and Turks, Azimitae[13] and Saracens, Kurds and Publicani and many others from various nations. There were three thousand Agulani, who carried no arms, not even swords: completely covered with iron, they had no fear of enemy arms. Their horses flatly refused to carry standards and lances and went berserk at those who did.[14] Having assembled together, they sent scouts to the city to provoke our men to fight and persuade them to leave the city. Our men, however, were tired from the previous day's fight and judged it safer to stay within the walls than to come out and fight. The Turks swarmed over the fields and plains, challenging our men to fight and heaping shocking insults on them. They flung their lances and swords up into the air and caught them.[15] Eventually, having failed completely to entice any of our men out, they decided to return to their camps.

---

[10] Chapters VII and VIII parallel Gilo VII.223–77.

[11] Gilo's wording is closely similar (VII.223–5).

[12] Kiwam ed-Daula Kerbogha the Atabeg of Mosul. See Ibn al-Athir, *Histoire des Atabegs de Mosul*, *RHC Or.* vol.II.II, 28–31. He came to symbolise the Saracen opposition to the Crusaders, acquiring a branch of the Old French Crusading Cycle of his own: *La Chrétienté Kerbogha*, in *The Old French Crusade Cycle: the Jerusalem Continuations*, vol.VII part I, ed. P. R. Grillo (Alabama, 1984).

[13] A term for Saracens derived from those who use unleavened bread in Communion: *GF* 45, n.1.

[14] The corresponding passage from *GF* 49 is inserted in the middle of parallels with Gilo: 'neque lanceas neque sagittas neque ulla arma timebant, quia omnes erant undique cooperti ferro et equi eorum, ipsique nolebant in bellum ferre arma nisi solummodo gladios', ('they fear neither spears nor arrows nor any other weapon, for they and their horses are covered all over with plates of iron. They will not use any weapons except swords when they are fighting'). The *Antioche* 6570 follows what seems to be a mistranslation by Robert. This passage appears near-verbatim in the other *GF* derivatives: GN 209, BB 60.

[15] Gilo VII.240 has a similarly vivid vignette.

Chapter VIII: how Roger [of Barneville] rode out of the city with three others

The killing of Roger occasions considerable grief.

As they retreated, one of our men – Roger of Barneville – followed them with another three soldiers, hoping to spark them to some reaction;[16] however, they refused to fight on equal terms, having already heard all about Frankish battles. Instead they set an ambush behind them, hiding beneath a rock, and sent some of their soldiers to appear to be tempting the Franks to fight. When our men ran into the ambush, the brigands leapt from their cave and attacked them from behind; and those riding ahead turned round and rode swiftly towards them. When Roger and his companions realised they were trapped, they swung round hoping to find safety in flight, but found none. Roger pushed his companions in front of him and, slinging his shield behind his back, withstood the ferocious blows of the Turks himself. He had almost got away, nearly reaching safety, when his horse tumbled to the ground and, clinging as it went down, he fell with it. He was completely unable to get up because he was trapped by the weight of the horse. Alas! What grief and gnashing of teeth on the walls of Antioch, as the open-handed youth of the Franks saw the outstanding soldier thus torn in pieces by rabid dogs! They looked away, unable to watch as the Turks ripped Roger limb from limb. Eventually they hacked off his head and, impaling it on a stake, carried it off to their camps as a kind of triumphal standard. (Their camps were next to the Iron Bridge.)

Chapter IX: about Sensadolus[17]

Sensadolus weeps and, prostrate, grovels to Kerbogha. He asks for help and promises obedience.

Sensadolus, the son of the recently dead King of Antioch, had made his way to Kerbogha.[18] Flinging himself prostrate at his feet, he had begged for pity and for

---

[16] Roger of Barneville came from Sicily (Riley-Smith, *First Crusaders*, 100–101; Jamison, 207–8). The *GF* mentions his arrival at Nicaea (15–16) but does not give the episode. However it appears in other sources as well as Gilo (RA 66, AA 407–8, 411 where he is avenged by Tancred; it also appears in Anselm's second letter to Manasses of Reims if we may identify Rogerius de Bithiniacavilla with him (*Kreuzzugsbriefe*, 159). The episode is also found in the *Antioche* 6682–724 closely following Robert's version.

[17] Robert returns to the *GF*. Unless we are to assume more than one son for Yaghi-Sian, this is inconsistent: the son was killed in an earlier battle at IV.21. This suggests strongly that Robert has made a rare error in combining his sources. The cluster of episodes which follows – the embassy of Sensadolus, the useless weapons, Kerbogha's letter and the prophecies of his mother – occur in virtually the same form in all the *GF* derivatives: GN 209–16, BB 60–64.

help against the Franks, who had killed his father and disinherited him from the renowned city. He had no place to go other than the citadel of the city, because the whole of the rest of it was now subject to the Franks.[19]

'My father sent you an embassy seeking help whilst he was still alive,' he said, 'promising either to enrich you with great gifts or to hold Antioch and the whole kingdom from you as a fief. I make the same promise to you. If you can recover Antioch, I will hold it from you and promise you complete fealty. If you cannot, you should flee along with every man from our nations. For neither Anatolia, nor Syria nor Chorazin[20] are enough for the Franks: they claim that Jerusalem is theirs, and the kingdom of Damascus.'

The kings of those provinces were there listening to these words. Kerbogha replied:

'If you want me to help you and restore you to your kingdom, give me the citadel you still have, because it is the key to getting Antioch back for you.'

Sensadolus replied:

'If you can manage to get the Franks out of the city and give me their severed heads,[21] I will hand over the citadel and will do homage to you.'

They reached agreement. The citadel was handed over, and Kerbogha handed it over to one of his lieutenants to guard. He took it over on condition that if the Franks were defeated he should keep it; if they were victorious he would desert it and flee like the others. To this Kerbogha replied:

'And what would we do with the citadel anyway if we were defeated? It is fitting that the victors should have it, since victory will be a greater prize than any citadel.'

---

[18] Shams-ed-Daula: his name was rendered by Western chroniclers as Sensadolus. The episode is found in the *GF* and its derivatives, e.g. PT 89–90. As Sansadoine he plays a prominent role in the *Antioche*, acting as ambassador to the Sultan of Persia and eventually being killed by Hugh of Vermandois.

[19] The citadel in Antioch is on a high mountain with the rest of the town on the slopes and the floodplain of the Orontes. The Turks took refuge there and continued hostilities against the Christians from inside. See Runciman, *History*, vol.I, 236–8 for further description.

[20] A town on the shore of Lake Tiberias, modern Tell Hum or Kerazah. *GF* 50 refers to 'Corrozani'. This is Khorasan in Persia; used generally to refer to the home of Saracens, for example at *Antioche* 4790, 5080): see A.V. Murray, 'Coroscane: homeland of the Saracens in the *chanson de geste* and the historiography of the Crusades', *Aspects de l'épopée romane. Mentalités, idéologies, intertextualités*, ed. H. van Dijk and W. Noonan (Groningen, 1995) 177–84. The *GF*'s reading makes more sense in context. However Chorozaim is one of the places cited as the birthplace of the Antichrist (Emerson 80–81). It is not clear whether this is a deliberate or accidental change by Robert. Interestingly the *GF* manuscripts show variants: 'Corozana' in ms. D, 'Corozanae' in ms. X. Robert may have dealt with a defective source here by supplying a term familiar from elsewhere.

[21] Again.

Chapter X: the useless sword and lance which were brought to Kerbogha

Having arranged these things, Kerbogha brought the business to an end and turned his attention to dealing with other matters. As he sat on his throne, they brought him a Frankish sword which was in abysmal condition, blunt and covered in filthy rust. They also brought a lance in equally bad state – indeed it made the sword look good in comparison. When Kerbogha saw these, he said:

'Who can tell us where these arms were found?[22]

And why have they been brought into our presence?'
Those who had brought them replied:
'Glorious prince, ornament of the Persian kingdom, we took these arms from a Frank and brought them to you so you could see and understand what weapons these ragtag people are using to threaten us and ravage our kingdom – or indeed devastate the whole of Asia.'
Kerbogha smiled and said:
'It is quite obvious that these people are completely mad. If they think they can conquer the Kingdom of Persia for themselves with this kind of weapons they are not in their right minds. They are a presumptuous race and too ambitious for the possessions of others. Doubtless they have every confidence in their courage. But, by Mahommed, it was a bad day for them when they entered Syrian territory and took the walls of the royal city of Antioch.'

Chapter XI: what Kerbogha said

Kerbogha's words come from arrogance.

Having spoken, he ordered his secretary to be brought and said to him when he arrived:
'Take several rolls and ink, and write to the Pope of our religion, the Caliph; to the King of the Persians, the Sultan glorious above all others;[23] and to the great lords of the Kingdom of Persia. Wish them a long life, continuing peace and health every day. A happy fortune smiles on us benevolently, and grants us favourable success – I have the army of the Franks cooped up inside the walls of Antioch, and the citadel which dominates the city is now in my hands. So you can rest assured that, whatever the rumours you may have heard about them, they do not live up to them: the wolf never does as much damage as the cries which follow him

---

[22] Interestingly this hexameter is in the middle of borrowings from *GF* and not Gilo.

[23] Al-Mustachir, Abbasid caliph of Baghdad 1094–1118; Sultan Berkyaruk, 1094–1105. Robert is unlikely to have known the identity of either. The Saracens are described as mirror images of the Christians: cf. Daniel, 152, who remarks that the Christian background was so strong that it served as a template for the portrayal of non-Christian concepts.

suggest.[24] Although you instructed me to obliterate all of them entirely from the face of earth and kill them with the sword, do not hold it against me if I send some of the best to you in chains: you can then decide whether you want them to live or die. It seems right to us that those who came to take us prisoner should become prisoners, and suffer the rigours of servitude amongst us. It would be a real honour to the kingdom of Persia if the brother of the King of France were held there.[25] Live on in peace and complete tranquillity, and deliver yourselves up to every pleasure of the flesh; father sons non-stop who can resist other Franks if necessary and come to the rescue when our strength fails. I will not see you face to face until I have subjugated all of Syria and Anatolia and Bulgaria to your rule.'

Thus spoke Kerbogha with misguided pride, which turned to ignominy and confusion.

Chapter XII: what Kerbogha's mother said

Kerbogha scorned the advice of his mother, spurred on by black rage, and his anger grew. Nobody should be surprised that a woman should speak in this way, since she knew well the books of Moses and the prophets.

After this his mother came to him upset and worried, with a long face.[26] They met in a secret room, and she said to her son:

'My son, consolation of my old age and the only sign of all my love, I come to you in haste, exhausted by a long journey. I was in the great city of Aleppo when worrying news of you reached my ears and struck my heart with overwhelming grief. For I was told that you were drawing up your battalions and intended to fight the Christians. So I have come hurrying to find out from you yourself whether that is true or not.'

The son said to his mother: 'Mother, you have never heard anything more true.' She replied:

'Whatever wicked person advised you to do that, my son? You have no experience of the strength of the God of the Christians, and especially of the race of the Franks. If you had read the writings of all the prophets and the sages of old, you would not be ignorant of the fact that he is the All-Powerful and God of all gods. If you fight the Christians, you will be fighting him and his angels. But it is the act of a lunatic to take on the All-Powerful, tantamount to self-destruction. A prophet said of this same invincible God: *I kill, and I make alive; I wound and I*

---

[24] Proverb.

[25] Another compliment to Hugh of Vermandois.

[26] Kerbogha's's mother and her prophecies feature prominently in *GF* 53–56, and the episode is found in its derivatives e.g. PT 93–6, GN 212–16. In the *Antioche* 5252–68 she is called Calabre and described as 140 years old and more learned in magic than Morgan; she has two dialogues with Kerbogha (5377–95; 6837–959, following Robert's text). The Saracen reliance on divination contrasts with the Christian certainty of victory through God's power. See Bancourt, 600–20, on the association between Saracen women and magic.

heal: neither is there any that can deliver out of my hand.[27] *If I whet my glittering sword, and mine hand take hold on judgement; I will render vengeance to mine enemies, and will reward them that hate me. I will make mine arrows drunk with blood, and my sword shall devour flesh.*[28] It is terrifying to fight him who knows how to sharpen his sword thus, when sharpened to sate it, and when sated to mince flesh. Who, my son, sank Pharaoh, King of Egypt, into the Red Sea with his whole army?[29] Who disinherited Seon, King of the Amorites and Og, the King of Bashan,[30] and all the kingdoms of Canaan and gave it to his own people to inherit? The same God shows how much he loves his people and how assiduously he surrounds them with his protection when he says: *Behold, I send an angel before thee, to keep thee in the way, and to bring thee to the place which I have prepared. If thou shalt indeed obey his voice and do all that I speak; then I will be an enemy unto thine enemies, and an adversary unto thine adversaries. For mine Angel shall go before thee.*[31] That is the God who is angry with our race because we have not listened to his words or done his will; that is why he has stirred up his people against us from the far-flung lands of the West, and has given all of this land into their possession. There is nobody who can turn this race away from them; nobody who is strong enough to exterminate them.'

After all this Kerbogha said to this mother:

'Mother, I think you are either insane or being tormented by the Furies of Hell.[32] Who told you' (he said) 'that these people cannot be exterminated? I have more lords and emirs with me than the Christians put together. Tell me mother: are Hugh the standard-bearer and Bohemond, the Apulian, and the swordsman Godfrey their Gods? They eat earthly food like us, don't they? Their flesh can be slashed by iron the same as ours, can't it?'[33]

To this his mother replied:

'Those you name are not gods but men, and outstanding soldiers of God who gives them courage, bolsters their strength and gives them magnanimity just as he said through the prophet: *how should one chase a thousand, and two put ten thousand to flight?*[34] That is what has come to pass in the person of these men who have made our people flee from all of Anatolia. So, my son, I beg you in all the names of our divinities to turn away from them and not to attack them. I have already told you that it is foolish to attack the Omnipotent and fight his people.'

Her son replied:

---

[27] *Deuteronomy* XXXII.39.

[28] *Deuteronomy* XXXII.40–41.

[29] *Exodus* XIV.

[30] *Numbers* XXI.21–9 and *Deuteronomy* II.26–35 for Seon; *Numbers* XXI.33–5 and *Deuteronomy* III.1–7 for Og; *Deuteronomy* XXIX.7, XXXI.4 for both; *Psalms* XXXVI for the same sequence of references to the Israelites, Seon and Og.

[31] *Exodus* XXIII.20, 22–3.

[32] Classical reference.

[33] Robert tones down the extravagant claim of *GF* 55–6: 'manducant in uno quoque prandio duo milia vaccas et quatuor milia porcos' ('and do not they eat two thousand cows and four thousand pigs at a single meal?', Hill's translation).

[34] *Deuteronomy* XXXII.30.

'Do not weep, dearest mother, or wear yourself out with deep groaning. Even if I knew I was to die in battle, you could not keep me back by any art or device.'

His mother, even more upset, spoke again to her son:

'I know that you will fight but not die now; however you will lose your life before the end of the year. Now you are known, praised and famous throughout the Orient, second to none in the palace of the King of Persia: once you have been defeated your infamy will be as great as your glory now, for the more someone has excelled the rest, the more his name suffers when he falls shamefully. You may be surrounded now with every efflorescence of royal Oriental riches, surrounded by an enormous crowd of innumerable acolytes: if you are overcome how will you fight in future with the same or different numbers? You used to be the one who could put many to flight with a few men: now you will learn how to run ahead of few with many like hares fleeing a dog.'

Her son, sparked to anger, lost patience with the meanderings of his mother. He interrupted her and said:

'Mother, why are you talking so much hot air and boring me to death with ill-judged comments? No soldiers are strong enough to resist us and no other army is strong enough to prevail. But tell me, mother, how did you discover that we are to be defeated in this battle? and why I am supposed to die not here but meet a sudden end before the end of the year? and that the Christians will take over our lands?'

His mother replied:

'Our forefathers discovered a hundred years and more ago through the sacred oracles of the Gods, in their casting of lots and their divinations and the entrails of animals, that the Christian race would come upon us and defeat us. The soothsayers, mages and diviners, the oracles of our divine powers and the words of the prophets (in which it is said: *from the east and from the west, from the north and from the south*[35] *shall your coast be. There shall no man be able to stand before you*)[36] all agree. So we believe that all this will come to pass, but we do not know whether it will be now or later. However it seems likely to some of us to be imminent, because the continuing ruin of the things of this world foretells it and the configurations of the stars show it. I am telling you the truth such as I have it about this battle you are to fight and about your death. From the moment when you began to get your soldiers together to fight, I have been scrutinising anything which could give me an inkling of the future with anxious care; and everything indicates that absolutely nobody can overcome the Christians. I have examined the courses of the stars, the seven planets and the twelve signs, in my wisdom with the astrologers, and I have examined with the diviners whatever can take physical form in the entrails and shoulder-blades of animals;[37] I have cast lots with the

---

[35] *Psalms* VII.3.

[36] *Deuteronomy* XI.24–5; see also *Joshua* I.4–5, ... *shall be your coast. There shall not any man be able to stand before thee.*

[37] For everything one could possibly wish to know on twelfth-century use of shoulder-blades in divination see Gerald of Wales, *Itinerarium Cambriae* I.11, *Giraldi Cambrensis Opera* VI, ed. J. F. Dimock (London, 1868).

soothsayers. All this points to one conclusion: it promises the title of victors to the Franks and death to you as I have already said.'

He said: 'Mother, no more of this: I will fight the Franks as soon as I can.'

So, seeing that she could do nothing more, she returned without delay to where she had come from, carrying with her all the spoils she could.

Chapter XIII: what was happening inside the city

The troops are constantly engaged in battles in the city.

Now let us describe what had been going on in the city in the mean time. The Turks were freely going in and out of the citadel; they were provoking our men day and night to battle by throwing missiles and shooting arrows; and when their soldiers began to weaken, new and fresh ones came in support such that whilst their strength was continually replenished the strength of our men diminished through daily exhaustion. They could never rest or put down their weapons, but had to be always ready to fight. The squares of the city were cluttered with missiles and arrows, and the roofs of the houses were weighed down with them. There was a new fight every day in front of the citadel, with our men and theirs mingling in combat each time. However, under the protection of God few of ours died, whilst theirs perished in droves.

Chapter XIV: the tortures of hunger in Antioch[38]

Here is described the great famine inside the walls.

As time slipped by, hunger, more cruel than any enemy, crept up on our men and weakened them day by day. Their faces grew gaunt, their arms weak; trembling hands barely had the strength to tear up grass, pull leaves from the trees or roots of turnips from the woods.[39] All these things were cooked and eaten as if inestimable riches. The leg of a donkey fetched 60 solidi, and the one who paid that price for it was by no means considered extravagant. A small loaf cost a bezant; the flesh of donkeys, horses, camels, oxen and buffaloes was eaten, cooked with the hide still on. Mothers starving with hunger latched their children to the breast, but the babies found nothing there and lay shaking with eyes closed for want of milk. One day

---

[38] The description of famine interweaves elements of *GF* 62 and Gilo VII.299–316. Robert then jumps back to *GF* 56 which he follows, with some variations, until the end of Book VI.

[39] Compare Gilo VII.299–300: 'vulgus iners herbas dubias letumque minantes/vellit' ('the helpless common folk plucked plants of doubtful nature, threatening death', Grocock and Siberry's translation). A reminiscence of Lucan VI.112–13: 'foliis spoliare nemus letumque minantes/vellere ab ignotis dubias radicibus herbis' ('busily stripping leaves from bushes and trees and grubbing up poisonous-looking roots for food', Graves' translation).

Kerbogha did tempt our men to fight outside the city near the part with the citadel; but the soldiers and horses, tortured with hunger, were unable to withstand his swift attacks. So our men gathered together thinking it safer to return to the city. However they were pressed by the Turks and found the gate too narrow so that some were crushed to death at it. And so battle continued inside and out, and our men – starving to death – were unable to rest. Some of our soldiers, scared out of their wits by these and similar privations, gave up and fled that night, tying ropes to the battlements and skinning their hands as they slid down, then running to the sea.[40] When they reached the coast they told the sailors to flee because all the Christians were either dead or taken prisoner. So the sailors reluctantly put to sea to ensure that they did not fall into the power of the Turks.

Chapter XV: how Count Stephen fled

The Count of Chartres, a famous city and dear to those who know it, flees in terror and abandons the fight and his allies.

Stephen, Count of Blois, who was considered one of the great princes, shrewd in council and well considered for his integrity, had been kept behind by a serious illness before the fall of Antioch and had retreated to a castle which belonged to him, known as Alexandretta.[41] When he heard this tale from those of our men who had fled, he climbed secretly up the mountains which dominated the city so that he could see how things stood and whether their story was true. What he saw was innumerable Turkish tents in the distance, and he realised that our men were trapped in the city. He fled, panicking with fear, returned to his castle and stripped it bare, and set out to ride back to Constantinople. Those besieged in the city awaited his arrival with desperate longing, thinking that he would bring the Emperor with him and also help with necessary supplies. However, he came to Philomena[42] with a very different end in view. He found the Emperor there and had a secret conversation with him.

'My lord Emperor,' he said, 'our men have indeed taken Antioch. However the citadel which overlooks it is in the hands of the Turks, innumerable forces of Turks are besieging them outside and those in the citadel attack them from within. What more can I tell you except that by now they are either already dead or shortly all about to die? As for you, Reverend Emperor, if you accept my advice you should

---

[40] The so-called *funambuli*, named as William and Aubrey of Grandmesnil, Guy Trousseau and Lambert le Pauvre by *GF* 56. Robert drops the names.

[41] Modern Iskenderun. *GF* 63 says the illness was feigned; Robert is more favourably disposed to one of the great French lords. Stephen was to become a byword for cowardice: not only did he desert the Crusade but his intervention persuaded the Emperor not to send help at a crucial moment. See for example the mocking description at *Antioche* 5608–44. Fulcher of Chartres' rehabilitation of him after his death on the Crusade of 1101 was not widely followed (Epp, 146).

[42] Modern Akshehir.

go no further but return to your city. No human power can help them any further, whereas if you go there you risk death along with your army.'

On hearing this the Emperor was extremely upset. He repeated openly to his princes and magistrates what had been said to him in private. All were saddened and wept for the death of our men.

Chapter XVI: the lamentation of Guy

Guy weeps excessively and beseeches God through his tears not to be displeased with his people nor let them perish.

There was a particular soldier there called Guy, who had made a considerable name for himself in military matters and was a great friend of Bohemond's.[43] When he heard this news he was so grief-stricken that he fell to the ground as if dead. On regaining consciousness and rallying his thoughts, he began to weep passionately; tearing his cheeks with his nails and ripping at his hair with his hands he brought all to share his mourning. He said:[44]

'O Omnipotent God, where is your strength? If You are Omnipotent, why did you let this happen? Surely these were your soldiers and pilgrims? What king or emperor or powerful lord has ever allowed his household to be killed if there was any chance of helping them? Who will volunteer to be your soldier or your pilgrim in future? O Bohemond, honour of the other leaders, crown of the wise, glory of the soldier, consolation of the desperate, strong heart of the army and unparalleled glory of the whole world, how did such a misfortune befall you as to fall prey to the whims of the Turks? Alas! Why should I be allowed to survive you? For the short amount of time I survive you what light can be welcome to me, what beauty pleasant, what glory delightful, what life pleasing? O God – nay rather if you are God – if what this lightweight and fugitive count has come and told us is true, what will happen now about travelling to your Holy Sepulchre? Why were your servants killed as if they had no lord? O Bohemond, where is the faith you have always professed in your Redeemer, our Lord Jesus Christ? O Emperor and renowned soldiers, who weep with me for so many funerals and the funerals of so many, who could possibly believe that such a great army could perish in this way? It is certain that if they were surrounded in the middle of the battlefield by the entire peoples of the Orient, they would all have been avenged before being killed. And yet now even though they had a city to defend themselves in, have they have all been killed thus? O Emperor, you can be absolutely certain that if the Turks have killed our

---

[43] Bohemond's half-brother Guy of Hauteville, a long-standing member of the Emperor's entourage whom the Emperor had sought to entice with offers of marriage and wealth: AC 188. For details of his activities in Byzantium see AC 188–91, 406–10, 420.

[44] A set-piece lament: for references see note to V.7. Compare also laments in the *chansons de geste* e.g. William's lament over Vivien (*Guillaume* 1997–2010) or Charlemagne's over Roland (*Roland* 2898–2905).

men, precious few of them will remain alive either. So do not have any worries about going there, because you will be able to retake Antioch.'

The Emperor, though, refused to agree with his advice, believing instead the empty words of the lightweight Stephen. He decided to retrace his footsteps and gave instructions that the region of Bulgaria[45] should be ravaged so that if the Turks came to that area they would find nothing in it. Guy himself and those with the Emperor also returned with him, not daring to march any further. Thus our men were deprived of all human aid. For 25 days they struggled incessantly with enemies and hunger, with the sword and with famine.[46]

---

[45] See Duparc-Quioc, *Etude*, 108, for comment on what seems to be an error by Robert: there is no point ordering the devastation of Bulgaria at this point, and *GF* 65 clearly states what the Emperor actually ordered: to retreat to Bulgaria and follow a scorched-earth policy. *Antioche* 7102 reproduces the error.

[46] Robert ends the book, and the second section of his chronicle, with a cliffhanger.

Book VII

Victory at Antioch

June 1098–October 1098

Chapter I: How God appeared to a certain priest[1]

God appears to this man because he has no obvious fault and is not defiled by the stain of great vices. The words of God are sweet and the solace of great hope.

If supernatural pity had not provided for those bereft of all human help, not one of the Franks – now citizens of Antioch – would have survived. But now when they despaired of life and everything seemed to point to an imminent death, it pleased the Lord God of salvation, King of Kings, Jesus Christ, to appear to a certain priest whilst he was asleep one night in the church dedicated to His immaculate Mother.[2] With him were also the Blessed Virgin Mary herself and the apostle St Peter, to whom God himself gave the task of feeding his sheep.[3] He said to the priest: 'Do you know me?' The priest answered: 'No. Who are you, my lord?' Then a cross began to glimmer above the Redeemer's head, and he asked again: 'Now do you know me?' The priest replied further: 'I know you only by the cross I see on your head, which is like the ones I am used to seeing on images made in honour of Our Lord Jesus Christ the Redeemer'.[4] God then said to him: 'Look, it is I.'

When the priest heard that it was indeed the Lord, he immediately prostrated himself at his feet, humbly begging him to help his Christians struggling under the weight of hunger and enemy attacks. Jesus replied:

'Is it not obvious to you that I have been helping them all along? I gave them the city of Nicaea and helped them win every battle there was. I looked with pity on their sufferings at the siege of Antioch; eventually I granted them entrance to the city. I allowed them to suffer all these tribulations and difficulties because they have committed many sins with Christian women – and pagan women – which found grave displeasure in my eyes.'

At this the mother of mercy, the most devout Virgin, and St Peter the Apostle fell at his feet, begging him to take pity on his people. The holy Apostle added to his prayer, saying:

---

[1] Robert follows *GF* 57–61, 65–8 for Chapters I–VIII.

[2] His name was Stephen Valentine: see Runciman, *History*, vol.I, 244.

[3] St Peter is, of course, particularly appropriate to Antioch.

[4] The standard portrayal of Christ at the time: innumerable examples, e.g. the Last Judgement tympanum at Sainte-Foy de Conques.

'Lord, I thank you because you have given my church over to the power of your servants after allowing it to be shamefully soiled by the vice of the pagans who have dwelt in it for so many years. The holy angels and my companions, your Apostles, rejoice over it in the heavens.'

Then God said to his priest:

'Go and tell my people that they should turn back to me and I will turn back to them.Within five days I will send them ample help. They are to sing this response each day: *Our enemies are gathered and glory in their strength* right through with the whole verse.'

The vision ended and the reverend priest woke abruptly from sleep. Spreading his hands he prayed to God as *the Spirit gave* him *utterance.*[5] That same day, at the third hour, he made his way to the leaders of the army, whom he found fighting the enemy in front of the citadel with the two sides locked in battle. Calling them together, his face wreathed in beaming smiles, he said:

'O soldiers of the Eternal King, I bring you joy and exultation from our Redeemer; he sends his blessing on you and if you obey him you will know his grace.'

All listened attentively, a crowd gathering round him as he unfolded the sequence of events in his vision. When he came to the end, he added:

'If you do not trust in this vision and suspect it to be false, I shall prove its truth to you in any way you choose. If I am found to be a liar, inflict every conceivable injury on my body.'

Then the Bishop of Le Puy ordered a cross and the Holy Gospels to be brought, so that he might swear to the truth of his account in front of everyone: which he duly did.[6]

Chapter II: The vision of St Andrew

Another vision appears to a pilgrim by Divine will, which is proved to be truly divine.

Divine goodness wanted to pile good on good, and cheer its miserable servants more and more. So a certain pilgrim happened to be there, called Peter, who spoke out about this vision:[7]

'O people of God and outstanding servants of the Lord, hear my voice and *incline your ears*[8] to my words. During the siege of this city, Saint Andrew appeared to me one night in a vision saying: 'Hear and understand me, honest

---

[5] *Acts* II.4.

[6] Robert omits *GF* 59's description of the oath sworn by the leaders.

[7] Peter Bartholomew's discovery of the Lance is recounted in virtually all accounts of the Crusade. He was an Occitan in the service of one William Peter. See Runciman, *History*, vol.I, 141–6 for an account.

[8] *Psalms* LXXVIII.1.

man'. I replied to him: 'Who are you, my lord?' He replied: 'I am Saint Andrew the Apostle. My son, when you have entered this city and have it in your power, go quickly to the Church of St Peter and you will find there in a place I will show you the Lance which pierced the side of Our Saviour.' That was all the Apostle said to me. So I did not have the courage to tell anybody else, thinking I had seen an empty vision, But last night he appeared to me again and said: 'Come and I will show you the place where the lance is hidden, just as I promised. Hurry to excavate it from the earth, because victory will come to those who carry it.' And the holy Apostle showed me the place. Come with me to see it and dig it up.'His listeners were eager to run to the Church of St Peter, but he added:

'Saint Andrew orders you not to be afraid, but to confess and do penance for your sins, because five days from now you will triumph again over your enemies.' Then all gave glory to God, who stooped to console their troubles. They ran immediately to the Church of St Peter, desperate to see the place where the lance was to be found.

Chapter III: the Holy Lance is discovered[9]

Thirteen men dug there from dawn to dusk and, by God's will, they found the Lance.[10] The whole people rejoiced, loudly chanting the *Te Deum* and *Gloria in excelsis deo*. All swore unanimously that they would not flinch from any tribulation or from death, or give up on the journey to the Holy Sepulchre. The whole common mass rejoiced that its leaders had sworn this oath. They bolstered each other's courage and gloried in the prospect of divine help which each of them faithfully expected.

---

[9] Robert changes the order of *GF* to improve narrative flow, inserting this from *GF* 65. Gilo VII.317–26 also links the visions of Stephen Valentine and Peter Bartholomew, but in far less detail.

[10] The discovery of the Holy Lance was one of the most controversial episodes on the Crusade. It was found by the Occitan Peter Bartholomew and carried into battle by Adhemar; however doubts about its authenticity grew and it became a focus for growing Norman–Occitan enmity. Peter Bartholomew eventually volunteered to undergo trial by fire; he died in agony twelve days later. The episode is central to RA (68–72, 75–6, 81–2, 118–23); see also GF 59–60, 65; for a hostile account see RC 676–8 and 682. For discussion of the evidence see S. Runciman, 'The holy lance found at Antioch', *AB* 68 (1950), 197–209.

Chapter IV: fire from Heaven terrifies the enemies of our men[11]

Fire from the axis of Heaven disturbed the Turkish camp. Bohemond misjudges for once and burns the city.

The following night a flame appeared in the sky coming from the west and fell into the Turkish army. This sign deeply impressed everyone, particularly the Turks amongst whose tents it fell. They began to see glimmerings of what would come to pass: that the fire descending from heaven represented the anger of God; because it had come from the west it symbolised the armies of the Franks through whom he would make his anger manifest. The Turkish leaders began to cool their ferocity somewhat and their courage began to ebb away. However, given that the misguided fools had infinite numbers[12] and provoked our men to fight without respite day and night, the leaders of our army decided to build a wall between themselves and the Turks to give a little breathing-space. One day, for example, they attacked our men so fiercely that they trapped three of them in a tower in front of the citadel: two of them were wounded and forced to leave the tower, then decapitated; the other stayed there fighting fiercely until the evening, killing two of them, before then taking his own life with his sword.[13] Although Bohemond wanted to send help to them whilst they were still alive, he had trouble sending out even a few men not so much because they were under pressure from the enemy but because they were desperate with hunger. That made him angry and he ordered the houses in the part of town around Cassianus' palace to be fired: if men would not come out willingly that would at least make them come out against their will. At the moment the fire took hold, such a great wind arose that it fanned the flames to the point where 2,000 houses and churches were burned. When Bohemond saw the flames rising in this way, he was bitterly sorry for his actions, fearing for the churches of St Peter and of the Blessed Virgin Mary mother of God and many others. The fire lasted from the third hour of the day until the middle of the night when, the wind swinging round to the right, the flames were pushed back on themselves.

---

[11] See *GF* 62.

[12] Cf. *Ecclesiastes* I.15: *that which is wanting cannot be numbered.*

[13] Robert does not name the soldiers but adds the detail of the suicide. *GF* 61 names the third soldier as Hugh the Berserk, in the band of Godfrey of Monte Scaglioso. AA 413 says the three knights were from Malines. The episode reads rather like a doublet of VI.6, which is found in Gilo.

Chapter V: ambassadors – Peter the Hermit and Herluin – are sent to Kerbogha

The Franks, thirsting for war, send an embassy to the Parthians to tell them to prepare to fight.

As we explained above, the Lance was found by the will of God. The leaders and officials of the army agreed to the plan that they should send an embassy to Kerbogha and that their terms and views should be conveyed to him in his own language by an interpreter. Many were asked but nobody dared to convey the message until two were found: Herluin and Peter the Hermit.[14] Along with the interpreter they made their way to the Turkish camps and up to Kerbogha's tents. Turks gathered from all sides, itching to hear what the Christian messengers would say. Kerbogha was sitting on his throne, surrounded by royal pomp and wearing magnificent clothes. The ambassadors did not bow when they came into his presence but stood with heads unbowed. The Turks took this in bad part when they saw, and had they not been ambassadors the Turks would have punished them for the scorn they demonstrated by their proud reserve.[15] The ambassadors did not hesitate despite the fact that all about them were trembling with rage. They said to the proud prince:

'Kerbogha, the Frankish lords send the following message to you. What staggering audacity has possessed you that you should have marched against them with armed forces when in their view you and your king and your people are guilty of invading Christian lands with unbridled covetousness and insulting and killing them all. Your infernal gods could not make you do anything more shameful than when they sent you to fight the Franks. If you had any kind of rule of law and wanted to act fairly towards us, we would negotiate with you, reserving the rights of honour, and demonstrate to you with incontrovertible arguments what ought to belong to the Christians. If law and reason carry the same weight with you as the luxury of getting your own way, let a combat take place between your men and ours and this whole country be conceded to the victors without further bloodshed. If neither of these approaches finds favour with you, then either prepare to fly immediately or prepare your necks for our swords and halters.'

The interpreter came to the end of his speech. Kerbogha was so transported with anger that he could barely speak. Eventually he burst out as follows:

---

[14] The embassy of Herluin and Peter is found in *GF* 66–7 and the sources based on it. In the *Canso d'Antioca* Herluin goes alone and plays a rather different role, advising Kerbogha to flee; a similar role is played by the Saracen Mirdalis in RA. Herluin is not mentioned in all sources: AA 420 has Peter the Hermit as ambassador whilst in RC 664–5 Peter is the leader of five envoys. We know nothing about Herluin other than *GF* 67's comment that he was bilingual and acted as interpreter; Robert ignores this and sends an interpreter with them. The basic account is that of *GF*, but as ever Robert elaborates the detail and also adds extra speeches.

[15] The Christians also refuse to bow at Gilo VII.335–40; this is not in *GF*.

Chapter VI: what Kerbogha said

Kerbogha speaks, and insults our men.

'The Franks are certainly a proud people – but their pride will be curbed by our sword. Here they are demanding a battle between chosen men; whichever side wins victory will win the land, because they want it to be gained or freed from us without further bloodshed. They did not follow a sensible policy in taking up arms against us on behalf of an effeminate race. So go straight back and tell them that, if they agree to renounce their God and his Christianity, we will receive all of them with such good grace that we will give them this land – and land much better – and make all of them into mounted soldiers. If they decide not to, they will all die in short order or be led off in chains into our land.'

Chapter VII: what Herluin said

The servant of God insults him in return.

Herluin, who knew their language, then replied, saying:
     'O prince not of martial art but of the art of malice, if you only knew quite how ridiculous it is for Christians to say "I renounce God", such words would never have come out of your foul mouth. We know for a fact, by revelation from the very God whom you seek to persuade us to deny, that our salvation and your loss are imminent – joy for us, destruction for you. Who was it who sent you the fire yesterday evening, which frightened you all so much and disturbed you where you had fixed your tents? Let that sign be an omen of evil to you, of salvation to us: it gives us an absolutely clear message direct from God.'
     Kerbogha could no longer bear the plain speaking of Herluin and ordered him to be removed from his presence. Those who were standing around advised him to make a quick exit, because otherwise his status as an ambassador would cut no ice in ensuring his safety. So he left with his companions and returned to the city. I should not omit that, as they left, Kerbogha said to his followers:
     'Now you have heard those ragged and ill-favoured little men devoid of all presence speak without altering their views, not afraid of our anger or our dangerous weapons. They are all of one mind – desperate, seeking death and preferring death to capture. So, my brave men, when they march out to fight surround them on all sides and do not let even one escape or live a moment longer than necessary; if you leave them alive for a while, they will wreak havoc on our men before they are all killed.'
     That comment shows Kerbogha's stupidity, because it filled the minds of his men with terror. Indeed it is hardly surprising if he was foolish enough to utter

such idiocies, because the spirit of wisdom does not enter the souls of the perverse.[16]

Chapter VIII: the order in which they marched out to battle

The Bishop of Le Puy tells our men what to do, and all obey him. The battle lines are drawn up; there are six.

Peter the Hermit and Herluin returned to the princes of the army and told them what Kerbogha had said. In response the Bishop of Le Puy, with the assent and agreement of all, ordered a three day fast for everyone. Each confessed with a pure heart, and those who did have any food shared it amongst those who did not.[17] They spent those three days in complete humility and purity of heart, processing round the churches and begging God for mercy.

On dawn of the third day Mass was celebrated in the churches and all took communion of the sacred body of the Lord. By common agreement six columns were then formed up in the city and it was agreed which should go first and which after. The first column was that of Hugh of Vermandois and the Duke of Flanders. The second was that of Duke Godfrey. In the third was Robert of Normandy with his men. The fourth belonged to the Bishop of Le Puy, who carried the Lance of our Holy Saviour with him; he was accompanied by a considerable part of the army of the Count of St Gilles, who remained behind to guard the city. The fifth was Tancred's, and the sixth Bohemond's with the men best able to fight and the knights whom want had compelled to sell their horses.[18] The bishops and priests, monks and clerics, dressed in sacred vestments, marched out of the gate of the city with the soldiers; they carried crosses in their hands for blessing the people of God and sang loudly, hands raised towards the heavens: '*Save Thy people, and bless Thine inheritance: govern them also, and lift them up* now and *for ever*;[19] be to them a *strong tower from the enemy.*'[20] They chanted these and other psalms, particularly those fitting their difficult situation. Those on the walls and in the towers followed their example and sang likewise. And so the soldiers of Christ marched out against the acolytes of the Antichrist, through the gate in front of the mosque.

---

[16] Cf. *Proverbs* I.7: *fools despise wisdom and instruction.*

[17] Unity is a common theme in the Crusade chronicles: it recurs in Chapter X before battle starts. Compare FC I.13.5: 'qui linguis diversi eramus, tamquam fratres sub dilectione Dei et proximi unanimes esse videbamur' ('although we spoke different languages, we seemed of one mind like brothers and intimates inspired by the love of God').

[18] The order of the columns is that of the *GF*. The marching out of the army is a set piece found in most sources for the Crusade (e.g. RC 666, AA 42; GN 236–7, BB 75), reflecting both the fact that the Christians chose to offer battle rather than be attacked and the importance of the battle.

[19] *Psalms* XXVIII.9, slightly different in the Vulgate.

[20] *Psalms* LXI.3.

Chapter IX: how Kerbogha killed the apostate from Aquitaine

The villainous fool from Aquitaine meets his end.

Kerbogha watched them march out, standing on a small hill. As they came out he said: 'Hold back, men and let them all march out so that we can surround them more effectively.'[21]

Near him was a certain man from Aquitaine, known to us as Provençal, who was an apostate: he had been forced out of the city by his greed and had made his way to the camps of the enemy.[22] He had given a lot of misleading information which painted a bleak picture of the state our men were in, saying for example that they were dying of hunger, had all planned to save themselves by flight, had eaten their horses, were dwindling away with hunger, and that they had no option left other than to fly or to surrender to Kerbogha. Whilst the columns marched out of the city in ranks, Kerbogha asked what each one was and the Southerner told him in order. The sun threw its rays over mailed breastplates and lances which caught its glint, dazzling those who watched, and terrified the enemy: as Holy Scripture says, *terrible as an army* of siege.[23]

When Kerbogha saw them all together he shivered inwardly and said to those standing around him:

'This is a considerable and well-armed force. I can see no sign that they want to flee: on the contrary they seem minded to stand firm. Their aim seems to me not to be submission but pursuit.'

Turning to his apostate, he said:

'You criminal and arch-villain, what fairy-tales have you been telling us about these men – that they were eating their own horses, tortured by hunger and planning on flight? By Mahommed, this lie will be on your head, and you will pay by having your head cut off!'

Summoned by his order the sword-bearer of the imperial tyrant appeared and, pulling out his sword, cut off the apostate's head: and so he met a death worthy of his gabbling tongue and his apostasy. Then Kerbogha sent instructions to the emir who guarded his treasure. If he saw a fire lit at the head of his army, he should flee immediately and take all his possessions with him and order the others to flee,

---

[21] A standard part of the *GF* description: GN 238, BB 76. Crusaders and chroniclers alike were baffled by Kerbogha's failure to pick off the Christians as they filed out of Antioch over the bridge: the most likely explanation is dissension in the ranks (J. France, *Victory in the East: a military history of the First Crusade* (Cambridge, 1994), 285–94).

[22] The episode is not in other sources and the spy is not identified. However this may be a confused reminiscence of the role played by Herluin in the Occitan tradition preserved in the *Canso d'Antioca*; he briefs Kerbogha with the aim of demoralising him, but is not an apostate and escapes rather than getting executed. Gilo VII.357–60 describes Kerbogha threatening to behead Peter the Hermit for mocking him. The late twelfth-century manuscript G of BB, which is rich in variants, refers to an apostate (76). See Introduction, Chapter Three, for further discussion.

[23] *Song of Solomon* VI.4.

because he would know that the battle had gone to the Franks and victory had not been his.[24]

When our soldiers meanwhile came out into a flat area, they came to a halt on the orders of the Bishop of Le Puy and listened to his sermon in total silence.[25] He was wearing a breastplate and held the lance of the Saviour up in his right hand. He opened his mouth and said:

Chapter X: the sermon given by the Bishop of Le Puy

He gave a sermon to the people in case their terror might terrify the enemy.

'All of us *who were baptized into Jesus Christ*[26] are both sons of God and brothers together: we are bound by one and the same spiritual link and by the same love. So let us fight together in common purpose, like brothers, to protect our souls and bodies in such desperate straits. Remember how many tribulations you have suffered for your sins, as Our Lord God has seen fit to make plain to you in the visions he has sent. But now you are cleansed, and reconciled in full to God. So what should you fear? No misfortune can touch you. The man who dies here will be happier than he who lives because he will receive eternal joy in place of his mortal life. Conversely the man who survives will triumph over his enemies in victory; he will gain their riches and not suffer any need. You know what you have suffered, and the situation you now face. The Lord has brought the riches of the Orient right up to you – in fact, put them in your hands. So *fear not, nor be dismayed, be strong,*[27] because now God is sending the legions of his saints to avenge you on your enemies. You will see them today with your own eyes: when you do, do not be afraid of the terrifying noise they make. Indeed you should be used to the sight of them, since they have already come to your aid once; but human eyes do quail at the sight of citizens of heaven. See how your enemies are watching you march forward, necks straining forward like terrified stags or does, more inclined to flight than fight. You know their tactics well, and how once they have shot their arrows they place their trust in fleeing rather than fighting. So march out against them in the Name of Our Lord Jesus Christ, and may our all-powerful Lord God be with you.'

---

[24] The detail about the fire is from *GF* 68–9.

[25] Adhemar's sermon is at Gilo VII.378–99; it is not in *GF* or elsewhere.

[26] *Romans* VI.3.

[27] *Joshua* X.25.

Chapter XI: the start of the battle

As the sermon finishes the battle lines are drawn up. The warlike Hugh rides to help Bohemond, followed by the young entourage of Godfrey, famous for his prowess in war.

All responded 'Amen!' They deployed their forces in long lines. Hugh the Great rode first, carrying the standard – rightly called Great because he earned this privilege through his deeds and way of life.[28] The others followed in the order explained above; they spread out on a wide front, from the river to the mountains (a space of two miles). Kerbogha now began to fall back towards the mountains. Our men gradually followed him, all moving forward at a slow pace. The Turks now split into two: one section moved forward from the coast, the other – and larger – section remained on the battlefield. Their aim was to trap our men between them and shoot arrows into them from behind. So a seventh squadron was drawn up, whose task was to attack the part which had split off from the main army; it was pulled together from the soldiers of Duke Godfrey and the Count of Normandy and led by a duke called Rainald.[29] They sent him against the enemy; they fought and many fell on both sides. Meanwhile, the other six squadrons came within bowshot range of the Turks. The latter refused to advance further and shot off their arrows – in vain however because a side wind blew them off their target. When the Turks saw this they turned and fled. Thus the first squadron sought a fight in the battle and did not get one; they wanted someone to strike or be struck by, but had no luck finding anybody. Bohemond now sent a messenger to Hugh the Great seeking help, because he had come under heavy pressure from the Turks.[30] Hugh turned immediately to his men and said:

'Men, battle runs away from us so let us look for it and go to the famous commander Bohemond. That is where the battle is that you want and where the well-armed enemy you seek can be found.'

> Then, swifter than words, each follower flies there
> And the famous counts are joined in endeavour.

When Godfrey, leader of the leaders, saw that his friend [Hugh] the Great was heading that way with his men at high speed, he followed behind, also feeling deprived of an opportunity to fight. The heart of the Persian army and the greater part of its strength were based there, and so it was entirely appropriate that Godfrey and Hugh should join in. Each of them was a soulmate for the other, joined in equal friendship. Hugh the Great reached the *mêlée* first. He picked out one of the

---

[28] Gilo VII.369, 417–8. Robert returns briefly to *GF* 69 to describe the start of the battle.

[29] Rainald of Beauvais in some manuscripts of the *GF* (69). Rainald of Toul in WT; 'Rainaldus quidam comes', GN 239; Rainardus in PT 111.

[30] The description of Hugh and Godfrey and the death of Odo of Beaugency in chapter XII are closely paralleled in Gilo VII.431–59.

enemies who was bolder than the rest and was shouting to spur them on to fight. He spurred his horse, flecked with foam, towards him, thrust the lance into his throat and stopped him breathing. That was the end for the wretch. He fell immediately to the ground and yielded his soul to the infernal deities.[31]

Chapter XII: the death of Odo [of Beaugency]

At this point our men suffered a considerable setback. Odo of Beaugency, who was carrying the standard, was wounded by a poisoned arrow.[32] His strength failed from the pain of the wound and he fell to the ground along with the standard. William of Belesme hacked a way through the enemy with drawn sword and raised it from the ground.[33] No tongue can tell or hand write or page contain what the leader of leaders Godfrey achieved that day, or Bohemond, or the distinguished young soldiers. Not one of our men hung back or acted as a coward: there was no room for such behaviour and the enemy, far more numerous, pressed each hard. The more that were killed, the more they seemed to be; they swarmed from every side like flies on rotting matter.

Chapter XIII: help from the celestial army[34]

Squadrons of saints are sent to the help of our men from the summit of Heaven and bring aid.

As battle raged, and there was a risk of flagging in such a long fight with the number of enemies never growing less, an innumerable army of white soldiers was seen riding down from the mountains. Its standard bearers and leaders were said to be St George, St Maurice, St Mercurius and St Demetrius.[35] Once the Bishop of Le Puy saw them, he exclaimed loudly: 'Soldiers, here comes the help God promised you!' Our men would most certainly have been terrified had it not been for the

---

[31] The description is straight out of a *chanson de geste*: compare *Guillaume* 441–6: 'Puis refert altre sur la duble targe,/Tote lie freint de l'un ur desqu'a l'altre;/Trenchad le braz que li sist en l'enarme,/Colpe le piz et trenchad la curaille,/Parmi l'eschine sun grant espee li passe,/Tut estendu l'abat mort en la place', ('He... struck a pagan on the mail-shirt on his back; he thrust the spear right through his spine and out the other side: he skewered him well, and knocked him over dead', Bennett's translation). Hugh is the only prince to have an exploit of this kind described in detail during the battle.

[32] Hugh's standard-bearer; referred to here, in Gilo VII.452–9, and in the *Antioche* as Odon de Beauvais 8648–88 in a passage copied from Robert.

[33] Possibly William of Bohemia (Riley-Smith, *First Crusaders*, 225).

[34] Robert returns to *GF* 69.

[35] Robert adds St Maurice to the list given by *GF* 69. St Mercurius was martyred at Caesarea in Cappadocia; a hero of barbarian assaults against Rome, he was beheaded for refusing to sacrifice to pagan gods under the Emperor Trajan: for detail see the *Oxford Dictionary of the Christian Church*.

hope they placed in God. The enemy began to tremble violently; they turned away, covered their backs with their shields and each one fled wherever he could.

Chapter XIV: how the grass was set on fire

When the part of the Turkish army fighting near the coast saw their flight, they set the grass of the battlefield on fire: it burnt fast because it was dried out by the heat of summer. They did this as a signal to those in the tents to flee at once and take their most precious possessions with them. The part of the army in the mountains recognised the signal and fled immediately, taking as much as they could with them. However what use was that, since they were soon prevented from carrying it? When the Armenians and Syrians saw that they were overcome and that our men were in pursuit, they met them and killed them. Hugh the Great, Duke Godfrey and the Count of Flanders were riding together with their columns along next to the river, where the enemy army was at its most powerful and thickly massed. They began to press them so hard that the enemy were unable to return to their tents as they had intended. To pursue them more effectively our men mounted the horses of those who were dying and left their own horses – gaunt and suffering from hunger – on the battlefield, reins trailing from their heads. Amazing is the strength of Omnipotent God, and his power is boundless! Your soldier, weakened by long starvation, pursues enemies bulging with fat and flab so assiduously that they do not even dare to look back at the possessions they brought with them. Your benevolent spirit was in their minds, bolstering their physical strength and strengthening their resolve. Your soldier is not held back by the desire for plunder or avarice for any possession; for victory above all fills his mind. Our men were free to slice up the bodies of the Turks just as the corpses of beasts are cut apart in the abattoir. Blood spun away from the bodies of the wounded; dust spun away from the feet of the galloping horses.[36] The air was clouded and darkened as if at dusk. The fugitives managed to assemble on a hill somewhere, hoping to use it to marshall themselves against us.

Chapter XV: the death of Gerard of Melun

A man who acts rashly does himself no good. If this man had shown some moderation he would have lived for longer.

Gerard, the elderly Lord of Melun, who had lain ill for a long time during the siege, galloped up on a swift horse and flung himself against them out of the blue.[37] He was struck down by their missiles and thus died a good death.[38] When those

---

[36] Compare Gilo VII.479: 'pulvis ad astra volat morientium sanguine' ('dust flew up to the stars, foul with the blood of the dying', Grocock and Siberry's translation).

[37] Mentioned only here, in Gilo VII.484–7 and in the *Antioche* translating Robert.

[38] Gilo VII.484–7.

following close behind – Everard of Le Puiset, Pagan of Beauvais, Drogo and Thomas and Clarenbald and the rest of Hugh the Great's young troop – saw what had happened, they attacked without hesitating.[39] They met with stiff resistance. However, with God's help and reinforcements to their number, they valiantly prevailed. Much blood was spilt and many were decapitated who, if they had carried through their intention to flee, could have escaped safe and sound.[40] So they followed them as far as the Iron Bridge and Tancred's castle; they could pursue no further because nightfall brought an end. That day 100,000 knights died, and it would have been too great a task to count the number of those who died from the great multitude of footsoldiers. The tired soldiers, finding themselves some distance from the city, bivouacked in the tents which had belonged to their enemies, and found many things there which they could eat to their fill; before God sent terror into the hearts of the enemy they had all prepared supper in frying-pans and cooking-pots, cauldrons and casseroles; but the wretches managed neither to cook nor carry away with them what they had prepared.[41]

Chapter XVI: the Bishop of Le Puy and the spoils captured in battle

The reverend Bishop of Le Puy could be seen, wearing breastplate and helmet and carrying the Holy Lance, face flooded with tears through sheer joy. He exhorted them to thank God to whom they owed their victory, and said to them:

'From the day you became soldiers, nobody has stood comparison with you. Nobody has ever fought so many great battles in such a short time as you since you crossed the sea to Constantinople. Anyone who sees what you have seen today and is not affirmed in his love of God is a true stranger to the Christian faith.'

The reverend pontiff said these and other similar things; it was with such utterances that he instructed the people entrusted to him and tempered their horseplay and jokes. The sight of his presence and expression affected all so that nobody would dare to make stupid comments in his presence.

---

[39] A cluster of nobles from the Ile de France. See note to V.6 for Everard III of Le Puiset, viscount of Chartres. The passage is translated in *Antioche* 9145–71. Pagan of Beauvais is mentioned only here, in Gilo VII.468 and in the *Antioche*; Clarenbald lord of Vendeuil is mentioned a number of times in AA (293–5, 299, 304–5, 398) who suggests that Thomas, Drogo and Clarenbald came out in the contingent of Emicho of Leichingen; see too GN 239. Riley-Smith (*First Crusaders* 203) identifies Drogo as Drogo of Nesle, mentioned particularly in the *Antioche* and AA. He identifies Thomas as Thomas, Lord of Marle and la Fère (223); for details on his career see 156–7. Despite his proved reputation for violence, he was to mutate into an unlikely hero of the Old French Crusade Cycle: see Duparc-Quioc, *Cycle*, 39–44.

[40] Hugh's knights and their attack are also found in Gilo VII.468–75.

[41] A rare stylistic misjudgement by Robert: an attempt at vivid detail descends into bathos.

Chapter XVII: plunder and the surrender of the citadel

The celebrations were complete when the people of Antioch in the citadel surrendered without a fight.

The following day after that night 15,000 camels were discovered;[42] and who could count the numbers of horses, male and female mules, oxen, donkeys, sheep and animals of other kinds?[43] They also found many gold and silver vessels, an immense number of cloaks and all kinds of valuable plunder. They came in triumph with all of these to the city, and those who had remained there and the clerics, priests and monks received them in solemn procession.

Chapter XVIII: about the guardian of the citadel who wanted to convert to Christianity, and how he had a vision of the saints

When the Emir in the citadel saw his leader and those with him fleeing from the battlefield and the innumerable thousands of white knights scouring the plain with shining standards, he was so terrified that he asked for one of our banners to be given to him as a token of protection.[44] The Count of St Gilles, who had remained inside to watch over the citadel, passed him his banner. The Emir accepted it gratefully and fixed it on the wall of the citadel. However, when he discovered from some Lombards standing around that it was not a banner belonging to Bohemond – to whom the whole city had been granted – he returned the banner to the Count of St Gilles and asked for one from Bohemond, which Bohemond sent. When he received it, the Emir sent to Bohemond to ask him to come to him. Bohemond was following closely behind the envoys, and listened to what the emir had to say. The Gentile sought an agreement on oath that those who were with him and wished to leave should suffer no injury and receive safe conduct to the land of the Saracens; any who wished to turn Christian should be allowed to do so. Bohemond was overjoyed and said:

'My friend, we shall be delighted to grant what you ask. However please wait a moment while I go and tell our leaders, and I shall come back to you shortly.'

He ran off hastily and, having got the princes together, told them what the Gentile had said. All were delighted and thanked Almighty God. Bohemond returned to the Gentile, now on his side, and confirmed the acceptance of the agreement he sought. So the emir submitted to the Bishop of Le Puy and the might of holy Christendom with 300 of his soldiers, who were young and impressive. There was more rejoicing amongst the Christians over their conversion than over the fall of the citadel.[45] Bohemond took possession of it, and had those who did not

---

[42] Gilo VII.490 gives the same figure.

[43] Robert returns to *GF* 70.

[44] Ahmad ibn-Marwan according to Kemal ad-Din, III.583.

[45] Naturally.

want to be converted led to the land of the Saracens. After a fast of three days the gentiles were baptised amidst great rejoicing, to the greater renown of God and glory of Christianity. The converts often told later how, as they looked out from the citadel over the battle, they had suddenly seen innumerable thousands of shining white soldiers and been utterly terrified at the sight.[46] (That was no wonder, because the whole citadel had trembled from its foundations.) When they had then seen them fighting alongside the Christian squadrons and their own forces overthrown and put to flight, they had immediately realised that these were celestial forces and that they could not overcome the God of the Christians. So their hearts were touched and they promised to become Christians.

Chapter XIX: the date on which the battle of Antioch was fought

This battle was fought on 28 June, the Vigil of the Apostles Peter and Paul. The storm of troubles which had raged for nearly ten months, was appeased;[47] the royal city, long bent under the yoke of a diabolical captivity, regained the state of grace of its original liberty. The enemies who had held it captive became captives themselves and scattered to hiding-places in the forest, hollows in rocks and clefts in the mountains. The Armenians and the Syrians native to the country went out on their trail for several days. They found some half-dead, other wounded, others lacking part of their heads, others again clutching their stomachs to stop their entrails falling out. They took their possessions and killed them. And so the enemies of God were eradicated and the Christians, unparalleled servants of God, gathered rejoicing and happy in the glorious city of Antioch. They met on a given day and agreed that ambassadors should be sent to the Emperor of Constantinople and invite him to come and take possession of his city.[48]

Chapter XX: the death of Hugh the Great

What good of any kind could come once Hugh the Great left the scene? His death created great harm.[49]

What grief! All took the view that, since the embassy was to a king, a messenger of royal blood should go. Hugh the Great, royal indeed in blood and in his actions,

---

[46] Robert again emphasises the role of the celestial forces.

[47] Compare the Charleville poet at V.464.

[48] Also in *GF* 72: Robert hammers the message home again in Chapter XX: as made clear in book II, the crusaders' fulfilment of their oaths was entirely dependent on the Emperor meeting his promise. Despite the crusaders' offer he failed to do so; they were therefore justified in breaking their own oaths and Bohemond in retaining Antioch. It is hardly a coincidence that the justification is at this point in the text.

[49] Not very accurate: he died later, and arguably had less impact on the Crusade than many of the other leaders.

was therefore chosen – although had they known he would never return they would not have sent him. Once he had delivered his message to the king, he died unexpectedly and could not at the end of his life return as he had planned.[50] Meanwhile, the foxy Emperor of Constantinople was too cowardly to come and receive such a great city; he realised full well that he had violated faith with the Franks both in the oath sworn on the sacraments and in the tokens given and had not kept his promise. So all agreements reached between them were void.

Chapter XXI: how the princes split up to wait for the beginning of November[51]

The princes held council as to what they should do.

Meanwhile, the princes in the city began to discuss moving on to the Holy Sepulchre. What should they do? Should they set out soon and when should they set an end? There was common agreement that they should wait until the beginning of October to set out again:[52] the heat of summer was ferocious and the Saracen lands they were going to enter were arid and without water, so they waited for the wet season when springs would break out of the ground. There was also a need to decide what such a large multitude should do in the mean time, where and how it should live. Once they had reached a decision, they looked for a herald to announce what would be done. A herald was duly found; he found somewhere high and announced that those in need should stay in the city and reach agreement with the richer on entering their service; meanwhile the princes each went to their own castles and cities.

---

[50] An error by Robert: Hugh died on the Crusade of 1101: Runciman, *History*, vol.II, 27–9. It is surprising that Robert should make such a mistake given the prominence he affords Hugh. Bull, 'Capetian Monarchy', 42, suggests this may be a deliberate lie to bolster the prestige of the French court; if so it is a fairly blatant one in an area where the audience would be likely to have known better, but none the less possible for that.

[51] From here on, the battle of Antioch over, the relationships between Gilo, Robert and the *GF* alter. The remainder of the text is all in *GF* X, which is much longer than the preceding nine books and not focused on Bohemond. It corresponds to Books VIII and IX of Gilo, which unlike what precedes follow *GF* closely. Robert follows the *GF* for the remainder of his work although continuing to insert particular details also found in Gilo's text.

[52] Hagenmeyer sets the reassembly time at the beginning of November; so do *GF* 72 and Gilo VIII.6. So too does Robert in VIII.1. However, the reading of October here seems to be in all manuscripts cited by the *Recueil* and is presumably therefore Robert's mistake.

Chapter XXII: about the noble knight Raymond Pilet

Pilet's 'pilum' provokes Parthian weeping everywhere.[53]

Amongst the knights of the Count of St Gilles was Raymond surnamed Pilet, brave and physically impressive.[54] He was consumed by hatred of the Turks and could not bear the thought of leaving them unattacked for a long period. He collected around him a considerable force of knights and footsoldiers and led them to Saracen territory. They crossed the bounds of two cities and came to a castle known as Talamania under Syrian rule.[55] The Syrians received our men and surrendered to them very readily. Eight days later they came to another castle in which a large number of Saracens was lurking.[56] They arrived, attacked it, fought relentlessly all day and took it as evening fell. Once it had fallen they killed everybody other than those willing to convert to Christianity. Having successfully emptied it, they went back to the first castle which, as we have said, was called Talamania; they stayed two days, all left on the third and reached the city known as Ma'arrat-an-Nu'man. A large number of Turks and Saracens were gathered there from Aleppo and other towns and cities in the area, waiting for their arrival. As the Christians drew near, the barbarians came out against them; but they failed to fight against our men for long and fled back into the city. Our men certainly could not remain there because the immense heat of the summer was oppressive and they could find nothing to drink. So as evening fell they returned to their own castle of Talamania. Several Christians who were native to the country went along with them but scorned to return with our men; the Turks took them in an ambush and killed them. So they died as a result of their own stupidity: if they had gone back with our men none would have been killed. As the proverb has it, 'the unthinking man does not worry about anything until ill fortune strikes'. Raymond did not go back out as far as that city since he had no army to besiege it; he stayed in his castle until the agreed time of the beginning of October and spent his time harrying the Saracens.

---

[53] The pun on Pilet and 'pilum' is too tempting to miss, as is the heavy-handed alliteration; they are unlikely to be Robert's own, as argued in Introduction, Chapter Five. A 'pilum' is a javelin.

[54] Raymond Pilet, lord of Alès in the south of France. He features in most sources for the Crusade, both *GF*- and non-*GF*- derived: see Riley-Smith, *First Crusaders*, 220, for references. He is not mentioned in the *Antioche*, reflecting the prominence he was to assume near the end rather than the beginning of the Crusade. Gilo VIII.10–13 also praises him; the *GF* does not single him out.

[55] Tel-Mannas.

[56] The identity of this is uncertain.

Chapter XXIII: the death of the Bishop of Le Puy

In the sixth month the outstanding Bishop of Le Puy dies.

Those who had remained in Antioch led a tranquil and happy existence until they lost their lord the Bishop of Le Puy. The army was completely at peace when the Bishop began to sicken in the month of July; he did not linger for long because God did not allow him to suffer the torments of a protracted illness. On 1 August his holy soul was released from earthly bonds and transported to Heavenly Paradise to sit enthroned in glory. This happened on the feast of St Peter ad Vincula; to make it clear that it had happened by decision of divine judgement, the soul of the prelate was released from its earthly bonds on the very day on which the chains of the chief of the Apostles had been carried from Jerusalem to Rome.[57] There had never been such misery and grief in the army of God - no matter what the tribulation – as there was on account of the Bishop's death. All mourned him with good reason: he had brought counsel to the rich, consolation to the grieving, support to the weak, generosity to the needy and harmony to those who quarrelled. He used to admonish the soldiers:

'If you wish to triumph for God and be his friends, keep yourselves clean and take pity on the poor. Nothing will guard against death as much as charity does: it protects better than a shield and pierces enemies more effectively than any lance. Anyone who cannot pray for himself should give alms, and that will be as good as a prayer.'

He was dear to God and the whole people for these works and words of this kind. It would probably take us too far from the story if one were to list all the virtues he had been given by God.

Chapter XXIV: how a bishopric was founded at Albara ...

... something necessary once the city was captured

Once the Bishop had been properly buried, as was proper, in the Church of St Peter, the Count of St Gilles crossed into Saracen territory and went to a city known as Albara. He surrounded it with strong forces on all sides and fought it out for a long time with those on the walls using missiles and arrows. Realising, however, that he was having little impact, he had scaling ladders put up against the walls, sent armed soldiers up them and forced the enemy to flee:

> When the soldiers climbed onto the wall, they were higher than the enemies

---

[57] The play on the concept of release from bonds is shared with Gilo VIII.78–81. Adhemar is implicitly compared to St Peter.

Whilst the enemies were beneath them in strength.
They jumped down from the wall onto the rooves of the houses
And from the houses onto the streets.
Old, children and young fled here and there,
But flight was of no avail whatsoever to any.

The Count ordered that all should be put in chains, and those who refused to acknowledge Christ the Redeemer should be beheaded. So many heads were seen to fall; so many boys and girls were deprived of what should have been a long life. This was the judgement of God: the city had belonged to the Christians and had been taken from them with the same macabre behaviour.[58] None were spared from such a large crowd except those who voluntarily turned to Christ and were baptised.[59] Thus the city was cleansed and returned to the worship of our faith. The Count then discussed with his lords the question of ordaining a bishop to rule the city through his good counsel and help and to shore up faith in Jesus Christ in the hearts of those who had just been baptised. So an intelligent and well-known man was chosen, equally well versed in knowledge of letters and distinguished in other areas, and sent to be ordained at Antioch.[60]

Here ends the seventh book.

---

[58] Gilo's description at VIII.85–91 is similar. Yet more heads fall.

[59] Riley-Smith, *Idea*, 110, suggests that the savagery here may be based on a misreading by Robert.

[60]Peter of Narbonne, a priest in the army of Raymond IV. *GF* 75 and RA 91–2 also record his election. Runciman, *History*, vol.I, 257; see also B. Hamilton, *The Latin Church in the Crusader States* (London, 1980), 10–11, 22–3.

Book VIII

From Antioch to Jerusalem

November 1098–June 1099

Chapter I: why our soldiers returned to Antioch

The leaders and their forces assemble.

Summer was now over: the heat of the sun was weakening and the nights were longer than the days. The soldiers of Christ returned to Antioch from the places where they had spent the summer and gathered together on 1 November, All Saints' Day. They praised and glorified Eternal God, because the number of those returning was greater than when they had split up; a large number of outstanding knights and footsoldiers had followed in their footsteps from many parts of the world, and the Christian army daily grew in size.

Chapter II: the disagreement between Bohemond and Raymond

Count Raymond and Duke Bohemond lock horns.

Now that they were together and debating how they should make their way to the Holy Sepulchre, Bohemond sought the handing over of the city as they had agreed with him. The Count of St Gilles said that was impossible because of the oaths they had sworn through Bohemond's offices to the Emperor of Constantinople. So they held a meeting which lasted many days in the Church of St Peter, and there was a stormy debate. Since it proved impossible to reach any kind of agreement in full session, the bishops, abbots, and dukes and counts who had a more reasoned and sensible approach came into the place where St Peter's chair is found and discussed amongst themselves how they might both keep the promises made to Bohemond and the oaths sworn to the Emperor. When they left the meeting place they decided against making their views known to everyone. They took the Count of St Gilles aside to tell him their plan, and he approved of the proposed way forward on condition that Bohemond continued the journey already undertaken with them. Bohemond, asked for his views, was positive. Both swore on oath, their hands between those of the bishops, that they would not turn aside from the journey to the Holy Sepulchre and that it would not be thrown into confusion by any dispute between them. Bohemond then strengthened the defence of the citadel overlooking the city, whilst the Count strengthened the palace of Cassianus and the tower above the city gate nearest the port of St Simeon.

Since the tale of Antioch has detained us for a considerable period of time – exhausting our soldiers by eight months of siege during which it defied attempts to take it by any human force, art or device – let us now say something about its site and give some description for those who have never been there.

Chapter III: a description of the site of Antioch[1]

This chapter accurately describes the nobility of the city described above and [now] reconciled to the Lord.

As its history tells, Antioch was founded by 65 kings who all acknowledged its hegemony. It is surrounded by two walls. The first of these is made of large square stones, carefully polished; 460 towers are set in order round it. It delights those who see it by the orderliness of its construction, and is very broad and spacious. There are four mountains within the walls; these are high and stretch a long way up. The citadel is constructed on the highest of them, and is so well protected by its natural position that it is impregnable to any attack or any ingenious tactic. There are 360 churches in its territory, and the Patriarch oversees 153 bishops. On the eastern side it is protected by four large mountains; on the western side it is irrigated by a river known as the Farfar.[2] As I said above, King Antiochus founded it along with his 65 kings and named it after himself.[3] Our warrior pilgrims besieged this royal and extremely famous city for eight months and one day; they were trapped in it for three weeks by the Parthian race;[4] and, having defeated them with divine help, they then rested in the city for four months and eight days.

---

[1] This chapter, unlike Robert's other descriptions of places, is found in the *GF* and echoed in most of its derivatives albeit with slight changes in detail in each. See GN 249–50; PT 119–20; *GF* 76–7. It is not in Gilo.

[2] The Orontes. WT I.143 comments that it was also known as the Fer and confused with the Farfar in Damascus.

[3] It was founded by Seleucus: GN 250, typically, corrects the *GF* by reference to Trogus Pompeius.

[4] A rare description of the Turks in terms of classical literature. It is interesting that it comes in this passage, which stands apart from the narrative. See GN 83 on the difficulty of knowing whether to use classical or modern descriptions of peoples and places in writing history.

Chapter IV: how Chastel-Rouge and Albara were captured

Count Raymond (whose integrity was second to none) and his forces are the first to leave the city; they head for Ma'arrat-an-Nu'man, whose inhabitants attack them.

After all this, Raymond, the Count of St Gilles, was the first to leave Antioch with his forces and came to a city known as Chastel-Rouge. The following day he reached another city known as Albara. He had conquered both these cities with a small force and had brought them into the service of Christ. On the fourth day, at the end of November, he reached the city known as Ma'arrat-an-Nu'man:[5] his knight Raymond Pilet had originally taken it but had been forced to retreat under heavy pressure. The city was full of people, crammed full with people from the surrounding hinterland. The enemy saw our men in the distance; they were unconcerned about what seemed to them a small force in comparison to their own and tried to fight them outside the city. However, they soon realised that a small body can legitimately outfight a drunken multitude – especially when they are people who place their hope and trust in the name of God. When our men saw them preparing to resist, they buckled on their shields, aimed the points of their lances, attacked them in a charge and smashed through the middle of their troops. *There* the Lord *brake the arrows of the bow, the shield and the sword, and the battle.*[6] Once battle is joined with swords, bow and arrow are of little use. Those who were nearer the gate of the city thought themselves lucky; those further off wished with all their hearts either to get nearer the gate or that the gate would come to them. The city served as an excellent refuge since the combat had taken place near the door. Even so not all those who had marched out in one piece came back in a reasonable state. Those who had borne the brunt of the first attack of our men came back in particularly bad shape. They managed to shoot many of our horses with arrows, but left many more of their own riders sprawled on the ground. When they had retreated into the city, our men set up camp a bowshot away. They stayed awake all night, and when on the following day the morning star began to fade with the sun's rays, our men took up arms, surrounded the city on all sides and attacked it ferociously.

> Weapons, stakes and stones fly, and fires and torches
> Which set alight the rooves of the houses inside.[7]

Even so, the enormous multitude of enemies continued to resist. Our men achieved nothing that day and retired, exhausted, to their tents.

---

[5] 27 November.

[6] *Psalms* LXXVI.3.

[7] Compare Gilo VIII.136–7: 'Iactant saxa, faces flammas per inane ferentes/Quas herere volunt ad culmina suspicientes' ('they flung rocks and torches that carried flames through the void; they aimed them high, wanting them to stick to the battlements', Grocock and Siberry's translation).

Chapter V: Bohemond and several others follow the Count of St Gilles

Count Raymond and Bohemond are present at the same time.

The same day Bohemond, his men and a large number of others followed the Count On arrival they surrounded the city on all sides. When those inside saw this they were completely terrified, and blocked all the gates of the city by throwing boulders in front of them. The counts therefore decided on a change of tactic, since there would be no battle on equal terms. They had battering rams made, in other words iron-clad beams; these would be slung on ropes held by the soldiers, pulled back and smashed into the wall, so that the ramparts would crumble under the repeated blows. A wooden tower was also built which was taller than the stone towers and looked down on all the machines which were inside. It had three storeys and was well equipped with shields and pulleys. The two upper floors held armed men with weapons, stakes, pikes, arrows, stones, javelins and torches. Below were men no less well armed who pushed round the wheels on which they had rested the tower. Others in a tortoise formation came right up to the wall and filled in the ditch – which was huge – so that they could push the tower up to the wall and under its protection breach the wall. They did so. However, the wretched citizens fought back with some engine with which they flung large stones at the tower and also blasted Greek fire to burn it.[8] Nevertheless, with the protection of God's grace all their efforts and tricks were frustrated and came to nothing. For where the wooden tower was close to the wall, it dominated all those on the section in question and exposed them to view by dint of looking down on them.

Chapter VI: about William of Montpellier and Golfier of Las Tours

There is fighting on all sides, but as yet nobody gains the upper hand.

William of Montpellier himself was on the upper storey with many others.[9] With him was a hunter called Everard, who was skilled at blowing the trumpet; he terrified enemies and encouraged his own side to fight by the blast of its tumultous sound.[10] Whilst William and his men destroyed everything within reach, smashing in the rooves of the houses by throwing boulders, those beneath him were digging away at the wall; others again were putting ladders up against the battlements.

---

[8] Greek fire was a naphtha-based paste which stuck to and burned anything it touched, and could be extinguished only with vinegar. It was used, for example, at the siege of Acre in 1190: see H. E. Mayer, *The Crusades*, transl. J. Gillingham (Oxford, 1972), 141.

[9] William V, Count of Montpellier. He is not mentioned by fellow Occitan RA but is found in a number of sources: *GF* 26,78; PT 78, 123; Gilo VIII 170–2

[10] We know nothing about Everard beyond this reference, taken from the *GF* and appearing in most of its derivatives (*GF* 78; PT 122; BB 85, note; Gilo VIII.156–7; not in GN).

Once they were up, nobody wanted to be the first to the top. Golfier of Las Tours, a worthy soldier, did not wait but immediately went up onto the wall, followed by several brave men.[11] When the Gentiles saw them climbing onto the wall they reacted furiously. They rushed on them from all sides and obstructed them with so many darts and arrows that some of our men who had climbed up onto the wall flung themselves down and in trying to avoid death met it instead broken on the ground. When the celebrated young force of our men saw Golfier and a few others fighting on the battlements, they forgot about themselves and remembered their allies: they immediately climbed up and swamped part of the wall with weight of numbers. The priests and Levites, ministers of the Lord, were standing next to the wooden tower invoking Jesus Christ, Son of God as defender of the Christians, saying: *'O Lord be gracious unto us; be Thou our arm every morning, our salvation also in the time of trouble;*[12] *pour out Thy wrath upon the heathen that have not known Thee, and upon the kingdoms that have not called upon Thy name;*[13] disperse them in your strength and cast them down, Lord our protector.'[14]

In the mean time, whilst some were fighting, others weeping and singing psalms and others again undermining the walls, Golfier was sweating from the strain of battle: all the enemies were fighting him and his companions whilst he and they stood against all. His shield was the powerful bulwark which protected all his men, at least from the enemies on the wall. The short and narrow stretch of wall did not allow any ally to come and join him, or more than one enemy to approach. So not one of the enemy could overcome Golfier, whilst he overcame large numbers of them. In fact none dared to approach within striking distance any longer, each fearing for himself the fate Golfier's sword had inflicted on others. They flung weapons, arrows, stakes and stones at him; and his shield was so weighed down by them that it could no longer be lifted by one man alone.[15]

---

[11] Golfier, Lord of Las Tours in the Limousin. His heroism here is picked up in most sources for the Crusade: see for example *GF* 79, PT 123, RA 97–8, OV V.138–9. Gregory Bechada, who according to Geoffrey of Vigeois wrote a vernacular verse account of the Crusade, was in his household: the Occitan *Canso d'Antioca* preserves unique material on him both in the extant manuscript and in passages preserved in the later Spanish compilation the *Gran Conquista de Ultramar*. For full discussion and further references see 9–17, 34–40 in the *Canso* Introduction. Gilo VIII.188–211 has a similarly detailed description, suggesting that Robert inserted it in the middle of the *GF* from his other source.

[12] *Isaiah* XXXIII.2, slightly different in the King James version.

[13] *Psalms* LXXIX.6.

[14] Cf. *Psalms* LX.12: *through God we shall do valiantly: for it is he that shall tread down our enemies.*

[15] The account of Golfier's exploit is exceptionally vivid and detailed even by Robert's standards. Is it from an eyewitness source, perhaps Golfier himself? It also has overtones of Lucan's description of Scaeva (*Pharsalia* VI.144–262).

Chapter VII: how the city fell

The city is taken and all its people killed.

By now Golfier, strong though he was, was exhausted; sweat was pouring from the whole of his body onto the ground and he desperately needed someone to replace him. At that point those undermining the wall thrust their way forcibly into the city, and decapitated all those they came upon first. All up on the walls were petrified with astonishment at the unexpected turn of events:

> Immediately the warmth of life left their bones,
> And chilly fear stole over their hearts.

What help remained for people doomed to die and beside themselves, pressed on every side by enemies both inside the city and on the wall? Golfier, who not long before had been nearly fainting with exhaustion, now found a second wind: he now hastened in pursuit of the enemy as they fled, protected not by his shield or helmet but brandishing his blood-stained sword in his right hand. He killed several through sheer terror rather than at the point of the sword because they flung themselves down from the wall. Above the gate was one tower which seemed more imposing and stronger than the rest. Through an interpreter Bohemond ordered the richer citizens to flee to it: he would protect them from death if they bought their freedom from him. They did so, trusting in his good faith. Eventually the whole violent business came to an end, brought to a halt by the coming darkness of evening. The following day might well have been the Sabbath, but neither the victors nor the vanquished could rest. The Count posted sentinels round the city, inside and out, to ensure that nobody fled and took plunder from the city with them. When the following day dawned our men ran to take up arms and stormed savagely through the roads and squares and on the rooves of the houses, like a lioness deprived of her cubs:

> They slash apart and slaughter children and young people
> And those weighed down by their years and bent by old age.[16]

They spared none: on the contrary they strung several up at the same time to finish them off more quickly.[17] An astonishing turn of events and astonishing sight to see such a huge number of people – armed at that – killed with impunity and putting up no resistance. Each of our men took whatever he found. They cut open the internal organs of the corpses and pulled out gold bezants and coins. How detestable the desire for gold! All the streets of the city were dyed with rivers of

---

[16] The episode is in *GF* 79–80, but Robert betrays a certain ambivalence. The bloodshed is ascribed to the obstinacy of the Saracens and to 'detestanda auri cupiditas' rather than the Crusaders themselves, but the episode is portrayed in disturbing tones.

[17] Gilo VIII.259–63 gives more detail on the stranglings, which are not in *GF*.

blood and strewn with corpses of the dead. What a blind people, all destined to die then and there! Not one out of such a large number volunteered to confess the name of Jesus Christ. Bohemond eventually ordered those whom he had ordered to be shut in the palace tower to be brought to him. He ordered the old women, the men weakened by age and those rendered useless by physical disability to be killed. The youngsters, adults in the prime of life and good condition and the men were to be preserved and taken to Antioch to be sold. This butchery of the Turks happened on 12 December, a Sunday. Not everything could be completed that day. The following day various Turks were found lurking in various places, and were also killed. There was no place in the whole city and no ditch which was not defiled with their corpses or blood.

Chapter VIII: the disagreement between Bohemond and Count Raymond

Count Raymond and Bohemond disagree.

And so, with the city taken and freed from the Turkish rebels, Bohemond sought a truce with the Count of St Gilles: he wanted Antioch to be completely surrendered into his power and to be allowed to enjoy it undisturbed. The Count objected in response that this would involve perjury because of the oath given to the emperor at Constantinople through Bohemond's own offices. So Bohemond returned to Antioch with his own followers, where they stayed. The Frankish army lingered in Ma'arrat-an-Nu'man for a month and four days, during which time the Bishop of Orange died a worthy death.[18] They overwintered there for a long and dreary period, which meant they were unable to find anything to eat or take by force. They were so desperate with hunger that they ended up – a horrible thing to have to describe – cutting up the bodies of the Turks, cooking them and eating them. The Count of St Gilles was distraught by such difficulties, and sent to all the princes at Antioch to come to the city of Chastel-Rouge to decide how to go forward to the Holy Sepulchre.[19] They duly came together in Chastel-Rouge, but discussion centred on how to achieve peace and an agreement between the Count and Bohemond rather than any consideration of why they had actually come and were there. No agreement was reached, and all the princes returned to Antioch, abandoning both the Count and the journey to the Sepulchre. Meanwhile, the Count was left not only with his own men but a large force of young men, who were desperate to complete the pilgrimage. So the Count returned to Ma'arrat-an-Nu'man, where the pilgrims were awaiting them, placing more trust in God than in his princely colleagues. The whole Christian army was deeply demoralised by the disagreements amongst the princes. All knew that actually simple justice was on Raymond's side, and no desire or ambition could turn him aside from his duty.

---

[18] William, Bishop of Orange. Hagenmeyer (*Chronologie*) puts his death on or around 20 December.

[19] The *Recueil* text prints 'in sedi sponerent' for 'in se disponerent', a rare slip.

However when he realised that he was in fact the obstacle to moving on to the Holy Sepulchre, he was deeply upset, and walked barefoot from Ma'arrat-an-Nu'man to Kafartab. After four days there the princes came together yet again and embarked on the same arguments. Count Raymond said:

'Brothers and lords, you have renounced all your possessions and put yourselves last for love of God. Explain to me how I can be reconciled to Bohemond, as he wishes, without perjury. Alternatively, if that is not possible, explain whether I should perjure myself to keep him happy.'[20]

Nobody was willing to take a view on this proposition. All spoke in favour of reconciliation without any suggestions as to how it was to be achieved, went their separate ways and returned to Antioch.[21]

Chapter IX: how the Count of Normandy left Bohemond and went with Count Raymond

The King of Shaizar is terrified of our forces.

The Count of Normandy remained with Raymond along with his men, knowing quite clearly that justice was on the latter's side. The two counts drew up their forces and made for Shaizar;[22] the ruler of Shaizar had more than once sent word to the Count at Ma'arrat-an-Nu'man and Kafartab that he wanted to make peace with him and place his forces at the Count's disposal. So they made their way there believing him and set up camp near the city. However, when the king saw the Frankish columns actually next to his city, he was utterly horrified and dismayed; he gave orders that nobody should do business with them. The following day he sent two of his counts who were to show them how to ford the river and take them somewhere where they could forage. (The river was called the Farfar). They led the Christians to a highly suitable valley, overflowing with supplies. It was guarded by a very well-fortified castle.[23] Beneath its gaze they found some 15,000 animals grazing in the fertile valley, and rounded them all up. When they decided to besiege the citadel, its garrison surrendered and made a pact with the counts setting out an agreement in perpetuity: they promised by their faith and on their law that they would never again harm Christian pilgrims and would offer them shelter and the chance to buy food just as they would men of their own race. They remained there for five days. On the sixth they loaded the camels and pack animals with corn, flour, barley and cheese and other things to eat. They left the city, in good

---

[20] Raymond's pithy summary of the situation marks a change in approach by Robert. Previously he has been at pains to emphasise that the Emperor broke his promise and that the Crusaders' oaths are therefore void; it is surprising not to see the argument reiterated here. *GF* 80 does not put the issue so starkly.

[21] Robert's words suggest bitter experience of such meetings.

[22] Classical Larissa; on the Orontes.

[23] Masyaf.

heart, and came to a castle of Arabs. The commander of the castle took the sensible approach: he came out to meet Count Raymond and made peace with him.

Chapter X: the city of Caphalia

Here the inhabitants of Caphalia flee in haste from our swords.

They then reached a city built in an attractive and broad valley which was well fortified with walls and towers and said to be full to overflowing of all kinds of fruit. The inhabitants knew it as Caphalia.[24] Its inhabitants were terrified when they heard the sound of the Franks: they left their own homes and fled elsewhere. The fate which had overtaken Antioch and Ma'arrat-an-Nu'man scared them out of their wits and spurred the inhabitants to flee. So when our men came to put up their tents around it and besiege it on all sides, they were surprised that nobody came out to them from such a large city; nobody appeared on the tall towers or the battlements on the walls; inside was deep silence, and the sound of not one voice could be heard. So they sent scouts who were to find out exactly what was going on and report back. The scouts set out. As they approached near the gate they found a door left open, but saw nobody inside. Protecting their faces with their shields they went in through the gates with some hesitation, but found inside no man, woman nor beast of any kind. They discovered that the town had been left in good order: the granaries were full of wheat, the presses overflowing with wine and chests filled with nuts, cheese and flour. So they hurried back to the Counts of Normandy and Toulouse and told them what they had found out. There was no point setting up the tents, since God gave them the benefit of the work of others with no need for them to take up arms or fight. And so came to pass what is told in the proverbs of Solomon: *the wealth of the sinner is laid up for the just.*[25] They found gardens full of vegetables, beans and other pulses which were reaching their peak already. They rested there three days. Having chosen guards to watch over the city, they climbed a steep range of mountains and came down into a valley which was pleasant and full to bursting with all kinds of fruit and produce; they stayed there 15 days. Near the valley was a castle full of Saracens.[26] One day when our men went up close, the Saracens flung down onto them from the walls large numbers of sheep and a lot of other animals in the belief that all our men were after was supplies.[27] Our men were delighted to get them and took them to the tents. The next day they struck their tents and shelters and set off to camp outside the castle; but when they got there they found it devoid of people. All of them had fled overnight, but had left behind an abundance of fruit and produce, milk and honey.[28]

---

[24] Probably Robert's garbled rendering of Rafaniyah.

[25] *Proverbs* XIII.22.

[26] Hisn al-Akrad.

[27] Gilo VIII.356–7, a detail inserted in the narrative of the *GF*.

[28] Cf. *Exodus* III.8, XIII.5; *Deuteronomy* VI.3; numerous references.

Our men celebrated there the Purification of the Blessed Virgin Mother of God, exalting God for granting them so many good things.[29]

Chapter XI: the gifts which the kings of Hamah and Tripoli sent our men

The King of Hamah sends splendid weapons; many goods are sent as a gift from the city of Tripoli.

The King of the city of Hamah[30] sent his ambassadors to find the [two] Counts while they were there and asked them for peace, sending highly desirable gifts, horses and gold. He sent a golden bow, precious robes and glittering weapons. Our men accepted them all, but did not send back any clear response. The King of Tripoli was equally anxious. He sent ten horses and four mules, asking for peace in the same way. Although they accepted the gifts, our men sent back word that they would never make peace with him unless he became a Christian. (In point of fact the Count of St Gilles was very keen to get his lands, which were excellent, and his kingdom which enjoyed a higher reputation than the rest.)[31]

Chapter XII: the impregnable castle called Arqah

The castle of Arqah was attacked on all sides.

After 14 days they left the welcoming valley on the fifteenth day and made their way to a very ancient castle known as Arqah. Although it was called a castle, it could stand comparison with famous cities by virtue of its position, the extent of its ramparts and the height of its towers. A large number of people had congregated in it because of its strength; they had no fear of any weapons, enemies or siege machines. Our men quickly surrounded it and attacked it promptly, but the garrison beat them off effectively. They attacked [the castle] repeatedly with every kind of weapon and throwing machine, without success; in fact they lost more than they gained. Eventually 14 of our soldiers, not knowing what to do with their enforced leisure, marched out towards Tripoli. They encountered 60 Turks driving along a large number of captives and more than 1,500 animals which they had captured. When our men saw this they attacked despite their small number, raising their hands towards Heaven and calling upon the Lord of Hosts. With the help of God, succour of armies, they were victorious. They killed six of the Turks, took their horses and returned to the camp exulting with immense booty. The whole army

---

[29] 2 February.

[30] Robert uses the Crusaders' name of Camela, She-Camel.

[31] *GF* 83 is kinder about Raymond's motives, suggesting that he wanted the Emir baptised.

was absolutely delighted that such small numbers could win such a victory and take so much booty.

Chapter XIII: about the city known as Tortosa, which was found deserted

A few men slaughtered and despoiled many.

Others saw this, and some left Raymond's army inflamed with the desire to do what was right. At their head were Raymond Pilet and Raymond the viscount of Turenne.[32] They raised their standards high and rode towards the city known as Tortosa.[33] When they arrived they attacked it with determination, but without success, for a whole day. At nightfall they withdrew to a corner and spent the night tending immense flaming pyres to make it look as if the whole of the Christian army was stationed behind them. The inhabitants of the city were desperately scared by the billowing flames, believing that all of our men were there; they fled abruptly, leaving behind a city full of supplies. (This city never experiences any shortages, sited as it is on the best harbour of the coast.) The following day our men found it entirely empty when they came to attack it. They praised God very sincerely, entered it and remained there throughout the siege of Arqah.

Chapter XIV: the city of Maraclea

The city of Tortosa is also captured, vastly precious. The city of Maraclea[34] is not far off.

Another city not far off is known as Maraclea.[35] Its prince entered peace talks with them and took their banners into the city. How amazing are the strength and power of God! Whilst the princes whose role it was to rule and support their people were far off, God put in motion the defeat of kings through a few humble individuals. This was so that human arrogance could not say: 'It was we who conquered Antioch and other cities, and we who were victorious in so many great battles'. It is beyond doubt that they would never have defeated their enemies if He who rules rulers had not been at their side.[36] When Godfrey, Duke of Dukes and soldier amongst soldiers, heard about the happy turn of events and the impressive trophies

---

[32] Raymond, Viscount of Turenne. In the *GF* he carries out raids at 83–4, 87–8, followed in most of the derivatives (PT 129, 134–5; BB 91, 97; OV V.146, 158. PT 78 adds his presence in Raymond's garrison. His presence is independently attested in charters from Tulle: see Riley-Smith, *First Crusaders*, 220.

[33] Modern Tartus.

[34] Eraclea in the *Recueil* text.

[35] Modern Maraqiyah.

[36] Cf. *Proverbs* VIII.15: *by me princes rule.*

from the battle, he was sparked with a desire for victory. He, the Count of Flanders and Bohemond finally struck camp in Antioch and moved on to the city of Laodicea.[37]

Chapter XV: how Bohemond split off from our men

Here Bohemond split off from them and the main army of God. He had inherited the highest principles from his French father; but they were tainted by elements from his Apulian mother.[38]

Chapter XVI: the Duke and the Count head for the city of Jabala

Duke Godfrey, strong in faith as ever, and the Consul of Flanders, whose sword never fails, besiege the city of Jabala to subdue it.

The Duke and the Count of Flanders then led their forces towards the city known as Jabala and set up a siege round it. At that point a messenger arrived from the Count of St Gilles to say that the Turks were preparing to attack him and that the battle would be appallingly hard. So he sent an urgent message to the Duke and the Count of Flanders asking them to come as quickly as possible to the battle and give him help. When the Duke heard this he sent to the prince of the city offering peace, which the latter had been seeking for some time. With peace concluded and the gifts marking it received, they flew to the battle which was expected. They arrived at the siege around the above-mentioned castle and set up camp on the other bank of the river which flowed past it.

Chapter XVII: battle at Tripoli

Now they make their way to Tripoli, which they deluge in blood. Here they enter a pleasant valley to find something to eat, and happen on much-needed gifts of food.

When the Duke realised that he was wasting his time, he led his forces to Tripoli and found the enemy all ready and waiting. They faced up to our men with bows ready strung; but our men threw their shields in front of them and took as little notice of bows and arrows as if they were straws. Battle was joined, but not on equal terms. The enemy followed their normal tactic of turning tail once they had

---

[37] Modern Latakieh.

[38] An extraordinary comment which sits well with Robert's consistent praise of the French but oddly in a text supporting Bohemond's crusading appeal. The chapter is unusually short and it is tempting to wonder – in the absence however of any manuscript evidence – whether it is some kind of marginal comment which became incorporated into the main text.

shot off their arrows; our men had positioned themselves blocking the way between them and the city. Why waste words? So much human blood was spilt there that the water supplies of the city flowed red and their cisterns were full of it. The leaders of the city died there; those who were not killed were dismayed at the contamination of the cisterns. After all this slaughter our men were less than happy because they had taken no valuable spoils other than weapons and clothes. They ranged through the above-mentioned valley, Desen,[39] taking innumerable sheep, cows, donkeys and various kinds of animal and also plundering three thousand camels. They were completely mystified as to where such a large number of animals could have come from, since they had been in the valley for 15 days.

They returned to camp with an enormous amount of booty.

There were no problems of shortages in that siege because ships visited a port nearby and brought all the supplies needed. They celebrated our Lord's Easter there on 10 April. The siege lasted one day short of three months.

Chapter XVIII: the death of Anselm of Ribemont and various distinguished men

The death of our men puts an end to the siege because a number of good men died.

Anselm of Ribemont died at that siege.[40] He was a highly admirable man and outstanding soldier amongst his peers; whilst alive he did many things worth relating, above all the fact that he was a tireless defender of the monastery of Aix in all circumstances.[41] Another who died there was Pons Balazun, whose temples were smashed in by a stone flung from a catapult.[42] William the Picard[43] and Warren of Petra Mora died,[44] the first from a missile, the second from an arrow. Because of these and others our men gave up the siege, because the castle was impregnable and had no fear of being taken by any enemy attack.

---

[39] El-Bukeia.

[40] Anselm II of Ribemont, Castellan of Bouchain and Lord of Ostrevant and Valenciennes in northern France. An important figure on the Crusade, whose letters to Archbishop Manasses of Reims are a key piece of eyewitness evidence for events (*Kreuzzugsbriefe* 144–6, 156–60). His death is referred to in most sources (*GF* 85, PT 131, RA 108–9, RC 680–1; AA adds further details (315, 424, 452, 456).

[41] See Hagenmeyer, introduction to *Kreuzzugsbriefe*, 63.

[42] According to RA, Pons Balazun was his co-author until his death here (35, 75, 107); PT and Gilo also mention him (131; IX.82–3) although he is not in the *GF*, BB or GN.

[43] We know nothing of William the Picard beyond this reference nor why he should have been singled out for mention. His death is in *GF* 85, followed by PT 131, BB 93, Gilo IX.84.

[44] We know nothing of Warren of Petra Mora. He is mentioned only here and in Gilo IX.85.

Chapter XIX: the treaty with the king of Tripoli, and his gifts

Peace is formally agreed with the king of Tripoli. Now they take the fastest route to the city.

They struck their tents and headed for Tripoli, where they agreed peace terms long sought by the King and citizens. Having clasped right hands, the lords trusted them to a point where they went into the city right up to the King's palace. For his part the King freed 300 of our pilgrims from captivity and handed them over to the princes so that they would have more faith in his intentions to abide by the peace terms. He handed over 15,000 bezants and 15 horses with excellent equipment, and sent good quality supplies to the whole army which ensured that they had absolutely everything they needed. He furthermore reached agreement with them and swore that, if they could take Jerusalem and win the battle which the Emir of Babylon was threatening to fight, he would become a Christian and submit to the King of Jerusalem.[45] They spent three days at Tripoli. The lords and soldiers saw that the harvest for that year would soon begin; they agreed without exception to make the journey to Jerusalem and take the most direct route with no diversions. It was 4 May when they left Tripoli and, climbing up over some steep mountains, came to a castle known as Batrun. The next day they arrived at a city called Jebail, around which they were unable to find any water to quench their desperate thirst. (It was summer and the horses and all the large number of men were thirsty.) The next day they came to the River Nahr Ibrahim,[46] where they stayed overnight and drank their fill. The following night was that of the Lord's Ascension.[47] They made their own ascent, climbing a mountain on a very narrow path on which they were convinced they would meet the enemy. However, God, who was their only guide (and *there was no strange god with him*),[48] ensured that they crossed unharmed. They came thus to the city of Beirut on the coast; from there to another city called Sidon; and then to a further one, Tyre; then to Acre; from Acre to the castle called Haifa; and thus to Caesarea.

---

[45] A slip by Robert: as there was not yet a Christian King of Jerusalem (note he does not use the term 'Advocate') the Emir would find it hard to submit to him. In Book IX he refers consistently to Godfrey as 'King'.

[46] Robert renders these names in a slightly garbled form as Betelon, Zebaris and the River Braim. Jebail is the classical Byblos.

[47] 19 May. Note the symbolism of the Ascension.

[48] *Deuteronomy* XXXII.2.

Chapter XX: about Caesarea[49]

The city of Caesarea lies next to the sea.

Caesarea is a famous city of Palestine, reputed to be the home of the Apostle Philip: the house is still shown today, as is the bedroom of his daughters, who had the gift of prophecy.[50] The city is on the coast and used to be called Pyrgos, in other words the Tower of Strato. It was made more magnificent and beautiful by King Herod, who improved the sea defences; and it was named Caesarea in honour of Augustus Caesar. Herod constructed a temple to him in white marble: it was there that his nephew Herod was struck by the angel,[51] Cornelius the centurion was baptised[52] and Agabus the prophet was tied by Paul's belt.[53] Our men pitched their tents next to this city and celebrated the Lord's holy feast of Whitsun there.[54]

Chapter XXI: about the city of Ramla

They came next to the city of Ramla, which the Saracens had deserted in fear of them. Near this city could be found the famous church of the martyr St George, where his most sacred body was buried and which was on the very spot where he had undergone martyrdom for the name of Christ.[55] The Christian soldiers there chose a bishop because they reverenced the soldier of Christ; established the bishop there once chosen; and once established gave him a tenth of all their wealth.[56] And it was fitting that the undefeated soldier George, standard-bearer of their army, should be honoured by them in this way.[57] The Bishop accordingly

---

[49] A Robert addition in neither *GF* nor Gilo.

[50] *Acts* XXI.8–9.

[51] *Acts* XII. 19, 23.

[52] *Acts* X.1–33.

[53] *Acts* XXI.10–11.

[54] 29 May.

[55] As Robert says, this was one of the major churches in the Holy Land.

[56] Robert of Rouen, chaplain to Robert of Normandy. His election is referred to in *GF* 87 and RA 136. See Runciman, *History*, vol.I, 277; Hamilton, 11.

[57] Robert again alludes to the help given by the celestial forces.

remained there with his men, well supplied with gold and silver, horses and animals. The Christian army pushed on to the holy city of Jerusalem in the strength of the name of Him who lay there dead and rose again on the third day, whose power is equal with the Father and the Holy Spirit and whose glory is without end. Amen.

Here finishes the eighth book.

Book IX

The fall of Jerusalem and the battle of Ascalon

June 1099–August 1099

Chapter 1: how our men arrived at Jerusalem

O good King Jesus Christ, how your people wept when they saw Jerusalem near!

O good Jesus, when your forces saw the walls of the earthly Jerusalem, what rivers of tears poured from their eyes! They soon saluted your Holy Sepulchre by praying and bowing their bodies towards it; and they adored You who lay in the Sepulchre now seated at the right hand of the Father and who will come to judge all humans. Most certainly then did you take away hearts of stone from all and bring hearts of flesh, and put your Holy Spirit in their midst.[1] And so they fought against Your enemies who were there and had been for a long time, encouraging you to come to their help. They fought better with their tears than by throwing darts, because although they flowed abundantly over the earth they also rose up into Heaven before you, their Defender. Standing up after they had prayed, they hurried toward the royal city. Inside they found the enemies of the Eternal King, and set up camp around them as follows.

Chapter II: how the siege of Jerusalem was organised

On the northern side were the camps of the two Counts of Normandy and Flanders, next to the church of St Stephen the Protomartyr where he was stoned by the Jews. On the west were Duke Godfrey and Tancred. On the south was the Count of St Gilles, on Mount Zion around the Church of the Blessed Virgin Mary Mother of God where the Lord dined with his disciples. Once they had set up their tents around Jerusalem and whilst they were recovering from the fatigue of the journey and preparing siege machines to take the city, Raymond Pilet and Raymond of Turenne and several others left the camp to reconnoitre the surrounding region and ensure that the enemy did not come upon them unawares and catch them unprepared. They happened on 200 Arabs, fought them, overcame them, killed several and gained 30 horses.

---

[1] *Ezekiel XI.19: I will take the stony heart out of their flesh, and will give them an heart of flesh.*

Chapter III: the day of the first attack on Jerusalem

On the Monday of the second week in June, 10 June,[2] the Christians attacked Jerusalem. They did not get the upper hand that day, but their work did not go to waste because they knocked down the defences in front of the wall so effectively that they got one scaling ladder up against the main wall: had they had enough ladders that first effort would have been their last. Those who went up the ladder fought the enemy for a long time with darts and swords. In the fight many of our men died, but far more of theirs. The coming of evening, not a good time for fighting, brought an end and nightfall brought rest to both sides. That failure had serious and protracted consequences for our men, because for ten days they were unable to find any bread to eat until their ships came fully laden to the port of Jaffa. They also suffered terrible pain from thirst because the Pool of Siloam (which rises at the foot of Mount Zion) could hardly serve even the needs of humans; that meant that the horses and other animals had to be taken six miles to water and only under a large armed guard. So water was very expensive in the army and fetched a high price.

Chapter IV: how the ships which had arrived at the port of Jaffa were guarded, the outcome of the battle and the death of Achard of Montmerle

Here thirst and hunger afflict our men terribly. If Achard had not gone out in front, he would not have died in this way.

So they debated what they should do and chose soldiers to go to the ships and protect them from enemy attack. At dawn, therefore, 100 soldiers left the army of the Count of St Gilles: in particular Raymond Pilet (who was well used to all military vicissitudes and disinclined to shirk) and along with him another Raymond, of Turenne, Achard of Montmerle[3] and William of Sabran.[4] They went to the seaport ready to fight. On the way 30 of them split off from the others to scout the lie of the land and see whether they could find any enemies. After they had gone a little way they saw 700 Turks and Arabs in the distance; despite their

---

[2] Hagenmeyer suggests 13 June. Robert agrees with *GF* 88 on the day of the week but the date seems wrong.

[3] Achard of Montmerle was from Burgundy. His departure on Crusade is mentioned by *GF* 5; his death is in *GF* and derivatives (*GF* 88–9, PT 135, BB 98–9, GN 273, Gilo IX.193–205). The *Gran Conquista de Ultramar* gives an alternative version of the beginning of the Crusade in which he plays a leading role, starting the Crusade as revenge for a slap given by the doorman of the Temple when he was there on pilgrimage: although this has been ascribed to the Occitan version, the evidence suggests no more than that it was a variant thirteenth-century tradition: see Introduction to the *Canso d'Antioca* 41–2 for discussion and references.

[4] William I of Sabran near Arles. He is mentioned in the *GF* and derivatives (*GF* 88, PT 78 and 135, BB 98; also RA 141).

small numbers they attacked them immediately. However, the enemy were so numerous that our small number of men could not resist them. Even so our men consigned those who had borne the brunt of their first attack to eternal death. After this attack they had thought they would be able to wheel round but, surrounded by the multitude, were unable to do as they had intended. Achard met his end there, a brave and distinguished fighter, as did some of the footsoldiers. Before battle could begin, a messenger raced up to Pilet on a swift horse to tell him that Arabs and Turks had attacked our men. When Pilet heard this, he immediately spurred on his horse but arrived too late. In the mean time Achard had died, but before meeting his end had paid for his life with a great deal of blood and for his death by the death of large numbers. When the enemy saw our men in the distance,

> As doves flee the hawk with trembling wing[5]

just so,

> They flee, and turned their backs to our men.

Our men followed them and killed many. They kept one alive who was to describe to them the cunning plans of the Turks and give the Christians advance warning of the fiendish tricks they were preparing. They also kept 103 horses, which they sent back to the camp, and went on themselves to the ships to carry out their instructions. The ships, laden with food, put an end to their hunger but could do nothing to extinguish their desperate thirst.

Chapter V: the thirst the Christians suffered[6]

Their thirst was so great during the siege that they dug in the earth and put damp clods on their mouths, and licked damp marble.[7] They stitched together the fresh hides of oxen and buffaloes and other animals; when they took the horses down to water the soldiers went, armed, as much as six miles. They filled the skins with water, took them back to the camp and drank the foul water from them. Several starved themselves as much as they could bear because fasting brought some relief from thirst. Who would believe that hunger would be of some use and that suffering would expel suffering?

---

[5] Ovid, *Metamorphoses*, V.605.

[6] Reminiscent of the description of thirst at Xerigordon in I.8: the Crusaders are faced with thirst at the end as at the beginning. Symbolism of the thirst for God, the living fountain? Compare the description at Lucan IV.308–10: 'si mollius arvum/prodidit umorem, pingues manus utraque glaebas/exprimit ora super' ('wherever they found a patch of soft soil they snatched handfuls of it and squeezed the moisture into their mouths', Graves' translation).

[7] Gilo IX.231–4, added to the description of the *GF*.

Chapter VI: how Jerusalem was stormed and taken

Here two towers of wood are built which look down on the top of the walls. The Christians swarm up ladders and climb the heights of the wall.

Meanwhile the lords had wooden beams brought from a considerable distance to make towers and machines to take the city. Once the materials arrived Godfrey, Duke of Dukes, built his tower and ordered it to be moved to the plain on the east of the city. The respected Count of St Gilles likewise built a similar castle and set it up to the south of the city. On the Thursday our men celebrated by fasting and distributed alms to the poor.[8] On the Friday, by the serenely glowing light of dawn, the famous warriors climbed the towers and put the ladders up to the walls.[9] The false inhabitants of the distinguished city were amazed and trembled to see themselves surrounded by such a strong force. They saw all too clearly that their last day had come and death was hanging over their heads; they began to resist ferociously and to fight like men who knew death was imminent.

Chapter VII: about Duke Godfrey and his brothers, and the fall of the city

Duke Godfrey was up high in his tower, not as a soldier but as an archer; the Lord guided his hand in the battle and his fingers in the combat so that the arrows he fired pierced right through the chest of the enemies, in at one side and out at the other. His brothers Eustace and Baldwin[10] were next to him like two lions next to a third; they withstood the hard blows of darts and stones and paid them back with fourfold interest.[11] Who could rise to telling the deeds of all when the eloquence of all those who are philosophers today would not suffice in such praises? While this battle was taking place on top of the walls, there was a procession around them in which the crosses and relics and holy altars were carried. They rained blows on each other the whole day. When the hour at which the Redeemer of all submitted to death on the cross was near, a certain soldier called Lethold, from the Duke's garrison, was the first to leap onto the wall.[12] He was followed by Wicher, the one

---

[8] 14 July.

[9] 15 July.

[10] Eustace III, Count of Boulogne, elder brother of Godfrey, well attested on Crusade: for references see Riley-Smith, *First Crusaders*, 205. Baldwin was Godfrey's younger brother. He is not elsewhere attested at the siege of Jerusalem, being in the County of Edessa which he had conquered at the time: error by Robert or deliberate legitimation of the next King of Jerusalem?

[11] Compare Gilo IX.274–5: 'stans comes Eustachius in castro cum Godefrido/Susceptos ictus reddit cum fenore duro' ('Count Eustace stood firm on the siege castle with Count Godfrey and paid back the blows he received with hard interest', Grocock and Siberry's translation).

[12] Lethold of Tournai in Flanders. His entry to Jerusalem is recorded in the *GF* 91 and derivatives, e.g. PT 140, BB 102; he is also referred to in RC 693, AA 472, 477, but not in RA.

who knocked flat and killed a lion with his bare hands.[13] The Duke immediately followed his soldiers, and all the other soldiers followed their Duke. Bows and arrows were now discarded and glittering swords drawn. At this the enemy deserted the wall immediately and leapt to the ground; the soldiers of Christ hastened in pursuit shouting at the tops of their voices. When Count Raymond heard them whilst in the process of moving his camp nearer the wall, he immediately realised that the Franks were in the city. He told his soldiers:

'What are we standing here for? We are wasting our time doing this. The Franks are taking the city and making it ring with loud voices and blows.'

Then he made his way swiftly with his men to the gate near the Tower of David, and called up to those in the citadel to open it to him.

Chapter VIII: the Tower of David is surrendered to the Count of St Gilles

Nothing like this happened in other battles. The Temple of Solomon is foul with the blood of Turks and severed limbs float on the paving.

As soon as the Emir guarding the tower realised who it was, he opened the door to him, and threw himself and his men on Raymond's good faith seeking protection from death. The Count replied that he would do no such thing unless the tower was surrendered to him. The Emir handed it over with alacrity, upon which the Count gave him all the surety he sought. Meanwhile Duke Godfrey had no desire for the citadel, the palace, gold, or silver or any kind of spoils. Instead at the head of his Franks he was desperate to make the enemy pay for the blood of the servants of God which had been spilt around Jerusalem, and wanted revenge for the insults they had heaped on the pilgrims. In no battle had he ever found so many opportunities to kill, not even on the bridge at Antioch where he had cut in half the Turkish giant.[14] Now he and Wicher (who had cut the lion in half) and many thousands of chosen soldiers slashed human bodies from head to abdomen, to the right and the left and both sides. Not one of our men hung back or showed any fear; there was no resistance; on the contrary each fled as best he could – though in fact nobody could flee because the crowd, confused by its own movement, became its own worst obstacle. Those who did manage to get away from such butchery and slaughter made their way to the Temple of Solomon and defended themselves there for a long day. When day seemed to be drawing to a close, our men – worried that the sun would set – found a new rush of courage, broke into the temple and put its occupants to a wretched death. So much human blood was spilt there that the bodies of the slain were revolving on the floor on a current of blood; arms and hands which had been cut off floated on the blood and found their way to other

---

[13] Probably Wicher the German, Ministerialis of Fulda. Gilo IX.289–90 also refers to the legend about the lion. This is picked up in ms G of BB (92, n.8). Wicher is referred to in other texts e.g. AA (507, 522, 526, 531, 533) and BB (47, 50).

[14] Recounted in IV.20.

bodies so that nobody could work out which body the arm had come from which was attached to another headless body. Even the soldiers who were carrying out the massacre could hardly bear the vapours rising from the warm blood.[15] Once they had finished this indescribable slaughter their spirits became a little gentler; they kept some of the young people, male and female, alive to serve them. They ran through streets and squares, plundering whatever they found; and each kept what he plundered. Jerusalem was full of earthly good things, and nobody lacked any delight other than spiritual.[16] She made her sons, come from afar,[17] so rich that none remained poor in her.

Chapter IX: the great devotion with which they approached the Lord's Sepulchre

With peace achieved and the slaughter of the wretched [inhabitants] complete, the people run to bow to the beautiful Sepulchre of the Lord. Those who climb up in the temple plunge shamefully down.

Made thus immensely rich, they made their way joyfully to the Lord's Holy Sepulchre. They thanked Him who was buried there, and laid down their mortal sins. On that day the Sepulchre of the Lord was glorious as the prophet foretold;[18] all approached it not on foot but on their elbows and knees and flooded the floor with tears raining down. It was there that the humility of the Redeemer was triumphant and the pomp of the Deceiver soundly defeated. The people of Christ humbly worshipped Christ the humble, and the old Lucifer who wanted to rival the creator was shamed.[19] Once they had completed this act of solemn devotion, they returned to their houses which the Lord had destined for them; surrendering to the needs of nature they gave their exhausted bodies food and rest in sleep.

The following day, when dawn rose above the horizon, they armed themselves and ran to the Temple of Solomon to ensure that no place was left from where they could be ambushed, aiming to exterminate those who had climbed up to the pinnacles of the temple. A very large number of Turks had in fact climbed up there, and would have been all too grateful to flee if they could have grown wings and flown away; funnily enough nature failed to provide wings, giving instead a miserable exit from their wretched lives.[20] When they saw our men running to

---

[15] This horrendous little vignette is also in Gilo IX.317–22. The remainder of Chapter VIII and Chapters IX and X follow Gilo's text (IX.334–71) and not the *GF*. One detail in both Gilo and the *GF* but omitted by Robert is that Tancred and Gaston of Béarn gave their banners as protection. RA and *GF* give broadly similar accounts: Robert as ever piles on the horror.

[16] The frequent sentiment about poor Crusaders becoming rich is given literal truth.

[17] *Isaiah LX.4: thy sons shall come from afar.*

[18] *Isaiah XI.10: his rest shall be glorious.*

[19] *Isaiah XIV.12–17.*

[20] Rather heavy-handed humour.

attack them high up in the temple they came to meet the drawn swords, preferring to die quickly rather than suffer a long-drawn out death under the yoke of slavery. They flung themselves to the ground, finding death on the soil which provides all things needed to sustain life. The Christians did not kill everyone, but kept many to serve them. It was then decided that the city should be cleaned. The Saracens who remained alive were ordered to drag the dead outside and cleanse the city immediately of all the filth created by such a large-scale massacre. They obeyed promptly, weeping as they dragged the corpses outside, and built huge pyres outside the walls like fortifications or defensive structures. They collected up the severed limbs in baskets and took them outside the city; and washed the paving of the temples and houses clean of blood with water.

Chapter X: Godfrey is elected King by all

The law is observed as the Duke is consecrated King.[21]

Having thus exterminated all the enemies from the city known as the City of Peace, it became necessary to debate the question of who should be King; one individual needed to be chosen from amongst them all to rule such a great city and population. Duke Godfrey was chosen by unanimous agreement of all in a clear vote and with general agreement, on the eighth day after the taking of the city. This proved to be a good decision by all, because Godfrey comported himself so well in his regal role that he added to the dignity of royalty rather than royalty adding dignity to him. It was not a case of the honour adding to his reputation; the worth of the honour was greater because of him He was so outstanding and effective in his royal status that – if it were possible to set up all the kings of the earth alongside him – all would judge him to be the foremost in terms of his merit and integrity as a knight, his elegant bearing and the clear signs of his noble way of life.[22]

---

[21] Robert is clear in this chapter and the rest of his work that Godfrey was elected as King. Godfrey in fact took the title of Advocate of the Holy Sepulchre; his successor Baldwin was known as King (Runciman, *History*, vol.II, 72). The shift in status seems to have taken place in the first few years of the Latin Kingdom, if indeed the title of Advocate was ever more than a convenient fiction: see 'The title of Godfrey of Bouillon', J. Riley-Smith, *BIHR* 52 (1979), 83–6. *GF* 92 calls Godfrey 'principem'. Gilo by contrast stresses his role as King, using 'rex' and its derivatives four times in three lines (IX.368–70).

[22] Gilo's text stops here.

Chapter XI: the election of the Patriarch

The King, people and clergy choose a Patriarch.

It was also appropriate that, having properly elected a proper temporal ruler, they should choose a spiritual ruler in the same way. So they elected a cleric called Arnulf who was well versed in divine and human law.[23] He was *instructed unto the kingdom of heaven*, namely in the Holy Church, well able to bring forth *out of his treasure things new and old.*[24] His election was on the feast of St Peter ad Vincula, a feast day highly appropriate to a city in chains and which had long been tied up in diabolical bonds until it was freed and absolved from on the same day as that on which it acquired a suitable priest.[25] Let us therefore thank God, the Redeemer and Liberator of his people, who allowed Jerusalem to be so often destroyed and enslaved, to be rebuilt so many times after being destroyed, and freed it from slavery by his wonderful power. And so, as I have explained, the Frankish people penetrated the lands of the East by one battle after another, and with the help of Divine Grace cleansed it of the filth of the Gentiles by which Jerusalem had been soiled for some 40 years.[26] With a priest canonically consecrated and a king crowned in the city, the famous name of the Franks was known throughout the Orient and the all-embracing power of Jesus Christ, who had been crucified there, shone even in the eyes of the infidels.

Chapter XII: about the citizens of Nablus who surrendered to the power of the King

Come and join our men, citizens of Nablus.

When the ordination of the priest and the king had been publicly celebrated with solemn rejoicing, in the splendour of grace shining forth, envoys came to King Godfrey from the city of Nablus,[27] mandated by the citizens to ask him to send some of his men to them and take both citizens and city under his rule and into his dominion; they wanted his empire to extend to them, preferring his government to that of others. (Nablus is a city of Caria, a province of Asia.) The King agreed and

---

[23] Arnulf Malecouronne of Chocques. Chaplain of Robert of Normandy (Riley-Smith, *First Crusaders*, 174), he was elected Patriarch but had a colourful career: see Runciman, *History*, vol.I, 290, 294. It is interesting that Robert should speak in such glowing terms of a cleric criticised by some.

[24] *Gospel of Matthew* XIII.52.

[25] 1 August, the anniversary of Adhemar's death. Robert compares Arnulf explicitly with St Peter and implicitly with Adhemar; a link also to the Papacy.

[26] In fact 400: it fell to the Moslems in 628. A further error by Robert, presumably from misreading his source (which here is neither *GF* nor Gilo's source).

[27] Classical Neapolis, the name used by Robert.

sent them his brother Eustace and Tancred with a large band of knights and footsoldiers: the citizens received them with a great show of reverence and handed themselves and their city over into his power.

Chapter XIII: about Clement, the Emir of Babylon, who assembled a large army to fight the Christians

The Emir of Babylon, opposed to everything good, wanted to destroy the Sepulchre of the Lord, and ranted against it to the arrogant people.

As these things were going on, that writhing serpent and slippery eel (who is always bitterly envious when he sees the faithful happy) was wretched when he saw the name of Christianity so magnified and the rule of the restored city of Jerusalem so extended.[28] So in his venom he stirred up the Emir of Babylon, Clement (better described as the Demented), against them and along with him the whole of the Orient.[29] The root of all malice hoped thus to destroy all the Christians and their city and to eradicate all memory of the Sepulchre of the Lord. However, just as human thoughts are vain, so their power vanishes. Clemens gathered together as many men as he could and came to the city of Ascalon in pompous array. When they arrived a messenger hastened to the king to tell him the situation. Godfrey did not delay but sent word to those he had sent out, asking them to hurry to the battle looming with the Emir of Babylon. The latter was now at Ascalon with an innumerable force, getting ready to lay siege to Jerusalem. When Eustace, Tancred and the other warriors heard this, they explained to the citizens of Nablus that a fight was imminent, bade them farewell and left them rejoicing and on friendly terms. Our men were keen to take on the Turks: they went up over the mountains and without sleeping or taking rest throughout the whole day and night reached Caesarea. The following day they made their way along the coast and came to a city known as Ramla, where they found many Arabs ahead of the main army. They pursued them vigorously and captured several, who told them the truth about the whole military situation. When they realised the situation they were in, they immediately sent messengers mounted on swift horses to the King

---

[28] The serpent is the devil: *Revelations* XX.2. Robert explicitly identifies the Saracens with diabolical forces and opposes Jerusalem to Babylon.

[29] Historically the ninth Fatimid Caliph of Egypt, al-Musta'li (1094–1101); his vizier was al-Afdal Shahanshah, the Lavedalius of Fulcher of Chartres (I.31). Babylon describes Cairo. Robert embroiders his role considerably and plays on the pun 'clemens – demens'. The name 'Clemens' is unique in the sources and is unusual for Saracen leaders, who tend to have fanciful names such as Falsaron or Corsablis (respectively *Roland* 879, 1213; 885, 1235). It is interesting that the Antipope between 1080 and 1100, Wibert of Ravenna, took the title of Clement III; as a Benedictine was Robert particularly keen to denigrate a Pope set up in opposition to the Cluniac Urban II? See discussion at Epp, 173. If so, it is appropriate that Clemens should be Emir of Babylon, abode of the Antichrist; and appropriate too that Robert should ascribe his machinations so pointedly to the Devil.

asking him to tell his troops the situation without delay and march to fight at Ascalon.[30]

Chapter XIV: about Ascalon, which had always been at loggerheads with Jerusalem

Nothing good was to be found in Ascalon.

Ascalon is a famous city in Palestine, 25 miles from Jerusalem. It was built by the Philistines, who called it Ascalon after Celon (the nephew of Cham and the son of Mizraim).[31] It was always the rival of Jerusalem and, despite its nearness, never wanted to engage in friendly relations.[32] That was where the Emir of Babylon was when the messengers arrived to see the King and relay the message described above. When the King heard it, he ordered the Patriarch to be called and accepted his advice: that it should be announced throughout the city that all should gather at church at crack of dawn the following day; that all should take communion of the Body of Our Lord after hearing Holy Mass, and that they should ride out to fight at Ascalon. The news did not bother those who heard it. However the following night seemed slower and longer to them than others.

Chapter XV: the Christians went to church hoping for safety in battle

> When dawn first showed its head in the morning,
> The sound of the bell called all to Mass.
> Mass was said and the people joined with God.
> Receiving a blessing and the sacred gifts,
> The people left the church and ran to take up arms,
> And marched despite their fasting against their enemy.
> Once the king left the city the trumpets, brass instruments and horns
> All sounded at once; their sound
> Made all the mountains and valleys around echo
> And struck terror into their enemies.[33]

And so the Christian forces marched out to fight, with God the bringer of victory in their bodies and minds. No number of men held any terrors for them because they

---

[30] Robert drops the details of the Bishop of Martirano given at *GF* 94.

[31] *Genesis* X.13–14, although Celon is not listed among the sons of Mizraim.

[32] Rather heavy-handed symbolism for the coming battle.

[33] Gilo's text ends with the election of Godfrey (IX.10 in Robert). Given that all Robert's hexameters coincide with passages in Gilo, it is interesting to find these hexameters describing events after the end of Gilo's account. That further confirms the hypothesis that Robert is not borrowing directly from Gilo or Gilo from Robert. It also suggests that their shared source, whatever it may have been, continued beyond the end of Gilo's text.

trusted not in their own strength but the strength of the Lord. The Patriarch left Peter the Hermit to carry out his functions, arranging for Mass to be said, prayers to be offered and processions to the Holy Sepulchre to be organised so that the God, who had become man, and who once lay in it would protect his people.

Chapter XVI: the King finds a large amount of booty on arriving at the river

Now the troops of footsoldiers are first to leave the city; the King follows more swiftly with the knights. They immediately plundered what they found. Our forces march out on a Friday.

When the King and his army came to the river on the near side of Ascalon, he found many thousands of oxen, camels, donkeys, male and female mules which came not only from the city but also the Emir's army. All these were guarded by 100 Arabs; as soon as they saw our men they left the booty to them and fled to seek somewhere to take refuge. Our men pursued them but managed to capture only two; anyway they took possession of all the spoils, which provided rich provision for Jerusalem. Day was now waning and the King ordered it to be broadcast throughout the army that all should rest, should rise at first light and should prepare for battle. The Patriarch pronounced an anathema against anyone who should take any plunder in the fight before victory was certain. Night passed; dawn broke with more than usual brilliance and awoke our men from sleep. It was the Friday on which the Redeemer of the human race defeated utterly with the victorious symbol of the cross the Devil of the human race, the King of Babylon;[34] now in the same way the Lord overcame the Emir of the Devil's Babylon through his followers. As we explained earlier, the King crossed the river; the Patriarch remained on the nearer side with the bishops and other clerics, Greek as well as Latin.

Chapter XVII: the lines are drawn up for battle beside the sea

The King then came down into a wide attractive valley with all his forces and reached the coast, where he drew up his ranks to fight. He took personal charge of the first; the Count of Normandy led the second; the Count of St Gilles the third; the Count of Flanders the fourth; Count Eustace, Tancred and Gaston of Bearn the fifth.[35] All the footsoldiers positioned themselves in front of the knights, armed with arrows, javelins and weapons. And that was the order in which they marched to meet the Babylonians.[36] The Count of St Gilles was on the right, next to the sea;

---

[34] 12 August. Robert makes the most of the symbolism of Friday.

[35] Gaston IV, Viscount of Béarn: well attested on Crusade, particularly in PT and AA: for references see Riley-Smith, *First Crusaders*, 206.

[36] The description is as at *GF* 95, but Robert enumerates the columns in the same way as at the battle of Antioch (VII.8).

the King was on the left, where the enemy were to be found in greatest numbers; all the rest were between these two.

Chapter XVIII: The emir was dumbfounded when he heard that our men were marching towards him

We should not pass over in silence what the Emir Clemens said when he was told that our men were riding out to fight him. Nobody had told him about the booty our men had taken the previous day, since nobody dared tell him anything other than good and welcome news – he liked to be happy. Anyone who announced anything unpleasant to him found themselves permanently out of favour. However, he was not particularly disturbed if he did lose any of his possessions because what remained was so valuable. In case anyone is tempted to dismiss what we are about to describe as an unfounded tale, the story came from someone who told it in Jerusalem, who chose to become a Christian and took the name of Bohemond at his baptism.[37] Clemens was told early in the morning that the Franks were indeed ready to fight and were not far off, marching towards him. Clemens is reported to have replied to the messenger: 'I cannot bring myself to believe what you say, because I do not expect to find them awaiting me even inside the walls of Jerusalem.' The messenger replied: 'My Lord, Your Eminence should be under no illusion: they are coming ready to fight and are close at hand.' Then Clemens ordered all his men to take up arms and prepare to fight. When all were standing drawn up to fight and he could see our men for himself, he said:

'O Kingdom of Babylon, pre-eminent over all other kingdoms, how you are shamed today with such a mean people daring to march against you! I had not expected to find them even skulking within the ramparts of a city: now here they are daring to march out against me by the equivalent of a day's march! Either they have lost their senses, or they love death as much as life. So I order you, warriors of Babylon, to exterminate them from the Earth, to let your eye spare none and to pity none.'

And so battle was joined.

---

[37] Robert lays some stress on this rather unlikely eyewitness, who does not recur in other sources at this point. Other sources do, though, refer to a convert taking the name of Bohemond. GN 251 says that the traitor Pirrus took the name Bohemond and went to Jerusalem before returning to Antioch. The apostate is mentioned at AA 381-2 and identified with Pirrus at 399–403. The closing sentences of RA are devoted to the same character. He reappears at IX.20. Robert mentions eyewitnesses at only one other point, the Council of Clermont (himself); it is interesting that he should be so emphatic about this distinctly dodgy eyewitness.

Chapter XIX: battle is joined on both sides

Here the Duke of Normandy[38] *distinguished himself in battle. He kills the king's standard-bearer at the very feet of the [Emir of] Babylon.*

The Count of Normandy, a soldier without fear, was the first to join battle along with his column, aiming for the part where he could see the banner of the Emir (which they call 'standard').[39] He slashed a path through the squadrons with his sword, creating carnage; when he reached the standard-bearer he knocked him to the ground at the Emir's feet and took the standard. The Emir was lucky to escape. He fled to Ascalon and halted outside the city gate, where he unhappily watched the unhappy slaughter of his forces from a distance. The King and other counts, equally bold, rushed on the enemy and struck out to left and right, creating carnage amongst all those who got in their way. The Turkish bows were of no use because our men attacked so quickly and forcefully that the Turks had no chance to draw them: they thought only of flight. Many thousands died there who would not have died if they had been able to flee. The numbers were so great that those in the rear were squeezing those in front towards death on our swords. Tancred and Eustace, the Count of Boulogne, attacked the Turkish tents and achieved many feats well worth remembering if they were written down.[40] Not one of our men hung back or showed any fear: on the contrary all were inspired by the same spirit and joined in pursuing the enemies of the Cross of Christ. It is wonderful that the small number of our men had no fear of such a large number of armed men, instead growing stronger and more determined with the help of divine grace.

Chapter XX: the Emir is defeated at the hour in which Christ suffered

Battle continued thus the whole day until the sun climbed up to the centre of the heavens, the same time as when Our Lord Jesus Christ ascended the Cross.[41] At that very hour all strength deserted the pagans; they were stupefied to a point where they could not flee and were too weak to defend themselves. They climbed trees in the hope that they could hide there out of sight of our men. However, our men shot arrows at them like a fowler shooting down birds, and having dislodged them from their perch slaughtered them on the ground like butchers in an abattoir. Others with swords in their hands rolled at the feet of the Christians, grovelled on the ground and did not dare to stand up in front of them.[42] By now the whole first section of the Babylonian army was in flight, and the the rearguard was unsure who was victorious, having expected anything but the flight of their own troops and a Christian victory. When they saw their own forces running away across the

---

[38] Always described as the Count by Robert.

[39] Orderic Vitalis uses the same word 'stantarum' in the same story (V.80).

[40] *GF* 95 refers to the Count of Flanders and omits Eustace.

[41] Robert refers back to the symbolism of IX.16.

[42] A description of the Islamic prayer attitude?

battlefield, they thought they were pursuing the Christians to kill them. Once they realised that it was the Christians who had won, their joy turned to despair. So they fled in absolute terror, joined their colleagues in flight and overtook them. Our men blew away the flanks and wings of the army as easily as the north wind dissipates cloud or a sudden gust a heap of straw.[43] Whilst all this was going on and the soldiers of Christ were destroying the followers of the Devil, with the Count of St Gilles (who was fighting near the sea) killing innumerable enemies and forcing many more to plunge into the sea, let us hear what Clemens – now literally Clement the Demented - said as he stood in front of the gate of Ascalon. This story was told by the convert mentioned above at Jerusalem, who was beside Clement as his hanger-on and house slave.

Chapter XXI: the Emir's lament

Here is Clemens' lament, like the words of one demented.

As the Christians slashed his army to pieces Clemens, like one demented, said:[44]

'O Mahommed, our Master and protector, where is your strength? Where is the strength of the heavenly powers in which you glory? Where is the strong power of the creator which always comes with your presence? Why have you abandoned your people like this to be mercilessly destroyed and dispersed and killed by a wretchedly poor and ragged people, a people who are the scrapings of other races, the lees, rust and slag of the whole human race. These are people, I may say, who used to seek bread from our people when they had nothing but scrip and staff. How many times did we give them alms? How many times did we take pity on them? Alas, alas – why did we spare them? Why did we help them in their wretchedness? Why did we not kill them all? Now we are all too aware that they came here not as true worshippers but as cunning spies. They saw us glorying in our contentment, coveted our riches, carried that covetousness back to their own country and told those men everything. Now they thirst for our silver and gold and spill our blood mercilessly for its sake. Are those who have such power really men or are they in fact gods from Hell? Maybe Hell split asunder and let these men spew forth. The abyss cracked and these people erupted from it; they have no sign of innate human feeling and no sign of piety. If they were really men they would fear death; but as it is they have no fear of returning to the Hell from which they emerged. O glory of the kingdom of Babylon! How horribly you are shamed today, with the loss of warriors who used to be strong and are now feeble. What nation can resist this

---

[43] *Isaiah* LX.24: *the whirlwind shall take them away as stubble.*

[44] The lament of Clemens is the longest speech in Robert after Urban's preaching of the Crusade: although it is in the *GF* Robert expands and emphasises it. The two speeches thus frame his work: the Crusade begins with a speech by the highest authority of the Church and finishes with a lament by the defeated Emir of Babylon, the counterweight to Jerusalem (who coincidentally shares his name with the Antipope Wibert of Ravenna). Both speeches are relayed by eyewitnesses, albeit the second one rather dubious.

appalling race now, since your own race cannot withstand them at this hour? Alas, alas! Those who have never before known how to flee, are fleeing; those who have made it their custom to abase others are abased themselves. Oh, what grief! Everything is turning against us. We have always been the victors, and now others are victorious; we have always lived in a happy frame of mind but are now plunged into misery. Who could keep his eyes from weeping and stop deep sobs from bursting out? For a long time I have devoted my efforts to bringing this army together with considerable care; I have wasted a lot of my time. I have brought together the strongest soldiers of the whole Orient at an unthinkable cost and led them to battle here, and now I have ended up losing them and the money I paid for them. I had got wood ready for building wooden towers and machines of all kind to set up round Jerusalem at considerable expense so that I could besiege it; the Christians came right out to face up to me before I ever got there! What kind of a reputation shall I have now at home when a new and alien people destroys my honour in this way! O Mahommed, Mahommed, who has ever invested more in the magnificence of your worship with shrines ornate with gold and silver, decorated with beautiful images of you, and with the ceremonies and solemnities of every kind of rite? This is what the Christians say to insult us: that the power of the Crucified One is greater than yours because he is powerful on earth and in heaven. And it certainly seems to be the case now that those who place their trust in him win, whilst those who revere you are defeated. That is not a consequence of any negligence on our part: your burial place is ornamented with far more gold, jewels and precious objects than his. The city distinguished by your burial has never fallen from glory but has gone from strength to strength and has been radiant with the worship of all your servants. By contrast the city in which the Crucified One was buried received no honour as a result: it was destroyed and trampled and several times reduced to dust. So whose fault is it that we are reduced to this state? Why should we give you every honour and receive nothing in return? O Jerusalem, whore and adulteress of cities[45], if you ever fall into our hands I shall raze you to the ground and completely destroy the Sepulchre of the One buried in you.'

Whilst the Emir Clemens was rehearsing these and other similar complaints over and over in a trembling voice, our men, courageous as ever, rushed the Babylonians so fiercely in front of the city gate that they left all of them either dead or incapacitated under their blows. It was in this way that divine strength won this battle and gave our men the glory of victory. Who could tell in full how many lost their lives at the narrow entrance to the gate? Clemens had every reason to weep when he saw so many of his men lifeless corpses before him. Some were still quivering and with their dying breath vilified Clemens for leading them there. Clemens is reported to have wept and lamented and cursed our men.

---

[45] Cf. *Revelations* XVII–XVIII. A further example of mirroring technique: Jerusalem is described in the terms normally reserved for Babylon.

Chapter XXII: the sailors flee

In the aftermath of this battle, with the enemy totally defeated, the sailors who had come by sea do the sensible thing and disperse.

There were sailors and ships from the surrounding coastal regions lying at anchor off the city. By order of the Emir they had brought all kinds of goods needed for the siege of Jerusalem. When they saw their own side and their master flung into shameful confusion, they were overcome by terror: they hoisted their sails and hastened back out to sea. Our men raised their hands to the heavens and thanked God in their hearts. When they returned to their tents they found gold, silver, and immeasurable spoils of clothes, abundant food, many kinds of animals and all kinds of weapons. They found horses and mares, male and female mules, donkey colts and mares and a dromedary. And what more can I say about the ewes and rams and other flocks all ready to eat? They found there cauldrons and kettles, cooking pots, couches and their coverings, baskets full of gold and silver, golden clothes and all kinds of ornament. Those who had the tents of the Emir to plunder (which were reported to be full of royal wealth) were enriched with magnificent booty.

Chapter XXIII: the standard which was captured in the battle[46]

The Count takes an exceedingly beautiful gift to lay before the Sepulchre.

The Count of Normandy gave the standard to the Lord's Sepulchre: it had a golden ball at the top of a silver pole and was valued at a price of 20 marks. Another bought a sword for 60 bezants. As our men made their way back in triumph they happened across a column of peasants carrying jars of water and wine which they thought their masters would need to use in the siege. Like beasts they were too dazed to move aside; they bent their heads and waited for the swords of our men. Some rolled in the blood of the dead and hid like corpses amongs the bodies of the dead. Once our men arrived back at the river where they had left the Patriarch, they rested and slept as they were tired.[47] When day returned to the land and dawn broke they got up and hurried to continue their journey.

---

[46] Robert changes the order of the *GF* to improve narrative flow.
[47] Cf. *Psalms* LXXVII.5.

Chapter XXIV: the sweet sound of the trumpets

An echo resonates, bouncing off each side of the mountains.

When they were about two miles away from the city they began to sound trumpets, brass instruments and horns and all kinds of musical instruments in triumph, so that the hills and mountains echoed back the harmony in melodic tones and as it were joined with them in rejoicing in God.[48] And so what Isaiah says about the spiritual Church of the faithful came true in reality: *the mountains and the hills shall break forth before you into singing.*[49] The harmony was delightful, pleasing and sweet in all sorts of ways, with the sound of the soldiers' voices and the sound of the trumpets joined by echoes from the mountains, the hollows in the cliffs and the depths of the valleys. When they arrived in front of the city gates, those who had remained there made God's praises resound in divine terms not on earthly mountains but heavenly ones. And God was rightly praised because now his pilgrims were received with open arms and praises, whereas before they had been received only with great difficulty, with lots of insults and sometimes only by making gifts.[50] Isaiah says of these pilgrims and gates: *therefore thy gates shall be open continually; they shall not be shut day nor night.*[51] This prophecy was fulfilled in our time, because now the gates of Jerusalem were opened *to the sons of pilgrims*[52] which used to be closed in their faces day and night. This battle took place to the praise and glory of Jesus Christ Our Lord on 12 August.

Chapter XXV: the first founder of Jerusalem, the next and the one after

[The name of] Jerusalem indicates who was its original founder.r

Since this historical sermon took its beginning and its end and its middle from Jerusalem it seems fitting at the end of the work to set down who founded it originally and gave it its name.[53] Melchizedek is said to have founded it after the flood (the Jews say he was the son of Noah). He founded it in Syria and called it Salem, going on to reign there for a considerable length of time.[54] Afterwards the

---

[48] Cf. *Isaiah* XLIX.13: *Sing, O Heavens; and be joyful, O earth; and break forth into singing, O mountains.*

[49] *Isaiah* LV.12.

[50] A reiteration of one of the twin justifications of the Crusade: safeguarding pilgrims to Jerusalem.

[51] *Isaiah* LX.11.

[52] *Isaiah* LXI.5. The King James version here reads 'of the alien'. The Vulgate reads 'filii peregrinorum': this means literally 'the sons of strangers', but by the twelfth century had come also to mean 'sons of pilgrims'.

[53] Compare Fulcher I.26 for a much more literal description of the city. For the twin significance of Jerusalem as spiritual and earthly city see Alphandéry, *La Chrétienté*, 22—3.

[54] *Genesis* XIV.18; XXXIII.18.

Jebusites held it and added a part of its name, Iebus; when the names were put together B was changed to R and the city was called Jerusalem.[55] Later on, when it had been improved by Solomon with the building of the Temple of the Lord, his own royal palace and a large number of buildings, gardens and cisterns it was called Ierosolima and understood as Ierusalumonia as if in Solomon's name.[56] It was corrupted by poets into Solima and called Zion by the prophets: in our language that means 'watchtower' because it is built on a mountain and those approaching can be seen from afar. Meanwhile, Jerusalem translates into 'Peaceful' in our language.

Chapter XXVI: its former nobility

Omnipotent Jesus, who suffered for us on the Cross, gave this city a nobility above all others: he ennobled her by purifying her and redeeming her from her wrongs.

As for the former glorious opulence of the city, we find it written in the Book of Kings that King Solomon *made silver to be in Jerusalem as stones.*[57] It shone far more gloriously and richly when the Son of God endured the Cross for the salvation of all mankind in it; the sky obscured its stars and the earth shook, *the rocks rent; and the graves were opened; and many bodies of the saints which slept arose.*[58] What city has ever experienced such a wonderful mystery, from which stemmed the salvation of all the faithful? It follows from this that, because the Son of God conferred on it the distinction of his glorious death, if the Church Fathers had so chosen the city should have been called not Jerusalem but, changing the R into S, 'Jesusalem', such that in our language it could be translated as Peaceful Salvation. Through these and similar symbolism comes the form and mystic sacrament of that heavenly Jerusalem of which it is said *we have a strong city; salvation will God appoint for walls and bulwarks. Open ye the gates, that the righteous nation which keepeth the truth may enter in.*[59] We cannot relay all the praises of Jerusalem uttered by the prophets and doctors of law. The earthly Jerusalem was forsaken by God in our era and held in odium because of the evil of its inhabitants. But when it so pleased God, he led the Frankish race from the ends of the earth with the intention that they should free her from the filthy Gentiles. He had long ago foretold this through the prophet Isaiah when he said: 'I shall *bring thy sons from far, their silver and their gold with them, unto the name of the Lord thy God, and to the Holy One of Israel, because he hath glorified thee. And the sons of pilgrims shall build up thy walls, and their kings shall minister unto thee.*'[60] We have found this and many other things in the books of the prophets which fit

---

[55] *II Samuel* V.6, 8; *Joshua* XVIII.28.

[56] *I Kings* V–VII for the building of the Temple and the palace.

[57] *I Kings* X.27.

[58] *Gospel of Matthew* XXVII.51–2.

[59] *Isaiah* XXVI.1–2.

[60] *Isaiah* LX.9–10. Again the King James text reads 'strangers'. See note 52 above.

exactly the context of the liberation of the city in our era. May God be blessed through all and above all; he strikes and wounds when he judges right, and equally through freely given goodness pities and heals when and how he sees fit.[61] Amen.

Here ends the ninth book.

---

[61] Cf. *Job* V.18: *he maketh sore and bindeth up; he woundeth, and his hands make whole.*

Appendix

Two letters calling Christians on Crusade

In around a third of the extant manuscripts of Robert's work two letters also appear: an almost certainly apocryphal letter from Alexius Comnenus to Robert of Flanders, and a letter of 1098 from the Patriarch of Jerusalem to the Churches of the West. The letters appear before Robert's text in some manuscripts and after it in others; in many the text of the Patriarch's letter is not complete. Both letters are *excitatoria* to Crusade and as such sit well with the hypothesis that Robert's work was commissioned to support Bohemond's abortive Crusade of 1106–7. I translate both here for easy reference using Hagenmeyer's text .

i) The supposed letter from Alexius Comnenus to Robert, Count of Flanders

Dating and purpose of letter

The letter of Alexius Comnenus to Count Robert of Flanders purports to be an appeal by Alexius to the West to save him from the Turks threatening to overrun his Empire. The letter has been edited by Riant and Hagenmeyer and translated into English by Joranson.[1] The letter appears in 36 of the Robert manuscripts and in three separate manuscripts; the *argumentum* at its head appears in 14, including the oldest manuscript of Robert.[2] An epitome also appears in Guibert's *Gesta Dei per Francos* with a few additional details.[3]

The letter starts by enumerating the suffering of the Eastern Christians in lurid detail. It emphasises the inability of the Emperor to fight, then lists the relics to be found in Constantinople which conveniently need protecting. It closes with an invitation to seek reward in the infinite riches of Constantinople.

The authenticity of the letter has been much debated. Views have ranged from seeing it as an authentic original translated into Latin to an outright forgery; most have taken a view somewhere between the two extremes, seeing it as having

---

[1] *Alexii I Comneni Romanorum imperatoris ad Robertum I Flandriae comitem epistola spuria*, ed. P. Riant (Geneva, 1879); *Kreuzzugsbriefe*, 130–136; E. Joranson, 'The problem of the Spurious Letter of Emperor Alexius to the Count of Flanders', *AHR* 55 (1950), 811–832. See also C. Cahen, 'La politique orientale des comtes de Flandre et la lettre d'Alexis Comnène', *Mélanges d'Islamologie: volume dédiée à la mémoire d'Armand Abel par ses collègues, ses élèves et ses amis* (Leyden, 1974), 84–90; M. de Waha, 'La lettre de Alexis I Comnène à Robert le Frison. Une revision', *B* 47 (1977), 113-25.

[2] Joranson 812.

[3] GN 100–04. See Joranson, 816, n.22.

perhaps some distant acquaintance with a real letter but heavily reworked as an *excitatorium* to Crusade.[4]

There is some slender basis in historical fact. Robert of Flanders set out on pilgrimage to Jerusalem in the late 1080s.[5] He sent 500 horsemen to support the Emperor in defending the borders of the Empire;[6] Ganshof argues that he took an oath of allegiance to Alexius and sent them as part of his feudal obligation[7]. So it is not inconceivable that Alexius may have sent a letter of this kind to the Count, although hard to see the context given that the horsemen were supplied. Anna Comnena mentions no such appeal for aid. As against that the circumstances alluded to in the letter show some match with what was happening in Byzantium in 1091 with pressure from the Turks and Petchenegs,[8] and the *argumentum* to the letter also points to 1091 as the date of composition. So some now lost letter from the Byzantine chancellery may lie behind this composition.

However, it does not convince as a piece of drafting. The style is tabloid. The Latin is loosely paratactic, plain to the point of baldness. At most it is fair to acknowledge that the rhetoric has a kind of crude effectiveness, with abundant use of hyperbole and a dramatic final demand to come before it is too late. As an *excitatorium* it has some merit, stressing the weakness of the Byzantines and the riches there for the taking – all the easier if their owners are too weak to defend themselves. But it is hard to believe that any self-respecting Byzantine civil servant would have dreamt of drafting a letter in this lurid style.

Neither does the content convince as a specimen of Byzantine diplomacy. It seems unlikely that an Emperor with previous experience of the Franks[9] would have held out the prospect of riches to be plundered in this way. Moreover, the sentiments it sets out are a commonplace of Western Crusading rhetoric. The emphasis on the riches to be gained on Crusade is common to many texts; so is the emphasis on the riches of Constantinople. The theme of Byzantine weakness coupled with the need to protect it as the home of Eastern Christianity are likewise widely found.[10]

In both style and content, therefore, the letter has far more in common with Western Crusade texts than the Byzantine court, taking its inspiration from a genuine event – and possibly, though unprovably, a genuine letter – in 1091.

What would have been the motive for producing it? There is no internal evidence on dating other than the reference to 1091, which in my view points at most to the date of a possible lost original. However, Joranson argues that the

---

[4] Helpfully discussed and summarised by Joranson, q.v.

[5] *First Crusaders*, 31.

[6] AC 229, 232, 252.

[7] F. L. Ganshof, 'Robert le Frison et Alexis Comnène', *B* 31 (1961), 57–74.

[8] Joranson, 831–2.

[9] See e.g. AC 162–73 on previous skirmishes with Bohemond.

[10] For emphasis on riches see Riley-Smith, *Idea*, 63: plunder was literally a matter of life and death on the Crusade, and it is hardly surprising it became a central theme; see e.g. Epp, 242–50. For attitudes to Byzantium see Riley-Smith, *Idea*, 145; Lilie 55–6, 'a restoration of the conquests to the Emperor meant the same as handing them over to the heathens' (56).

epitome in Guibert is followed by vicious anti-Byzantine rhetoric, which suggests that the letter should be seen as part of the anti-Byzantine recruiting campaign run by Bohemond in 1106.[11] This is borne out by the rhetoric the letter uses about Byzantium and by the fact that it occurs in Guibert and alongside Robert, both of whom wrote in the context of the same campaign.

To modern eyes this counts as a forgery. To a twelfth-century audience the concept of *auctoritas* was more important: if a document was accepted as genuine, it was by definition genuine. Arguably its inclusion in the works of Robert and Guibert would have conferred such *auctoritas*.[12] There are other examples: the so-called encyclical of Pope Sergius IV was probably produced by the Cluniac monks of Moissac to support the case for the First Crusade.[13]

Links between the letter and Robert's text

The link between the letter and the purpose of Robert's text is therefore clear. Moreover, Robert's account of Urban's speech and the letter share some details: the description of circumcision and sacrilege is common to both, and Robert refuses to recount in detail the sufferings of the women on which the letter lays stress. (Guibert, by contrast, dwells on the theme with lip-smacking relish.) The two texts also share an emphasis on the riches of Constantinople: at II.20 Robert's description of Constantinople refers to its riches, and lays heavy emphasis on the presence of relics and the protection it affords for them. Robert's text is virulently anti-Byzantine. And virtually all copies of the letter accompany Robert's text. All this suggests that the two texts were closely associated from the start, and strengthens the argument that Robert's text is intended as an incitement to Crusade.

Guibert also knew the letter. He gives an epitome, stating clearly that he had access to it but that his version is 'verbis ... vestita meis'.[14] Although the general thrust of his arguments is the same, the details are rather different. He states that churches were turned into mosques; he gives lurid details on the sufferings of women; he retains the sentiment about riches being a reason to help; he retains the reference to relics but comments with typical acerbity that if Constantinople has a head of John the Baptist there must be two in existence; and he offers the beauty of the women as an additional reason to help Constantinople.[15]

The rhetoric used by Baudry in his account of Pope Urban's speech hints lengthily and unspecifically at similar themes. There is much talk of the 'irrisiones'

---

[11] Joranson 825–6. De Waha dates it to 1095, arguing that it may be a paraphrase of a speech and citing the example of a Byzantine embassy to England at around this time.

[12] On the concept of *auctoritas* see Guénée 129–45. For an instance of use of forgeries compare the papal letters used (probably unwittingly) by Lanfranc, Archbishop of Canterbury in 1072 to assert his primacy over the Archbishop of York (Stenton, 664–5, who suggests the letters were prepared by Lanfranc's monks without his personal supervision.)

[13] 'Cluny and the First Crusade', H. E. J. Cowdrey, *RB* 83 (1973), 285–311, 301-2; 'The Genesis of the Crusades: the Encyclical of Pope Sergius IV(1009–12)', A. Gieysztor, *MH* 5 (1948), 3–23, 6 (1950), 3–34.

[14] GN 101–4; 101, 'clothed ... in my own words'.

[15] GN 103.

of the Saracens, the 'spurcitiam paganorum' and the profanation of churches: this is entirely in keeping with the themes of the letter, but the resemblances are not explicit enough to put it beyond doubt that Baudry had access to or used the letter.[16]

It is interesting that the letter should be associated with two out of the three Benedictine texts commissioned to improve the case for crusading made by the *GF*, embedded in Guibert's text and accompanying Robert's in virtually all manuscripts. This may suggest it was seen as part of the story alongside the need to rewrite the *GF*. What is not clear is whether Guibert or Robert wrote it. Guibert's comments suggest it was probably not him, and his elaborate prose style bears little resemblance to the simplistic style of the letter. Whilst there are clear parallels with Robert's own text, there is no evidence that Robert himself wrote it: in particular why would he pass over the suffering of women in his chronicle only to give abundant details on it in the letter? And although stylistic assessments are subjective, the crude style (in both senses) of the letter and the misjudgement of tone referring to the sufferings of Rachel are difficult to square with Robert's capable literary craftsmanship. Neither is there any evidence as to whether the letter preceded Robert's text, was written in parallel, or followed it later before being used by Guibert.[17]

Conclusion

To sum up, the letter is a simplistic but vivid excitatorium to go to the East and seek rewards from a Byzantium too weak to defend its riches, justified by the ostensible need to defend the Eastern Church and its relics against capture by the pagans. Whatever its basis in an original letter (perhaps dating from 1091) may have been, it very clearly fits the context of Bohemond's recruiting drive of 1106 to defend his territory against Byzantium. I have argued above that Robert's text needs to be seen in the same context . The close association between the letter and Robert's text is probably accounted for by its propaganda value and relationship to the process centred around reworking the *GF* rather than Robert's authorship.

---

[16] BB 12–15, particularly 13.
[17] The *Magdeburger Aufruf* casts no light on the relationship between Robert and the supposed letter of Alexius. All three share lurid rhetoric about the doings of the Saracens, but with differing details.

The letter of Emperor Alexius Comnenus I to Count Robert of Flanders[18]

The text of this letter was sent from the Emperor of Constantinople to all the churches of the West four years before the glorious journey to Jerusalem, and directed in particular to Robert Count of Flanders. The latter had now returned from his pilgrimage to the Lord's Sepulchre; the two had seen each other in the course of Robert's journey and talked amicably and pleasantly with each other. The Emperor was now – as he complains in this very letter – under heavy pressure from the wicked race of pagans under the leadership of the Old Soliman, father of Young Soliman. (The latter was later to be defeated by our men in battle, as that book tells, and forced to flee in shame). All this makes it extraordinary that the Emperor referred to above should always have been so venomously opposed to us and had no scruples about returning evil for good.

This is the end of the argument and the beginning of the letter.

To the Lord and glorious Count Robert of Flanders and to all the princes of the whole kingdom, lovers of the Christian faith holy and secular: the Emperor of Constantinople sends greetings and peace in Our Lord Jesus Christ and his Father and the Holy Spirit.

O most renowned Count and great defender of the Christian faith! The aim of this letter is to alert you, in your wisdom, to just how hard the most holy Greek Christian Empire is being pressed by the Petchenegs and Turks, pillaged daily and constantly raided, with Christians being murdered and mocked in various indescribable ways. The evils are many and, as we said, indescribable; so we shall limit our description to a few – which nevertheless are horrible to hear and disturb the air itself when recounted. For instance they circumcise Christian boys and youths above Christian baptismal fonts, pour the blood from the circumcision into the fonts in mockery of Christ, force them to urinate on it, and then drag them round the church and force them to blaspheme the name and faith of the Holy Trinity. Those who refuse are subjected to various punishments and eventually killed. Meanwhile they rob and mock noble women and their daughters, taking turns to defile them like animals. Others again as part of their corruption set virgins up in front of their mothers and force them to sing wicked and lustful songs[19] until they have finished their foul acts. This is the sort of thing we read about happening to the people of God long ago; the ungodly people of Babylon said to them, having mocked their various shrines, '*Sing us one of the songs of Zion.*'[20] And whilst their daughters are maltreated they now force mothers to sing dirty songs: their voices echo not in a song, in our view, but in a lament as is written about the Massacre of the Innocents: a voice was heard in Ramah: '*In Ramah was there a voice heard, lamentation and weeping, and great mourning, Rachel weeping for her children, and would not be comforted, because they are not.*'[21] However, although the

---

[18] The translation uses Hagenmeyer's text in *Kreuzzugsbriefe*, 129–36. I have compared my version against Joranson's.

[19] The mind boggles.

[20] *Psalms* CXXXVII.3.

[21] *Gospel of Matthew* II. 18; cf. *Jeremiah* XXXI.15.

mothers of the Innocents represented by Rachel could not be consoled for the loss of their children, they could at least be comforted by knowing that their souls were saved; these were in a worse case, inconsolable because they were lost both in body and in soul.[22] But this pales into insignificance compared to the worse things to come. They force men of all ages and stations into the sin of sodomy – boys, adolescents, young men, old men, nobles and servants and worse still and more terrible priests and monks; and – woe is me! The shame of it! – something which has never yet been told or heard of, bishops as well; they even claim that one bishop has succumbed to the lure of this appalling sin. They defile the holy places in innumerable ways, destroy them and threaten them with worse. Who does not lament at all this? Who does not sympathise? Who is not appalled? Who does not pray? By now virtually the whole area from Jerusalem to Greece has been invaded by them, as well as the whole of Greece with its upper regions (Cappadocia Minor and Major, Phrygia, Bithynia, Phrygia Minor which is Troy, Pontus, Galatia, Lydia, Pamphylia, Isauria, Lycia and the main islands Chios and Mitylene and many other regions and islands which we have not the heart to enumerate as far as Thrace);[23] almost nothing remains except Constantinople, which they threaten to take from us in very short order unless the help of God and the faithful of the Latin Christian Church come to our aid. For they have invaded the Propontis (this is also known as Avidus and flows out from Pontus besides Constantinople itself into the Aegean Sea) with 200 ships which the Greeks built and which they took and rowed here regardless of their wishes and are now threatening to capture Constantinople in short order both by land and via Propontis. We have written to you, Count of Flanders, as a lover of the Christian faith, to apprise you of these few highlights selected from innumerable evils. Let us pass over the rest so as not to offend our readers.[24]

So, for the love of God and the piety of all Greek Christians, we beg you to bring here whatever warriors true to Christ you can find in your lands, the powerful, the less powerful and the insignificant, to help me and the Greek Christians; just as you largely freed Galicia and the other kingdoms of the West from pagan rule last year,[25] now let your warriors try to free the kingdom of the Greeks for the salvation of their souls. Although I am Emperor I still do not know how to find any recourse or suitable way forward; I constantly flee the Turks and Petchenegs and stay in each city in turn until I know they are on their way. I would much rather bow down to your Latin shrines than those of the pagans.

Therefore, you should make every effort to stop them capturing Constantinople, thus ensuring that you will gain the joy of glorious and ineffable mercy in Heaven. Given the immensely precious relics of the Lord to be found in Constantinople, better that you should have it than the pagans. Here is a list:

---

[22] A rather heavy-handed and unconvincing piece of exegesis.

[23] Cf. *Acts* XIX.1.

[24] A distinctly unconvincing *praeteritio*.

[25] Joranson, 814, n.17 suggests this may refer to the expedition which Odo I, Borel, led to Spain in 1089. It could refer more generally to other battles of the Reconquista.

The pillar to which He was tied;

The whip with which He was scourged;

The crimson cloak in which He was wrapped;

The crown of thorns with which He was crowned;

The reed which was placed as a mock sceptre in His hand;

The clothes which were taken from Him before crucifixion;

A very large piece of wood from the cross on which He was crucified;

The nails by which He was hung;

The linen wrappings found in His tomb after the Resurrection;

Twelve baskets of fragments from the five loaves and two fishes;

The head of St John the Baptist complete with hair and beard;

Relics or bodies of many innocents and some prophets, apostles and martyrs – particularly St Stephen the Protomartyr – and confessors and virgins, which we shall not list in detail because of their sheer numbers.

It is more fitting for Christians than pagans to have all these. If they do have them all, it will be an important possession for the whole of Christendom. If they do not, it will be a major loss for which they will be held to account.

Now if [those from the West] should refuse to fight for this because they would rather have gold, they will find more in the city than in the whole of the rest of the world. The treasuries of the churches of Constantinople alone are overflowing with silver, gold, gems, precious stones and silken cloths or vestments, enough for all the churches in the world. Yet the inestimable treasure of the mother church St Sophia, or the Wisdom of God, far outweighs all these treasures and can without a shadow of doubt be compared with the treasures of the Temple of Solomon. Moreover, what can I say about the infinite treasures of the nobility, when nobody can guess at the value of the treasure held by common merchants? What waits to be discovered in the treasuries of past Emperors? I am certain no tongue would suffice to describe it because not only do they contain the treasures of former Emperors of Constantinople but also the treasure of all the past Roman Emperors was taken there and concealed in palaces. What more can I say? What men can see is little compared to what is hidden. So come quickly with all your forces and fight with all your might to prevent such a treasure falling into the hands of the Turks and Petchenegs. Their numbers may well be infinite, and 60,000 are already expected at any moment. I worry that they may undermine the determination of our soldiers by exploiting their desire for this treasure, just like Julius Caesar when he invaded the kingdom of the Gauls and just as the Antichrist will do at the end of the world when it falls into his power.[26]

So act now, while you have time. Do not let Christian lands – or, worse still, the Holy Sepulchre of the Lord – be lost. In so doing you will ensure yourselves mercy rather than judgement in Heaven.

Amen.

The letter ends here.

ii) The letter of the Patriarch of Jerusalem to those in the West

Hagenmeyer lists 32 manuscripts containing this letter, which he dates to January 1098.[27]

Like its companion letter, it is an *excitatorium* to Crusade, although noticeably more elaborate in style. Its sentiments can be paralleled not only in Robert's text but in those of other contemporaries:[28] the wonderment at Christian victory against overwhelming odds and its proof of the rightness of the cause; the link between events in the Bible and events on Crusade; and the comparison between living and dying for God. The reference to women being forbidden to go on Crusade is paralleled in Robert's account of Pope Urban's speech; however there is no reason to read a specific link into that or to suggest that Robert was the author.

The importance of the letter is as a concise and compelling statement of the religious justification for the Crusade; it has a clear logic as a companion piece for Robert's text and in bolstering Bohemond's appeal for crusaders. It is likely to have been put alongside Robert's chronicle for that reason, perhaps reflecting use by Bohemond as a recruiting tool.

The letter from the Patriarch of Jerusalem and other bishops to the Churches in the West[29]

The Patriarch of Jerusalem and all the bishops both Greek and Latin, all the armies of God and the Church: to the Western Church, brotherhood with the celestial Jerusalem and a share in the fruit of its labour.

---

[26] For Julius Caesar see Suetonius' *De Vita Caesarum*, ed. M. Ihm (Leipzig, 1908), *Divus Julius* ch. 51–4: Suetonius says a great deal about Caesar's lusts, and rather less about his covetousness. This may be a veiled implication in the letter. For use of bribery as one of the four wiles of the Antichrist see Emerson, 131.

[27] *Kreuzzugsbriefe*, 146.

[28] See discussion above in Chapter Four.

[29] The translation uses Hagenmeyer's edition in *Kreuzzugsbriefe*, 146–9.

We are well aware that you rejoice in the success of the Church, and believe that you are anxious to hear both favourable and unfavourable news of it, and so now we notify you of the growth in its fortunes. So know in your charity that God has triumphed in 40 major cities and 200 fortified places to the benefit of his church, both in Anatolia and Syria; and that we now have 100,000 armed men over and above the rank and file despite the fact that we lost many in the first battles. But what of it? What can one do against 1,000? Where we have one count the enemies have 40 kings; where we have a column they have a legion; where we have a knight they have a duke; where we a footsoldier, they a count; where we a castle, they a kingdom. So we placed our trust neither in numbers or strength nor any over-confidence but in the shield of Jesus Christ; protected in our cause by the soldiers of Christ who accompanied us – St George, St Theodore, St Demetrius and the blessed St Blaise[30] – we penetrated the wings of the enemy's force safe from harm, forced our way through (as we are still doing), and with God on our side were victorious on five battlefields. Why say more? I, the Apostolic Patriarch and the bishops and all the clerical orders of the Lord pray on our own behalf and on the part of God, and our spiritual mother the Church cries: '*Come, my dearest sons, inherit the kingdom prepared for you from the foundation of the world*[31] against the sons of idolatry who rise up against me.' So come, we beseech you, to fight on the army of the Lord in the very place where the Lord fought and where *Christ also suffered for us, leaving us an example, that ye should follow his steps*[32]. For did not the Lord die for us although innocent of sin? So let us die if need be, not for him but for ourselves, so that whilst we die to the world we may live in God. That said, there is no need for us to die or to fight to the death, for we have already succeeded in harder tasks and indeed the castles and cities we have taken have greatly diminished the opposition. So come; hasten towards a prize of double worth, a land of the living *flowing with milk and honey*[33] and with abundant food. See, men, the roads everywhere bear witness to the shedding of our blood, and you bring nothing with you other than what is rightfully ours. Let only men come and women be left behind; from a house where two dwell let one make his way swiftly to war. And in particular I, as Apostolic Patriarch and the bishops and all clerical orthodox orders, excommunicate those who took an oath but did not come and broke their promise; we remove them completely from communion with the Church. You are to do the same. Let them not be buried amongst Christians or remain behind except with good cause. Come and gain a dual glory along with us. It is in these terms that I write to you.

---

[30] In *GF* the saintly helpers do not appear until the battle of Antioch; they are invoked several times by Robert. However St Blaise – a physician and bishop of Sebaste in Armenia, where he was martyred – is found neither in the *GF* nor Robert.

[31] *Gospel of Matthew* XXV.34. The King James translation is slightly different.

[32] *II Peter* II.21.

[33] E.g. *Exodus* XIII.5.

Bibliography

Abbreviations for periodicals

AB: Analecta Bollandiana
AHR: American Historical Review
AOL: Archives de l'Orient Latin
B: Byzantion
BIHR: Bulletin of the Institute of Historical Research
JMH: Journal of Medieval History
MA: Le Moyen Age
MGH: AA: Monumenta Germaniae Historiae: Auctorum Antiquissimorum
MH: Medievalia et Humanistica
MJB: Mittellateinisches Jahrbuch
NM: Neuphilologische Mitteilungen
NMS: Nottingham Medieval Studies
R: Romania
RB: Revue Bénédictine
RHE: Revue d'Histoire Ecclésiastique
RHR: Revue de l'Histoire des Religions
RMS: Reading Medieval Studies
S: Speculum
SCH: Studies in Church History
SM: Studi Medievali
T: Traditio
ZFSL: Zeitschrift fur Französische Sprache und Literatur
ZRP: Zeitschrift fur Romanische Philologie

Dictionaries used

Du Cange	Du Cange, C., *Glossarium mediae et infimae latinitatis*, 6 vols (Paris, 1840–48)
Godefroy	Godefroy, F., *Dictionnaire de l'ancienne langue française*, 10 vols (Paris, 1880–1902)
Levy	Levy, E., *Petit dictionnaire provençal-français*, fifth edition (Heidelberg, 1973)
Lewis and Short	Lewis, C. T., and Short, C., *A Latin dictionary*, new impression (Oxford, 1987)

Texts and translations of the *Historia Iherosolimitana*

Texts of the Historia Iherosolimitana *in chronological order*

Veterum scriptorum, qui caesarum et imperatorum Germanicorum res per aliquot saecula gestas, litteris mandarunt, Reuber (Frankfurt-am-Main, 1584), 217–71
Gesta Dei per Francos, ed. I. Bongars (Hanover, 1611), 30–81
Patrologiae cursus completus. Series latina, J. P. Migne (Paris, 1844), vol.CLV, 669–758
Recueil des Historiens des Croisades (Académie des Inscriptions et Belles-Lettres, Paris, 1841–1906), 16 vols: *Historiens occidentaux* vol.III 717–882 *(Recueil, RHC Occ.)*

Translations of the Historia Iherosolimitana

Dutch:
Scoenre historie hertoghe godeuarts van boloen (Gouda, 1486)

French:
Collection des mémoires rélatifs à l'histoire de la France, F. P. G. Guizot (Paris, 1823–31) 30 vols; vol.XXIII (1825), 295–476

German:
Historia Hierosolimitana *von Robertus Monachus in deutscher Übersetzung*, B. Haupt (Wiesbaden, 1972)

Italian:
Historia di Roberto Monaca della Guerra fatta da principi christiani contra Saracini per l'acquisto di terra Santa, M. F. Baldelli (Florence, 1552)
La guerra per li principi cristiani guerregiata contra i Saracini corrente A.D.1095. Traslata in volgare per uno da Pistoia, S. Ciampi (Florence, 1825)
La prima crociata ... di Roberto monaco, tradotto ... con nota e schiarimenti, G. B. Cereseto (Nice, 1854)

Accompanying letters

H. Hagenmeyer, *Die Kreuzzugsbriefe aus den Jahren 1088–1100* (Innsbrück, 1901) *(Kreuzzugsbriefe)*

The apocryphal letter of Alexius is translated by Joranson in:
Joranson, E., 'The Problem of the Spurious Letter of Emperor Alexius to the Count of Flanders', *AHR* 55 (1950), 811–32

Munro's translation of Pope Urban's speech

D. C. Munro, *Urban and the Crusades* (Philadelphia, 1895), 5–8
A. C. Krey, *The First Crusade: the accounts of eye-witnesses and participants* (Princeton, 1958), 33–6
E. Peters, ed. and intr., *The First Crusade: the chronicle of Fulcher of Chartres and other source materials* (Philadelphia, 1971), 1–16 with other accounts of the speech

Primary texts

Latin and Greek

AA: Albert of Aix, *Historia Hierosolymitana*, *RHC Occ.*, IV, 265–713. A new edition by Susan Edgington was not available at time of writing.

AC: *The Alexiad of Anna Comnena*, transl. E. R. A. Sewter (Harmondsworth, 1969)

St Aldhelm: *De Virginitate* in *Aldhelmi Opera* ed. Ehwald *MGH: AA*, 15 (1919), 203–323

BB: Baudry of Bourgueil, *Baudri de Bourgueil: Oeuvres Poétiques*, ed. P. Abrahams (Paris, 1926)

_____ *Historia Jerosolymitana*, *RHC Occ.*, IV, 1–111

Carmen de Hastingae Proelio by Guy, Bishop of Amiens, ed. C. Morton and H. Muntz (Oxford, 1972)

Ekkehard: *Ekkehardi Uraugiensis Abbatis Hierosolymita nach der Waitz'schen Recension*, ed. H. Hagenmeyer (Tübingen, 1877)

FC: *Fulcheri Carnotensis Historia Hierosolymitana (1095–1127)*, ed. H. Hagenmeyer (Heidelberg, 1913); transl. H. S. Fink and Sister F. R. Ryan, *Fulcher of Chartres: a history of the expedition to Jerusalem* (Knoxville, 1969)

Gerald of Wales: *Itinerarium Cambriae* in *Giraldi Cambrensis Opera*, ed. J. F. Dimock, vol.VI (London, 1868)

GF: *Gesta Francorum et aliorum Hierosolimitanorum*, ed. R. Hill (London, 1962); also ed. L. Bréhier, *Histoire anonyme de la première Croisade* (Paris, 1924)

Gilo: *The Historia Vie Hierosolimitanae of Gilo of Paris*, ed. and transl. C. W. Grocock and J. E. Siberry (Oxford, 1997)

GN: *Gesta Dei per Francos*, Guibert of Nogent, ed. R. B. C. Huygens, Dei Gesta per Francos *et cinq autres textes* (Turnhout, 1996); transl. R. Levine, *The Deeds of God through the Franks. A translation of Guibert de Nogent's* Gesta Dei per Francos (Woodbridge, 1997)

HH: *Historia Anglorum: the History of the English people*, Henry of Huntingdon, ed. and transl. D. Greenway (Oxford, 1996)

Horace: *Q. Horati Flacci Opera*, ed. E. C. Wickham (Oxford, 1901); transl. *Horace for English Readers*, E. C. Wickham (Oxford, 1903)

Lucan: *Pharsalia*, ed./transl. J. D. Duff (Loeb, 1928); transl. R. Graves, *Lucan: Pharsalia: dramatic episodes of the Civil Wars,* (Harmondsworth, 1956)

Magdeburger Aufruf: 'Kreuzzug und Siedlung. Studien zum Aufruf der Magdeburger Kirche von 1108', P. Knoch, *JGMOD* 23 (1974), 1–33

OV: *The Ecclesiastical History of Orderic Vitalis*, ed. M. Chibnall (Oxford, 1969-75), 6 vols.

Ovid: *Metamorphoses*, ed. D. E. Hill (Warminster, 1985–2000), 4 vols.

PT: *Petrus Tudebodus: Historia de Hierosolymitano Itinere*, ed. J. H. and L. L. Hill (Paris, 1977); transl. J. H. and L. L. Hill, *Peter Tudebode: Historia de Hierosolymitano Itinere* (Philadelphia, 1974)

RA: *Le 'liber' de Raymond d'Aguilers*, ed. J. H. and L. L. Hill (Paris, 1969); transl. J. H. and L. L. Hill, *Historia Francorum qui ceperunt Jerusalem* (Transactions of the American Philosophical Society, 1968)

RC: *Gesta Tancredi*, Ralph of Caen, *RHC Occ.*, III, 587–716

Solymarius: 'Le *Solymarius* de Gunther de Pairis', ed. W. Wattenbach, *AOL*, I, 551–61.

Statius: *P. Papini Stati Thebaidos: Liber decimus*, ed. R. D. Williams (Leiden, 1972)

Suetonius: *De Vita Caesarum: Divus Julius*, ed. M. Ihm (Leipzig, 1908)

WM: *Gesta Regum et Anglorum*, William of Malmesbury, ed. and transl. R. A. B. Mynors, completed R. Thomas and M. Winterbottom (Oxford, 1998), 2 vols.
WT: *Willelmi Tyrensis Archiepiscopi Chronicon*, William of Tyre, ed. R. B. C. Huygens, *Corpus Christianorum* 63 and 63a (1986)

Vernacular

Baudry of Bourgueil, Old French poem based on: 'Un récit en vers de la première Croisade fondé sur Baudri de Bourgueil', *R* 5 (1876), 1–63 and *R* 6 (1877), 489–94
The Canso d'Antioca. An Occitan epic of the First Crusade, ed. L. M. Paterson and C. E. Sweetenham (Aldershot, 2003)
La Chanson d'Antioche, ed. S. Duparc-Quioc (Paris, 1976–8), 2 vols (I, *Edition*, II *Etude*)
La Chanson d'Aspremont, ed. L. Brandin (Paris, 1923–4)
La Chanson des Chétifs, ed. G. M. Myers, in *The Old French Crusade Cycle*, V (1981)
La Chanson de Guillaume, ed./transl. P. Bennett (London, 2000)
La Chanson de Jérusalem, ed. N. Thorp, in *The Old French Crusade Cycle*, VI (1992)
La Chanson de Roland, ed. I. Short (Paris, 1990)
La Chrétienté Corbaran, ed. P. R. Grillo, in *The Old French Crusade Cycle: the Jerusalem Continations I*, VII, Part I (1984)
Estoire d'Eracles empereur et la conqueste de la terre d'Outremer, RHC Occ., I–II
The Old French Crusade Cycle, ed. J. A. Nelson and E. J. Mickel (Alabama, 1977–96), 10 vols.
Gran Conquista de Ultramar, ed. L. Cooper (Bogota, 1979), 4 vols
Marie de France: Lais, ed. A. Ewert (Oxford, 1947)
Njal's Saga, transl. M. Magnusson and H. Palsson (Harmondsworth, 1960)
Pèlerinage de Charlemagne: The Pilgrimage of Charlemagne and Aucassin and Nicolette, ed. G.S. Burgess and A. E. Cobby (New York and London, 1988)
Raoul de Cambrai, ed. S. Kay, (Cambridge, 1992)
Ricketts and Hathaway: *Introduction à l'étude de l'ancien provençal*, F. R. Hamlin, P. R. Ricketts, J. Hathaway (Geneva, 1967)

Arabic sources

Ibn al-Athir: *Extraits de la chronique intitulée Kamel-altevarykh par Ibn-Alatyr*, RHC Or., I, 187–744
_____ *Histoire des Atabegs de Mosul*, RHC Or., II.II, 28–31
Kemal ed-Dîn:*Chronique d'Alep*, RHC Or., III, 571–732

Secondary works

Alphandéry, P., 'Les citations bibliques chez les historiens de la première Croisade', *RHR* 99 (1929), 139-57
_____*La chrétienté et l'idée de croisade* (Paris 1954-9), 2 vols.
Andressohn, J. C., *The Ancestry and Life of Godfrey of Bouillon* (Indiana, 1947)
Aston, S., 'The Provençal planh: lament for a prince', *Mélanges de philologie romane dédiées à Jean Boutière*, ed. I. Cluzel, F. Pirot (Liège, 1971), 2 vols., I 23–30
Baldwin, M., ed., *The First Hundred Years* (1969) in Baldwin, M. and Setton, K., *A History of the Crusades* (Madison 1969–89), 6 vols.
Bancourt, P., *Les Musulmans dans les chansons de geste* (Aix-en-Provence, 1982), 2 vols.

Bender, K. H., 'Des chansons de geste à la première epopée de croisade. La présence de l'histoire contemporaine dans la littérature française du douzième siècle', *VIe Congrès International de la Société Rencesvals* (Aix-en-Provence, 1974), 485–500

Blake, E. O. and Morris, C., 'A hermit goes to war: Peter and the origins of the First Crusade', *SC,* 22 (1984), 79–107

Bossuat, R., 'Sur un fragment de la *Chanson d'Antioche*', *NM* 32 (1931), 110–18

Brundage, J. A. , 'Adhemar of Puy: the bishop and his critics', *S* 34 (1959), 201–12

_____ 'An Errant Crusader: Stephen of Blois', *T* 16 (1960), 380–95

Bull, M. J., 'Overlapping and competing identities in the Frankish First Crusade', *Le Concile de Clermont de 1095 et l'Appel à la Croisade: actes du Colloque à l'Université Internationale à Clermont-Ferrand (23–25 juin 1995)*, ed. A Vauchez (Rome, 1997), 195–211

_____ 'The Capetian Monarchy and the Early Crusade movement: Hugh of Vermandois and Louis VII', *NMS* 40 (1996), 25–46

Cahen, C., 'La politique orientale des comtes de Flandre et la lettre d'Alexis Comnène', *Mélanges d'Islamologie: volume dédiée à la mémoire d'Armand Abel par ses collègues, ses élèves et ses amis*, ed. P. Salmon (Leyden, 1974), 74–80

Cohen, C., 'Les éléments constitutifs de quelques *planctus* des Xe et XIe siècles', *CCM* 1 (1958), 83–6

Cole, P. J., *The Preaching of the Crusades to the Holy Land 1095–1270* (Massachusetts, 1991)

Cook, R. F., *Chanson d'Antioche, chanson de geste: le cycle de la croisade est-il épique?* (Amsterdam, 1980)

Cook, R. F. and L. S Crist, *Le deuxième cycle de la croisade* (Geneva, 1972)

Cowdrey, H. E. J., 'Pope Urban's preaching of the First Crusade', *H* 55 (1970), 177–88

_____ 'Cluny and the First Crusade', *RB* 83 (1973), 285–311

Cross, F. L. and Livingstone, E. A., eds.,*Oxford Dictionary of the Christian Church*, second edition (Oxford, 1974)

Daniel, N., *Heroes and Saracens: a reinterpretation of the chansons de geste* (Edinburgh, 1984)

David, C. W., *Robert Curthose, Duke of Normandy* (Cambridge, Mass., 1920)

Dickerhof, G., '"Canum nomine gentiles designantur". Zum Heidentum aus mittelalterliches Bibellexika', *Secundam regulam vivere,* ed. G. Melville, P. Norbert Backmund, O. Praem (Windberg 1978), 41–71

Duncalf, F., 'The Peasants' Crusade', *AHR* 26 (1921), 440–53

Duparc-Quioc, S., *Le cycle de la croisade* (Paris, 1955)

Edbury, P. W. and Rowe, J. G., *William of Tyre: Historian of the Latin East* (Cambridge, 1988)

Edgington, S., 'The First Crusade: reviewing the evidence', *The First Crusade: origins and impact*, ed. J,. Phillips (Manchester, 1997) 55–77

Emerson, R. K., *Antichrist in the Middle Ages: a study of Medieval Apocalypticism, Art and Literature* (Manchester, 1981)

Epp, V., *Fulcher von Chartres: Studien der Geschichtsschreibung des ersten Kreuzzuges,* Studia Humaniora 15 (Düsseldorf, 1990)

Erdmann, C., *The origin of the idea of Crusade*, transl. M. W. Baldwin and W. Goffart, (Princeton, 1977)

Flori, J., 'Faut-il réhabiliter Pierre l'Ermite?', *CCM* 38 (1995), 35–54

France, J., *Victory in the East: a military history of the First Crusade* (Cambridge, 1994)

_____ 'The Anonymous *Gesta Francorum* and the *Historia Francorum qui ceperunt Iherusalem* of Raymond of Aguilers and the *Historia de Hierosolymitano*

Itinere of Peter Tudebode: an analysis of the textual relationship between primary sources for the First Crusade', *The Crusades and their sources. Essays presented to Bernard Hamilton*, ed. J. France, W. G. Zajac (Aldershot, 1998) 39–69

_____ 'The use of the Anonymous *Gesta Francorum* in the early twelfth-century sources for the First Crusade', *From Clermont to Jerusalem: the Crusades and Crusader societies 1095–1500* ed. A. V. Murray (Turnhout, 1998) 29–42

Ganshof, F. L., 'Recherches sur le lien juridique qui unissait les chefs de la première Croisade à l'empereur byzantin', *Mélanges offerts à M. Paul E. Martin* (Geneva, 1961) 49–63

_____ 'Robert le Frison et Alexis Comnène', *B* 31 (1961), 57–74

Gieysztor, A., 'The Genesis of the Crusades: the Encyclical of Pope Sergius IV (1000–12)', *MH* 5 (1948), 3–23; 6 (1950), 3–34

Glaesener, H., 'Godefroid de Bouillon était-il un médiocre?', *RHE* 39 (1943), 309–41

Grocock, C. W., 'Ovid the Crusader', *Ovid Renewed*, ed. C. Martindale (Cambridge, 1988) 55–69

Guénée, B., *Histoire et culture historique dans l'Occident médiéval* (Paris, 1980)

Hagenmeyer H., *Peter der Eremite* (Leipzig, 1879)

_____ *Chronologie de la première croisade* (Paris, 1901)

Hamilton, B., *The Latin church in the Crusader States* (London, 1980)

Hatem, A., *Les poemes épiques des croisades: genèse – historicité – localisation* (Paris, 1932)

Hatto, A. T., ed., *Eos: an enquiry into the theme of lovers' meetings and partings at dawn in poetry* (The Hague, 1965)

Hiestand, R., 'Il cronista medievale e il suo pubblico: alcune osservazioni in margine alla storiografia delle crociate', *Annali della Facoltà di lettere e filosofia dell'Università di Napoli*, 27 (1984–5), 207–27

Hill, J. H. and L. L., 'The Convention of Alexius Comnenus and Raymond of St Gilles', *AHR* 58 (1953), 322–7

_____ 'Contemporary accounts and later reputation of Adhemar, Bishop of Le Puy', *MH* 9 (1955), 30–38

_____ *Raymond IV, Count of Toulouse* (New York, 1962)

Horrent, J., *Le Pèlerinage de Charlemagne. Essai d'explication littéraire avec des notes de critique textuelle* (Paris, 1961)

Huygens, R. B. C., 'La tradition manuscrite de Guillaume de Tyr', *SM* 5 (1964), 281–373

Iorga, N., *Les narrateurs de la première Croisade* (Paris, 1928)

Jamison, E., 'Some Notes on the *Anonymi Gesta Francorum* with special reference to the Norman contingent from Southern Italy and Sicily in the First Crusade', *Studies in French language and medieval literature presented to Professor Mildred K. Pope* (Manchester, 1939), 183–208

Kleber, H., 'Wer ist der Verfasser der *Chanson d'Antioche?* Revision einer Streitfrage', *ZFSL* 94 (1984), 115–42

Klopsch, P., 'Prosa und Vers in der mittellateinischen Literatur', *MLJ* 3 (1966), 9–24

_____ *Einfuhrung in die Dichtungslehren des lateinisches Mittelalters* (Darmstadt, 1980)

Knappen, M. M., 'Robert II of Flanders in the First Crusade', *The Crusades and other historical essays presented to D. C. Munro by his former students*, ed. C. J. Paetow (New York, 1928), 79–100

Knoch, P., *Studien zu Albert von Aachen* (Stuttgart, 1966)

Kraft, F., *Heinrich Steinhöwels Verdeutschung der* Historia Hierosolymitana *des Robertus Monachus. Eine literarhistorische Untersuchung* (Strasbourg, 1905)

Krey, A. C., 'A neglected passage in the *Gesta* and its bearing on the literature of the First Crusade', *The Crusades and other historical essays presented to D. C. Munro by his former students*, ed. L. J. Paetow (New York, 1928), 57–78

La Monte, J. L., 'The Lords of Le Puiset on the Crusades', *S* 17 (1942), 100–18

Lacroix, B., '*Deus le volt!* Théologie d'un cri', *Mélanges offerts à Edmond-Réné Labande* (Poitiers, 1974), 461–70

Lambert, M., *Medieval Heresy* (London, 1977)

Lejeune, R., *Les chansons de geste et l'histoire* (Liège, 1948)

Lilie, R. J., *Byzantium and the Crusader States 1096–1204*, transl. J. C. Morris and J. E. Ridings (Oxford, 1993)

Manitius, M., *Geschichte der lateinischen Literatur des Mittelalters* (Munich, 1931), 3 vols.

Markowski, M., '"Crucesignatus": its origins and early usage', *JMH* 10 (1984), 157–65

Marquardt, G., *Die* Historia Hierosolymitana *des Robertus Monachus. Ein quellenkritischer Beitrag zur Geschichte des ersten Kreuzzugs* (Konigsberg, 1892)

Meyer, H. E., *The Crusades*, transl. J. Gillingham (Oxford, 1972)

Morris, C.: *The Papal Monarchy: the Western Church from 1050 to 1250* (Oxford, 1989)
    _____ 'The *Gesta Francorum* as Narrative History', *RMS* 19 (1993), 55–71

Munro, D. C., 'The Speech of Pope Urban II at Clermont 1095', *AHR* 11 (1905), 231–42

Murray, A., 'Coroscane: homeland of the Saracens in the *chanson de geste* and the historiography of the Crusades', *Aspects de l'épopée romane. Mentalités, idéologies, intertextualités*, ed. H. van Dijk and W. Noonan (Groningen, 1995), 177–84

Nicholson, R. L., *Tancred: a history of his life and career* (Chicago, 1940)

Norwich, J. J., *The Normans in Sicily* (Harmondsworth, 1992)

Oehler, H., 'Studien zu den *Gesta Francorum*', *MJB* 6 (1970), 58–97

Partner, N., *Serious Entertainments: the writing of history in twelfth-century England* (Chicago, 1977)

Poncelet, A., 'Boémond et St Léonard', *AB* 31 (1912), 24–44

Rieger, D., 'Zur Stellung des Tagelieds in der Trobadorlyrik', *ZRP* 87 (1971), 223–32

Riley-Smith, J., 'The title of Godfrey of Bouillon', *BIHR* 52 (1979), 83–6
    _____ *The First Crusade and the Idea of Crusading* (London, 1986)
    _____ *The First Crusaders, 1095–1131* (Cambridge, 1997)

Robinson, I. S., *Authority and Resistance in the Investiture Contest: the polemical literature of the late Eleventh Century* (Manchester, 1978)
    _____ *The Papacy 1073–1198: Continuity and Innovation* (Cambridge, 1990)

Runciman, S., 'The holy lance found at Antioch', *AB* 68 (1950), 197–209
    _____ *A History of the Crusades* (Cambridge, 1951–4) 3 vols.

Rychner, J., *La chanson de geste: essai sur l'art épique des jongleurs* (Geneva, 1955)

Skoulatos, B., 'L'auteur anonyme des Gesta et le monde byzantin', *B* 50 (1980), 504–32

Spiegel, G., *Romancing the past: the rise of vernacular prose historiography in thirteenth-century France* (Berkeley and Los Angeles, 1993)

Somerville, R., *Decreta Claromontensia: The Councils of Urban II* vol.I (Amsterdam, 1971)

Stenton, Sir F., *Anglo-Saxon England*, third edition (Oxford, 1971)

Swietek, F. R., 'Gunther of Pairis and the *Historia Constantinopolitana*', *S* 53 (1978), 49–79

Tellenbach, G., *Church, State and Christian Society at the time of the Investiture Contest*, transl. R. F. Bennett (Oxford, 1959)

Trotter, D., *Medieval French Literature and the Crusades* (Geneva, 1988)

Van Luyn, P., 'Les milites dans la France du XIe siècle: examen des sources narratives', *MA* 26 (1971), 5–51

Waha, M. de, 'La lettre de Alexis I Comnène à Robert I le Frison. Une revision', *B* 47 (1977), 113–25

Ward, B., *Miracles and the Medieval Mind* (London, 1982)

Witzel, H-J., 'Le problème de l'auteur des *Gesta Francorum et aliorum Hierosolymitanorum*', *MA* 61 (1955), 319–28

Wolf, K. B., 'Crusade and Narrative: Bohemond and the *Gesta Francorum*', *JMH* 17 (1991), 207–16

Yewdale, R. B., *Bohemond I, Prince of Antioch* (Princeton, 1924)

Index